BEYOND
GAY

BEYOND
GAY

"A powerful statement of a truly Christian struggle to deal with homosexual attraction."
—Fr. Benedict J. Groeschel, C.F.R.

DAVID
MORRISON

Our Sunday Visitor Publishing Division
Our Sunday Visitor, Inc.
Huntington, Indiana 46750

Our Sunday Visitor Publishing Division
Our Sunday Visitor, Inc.
200 Noll Plaza
Huntington, IN 46750

ISBN: 0-87973-690-9
LCCCN: 99-70512

Cover Design by Rebecca Heaston
PRINTED IN THE UNITED STATES OF AMERICA

To Richard and Michael,

two dedicated and long-suffering friends

without whose support this book would not

have been possible.

Acknowledgments

I could not have published this book without the support and encouragement of the following men and women:

Mike Aquilina, David Scott, Greg Erlandson, and all the folks from Our Sunday Visitor Publishing who let me borrow freely from their faith in this project during those times when I had none;

Steven Mosher and all the staff at the Population Research Institute who encouraged me to write it:

Dian Schlosser, Katherine Adams, and Matthew Gelis, who bore my discussion and worry about it stoically and with good humor;

the Andrew Schmiedicke family, who opened my eyes to what family love could be;

Michael Schmiedicke, whose belief in me, in turn, led me to believe; and Richard Hylton, a friend of more than fifteen years, who has borne all of my wackiness with a unique and generous strength.

Table of Contents

Introduction

Léon Bloy, the French Catholic writer and convert from Judaism, once said, "Man has places in his heart which do not yet exist, and into them enters suffering, in order that they may have existence." It's one of my favorite quotations. Just about all of Christian scholarship on the nature of suffering can be reduced to these few simple words. Suffering can bend and break us. But it can also *break us open* to become the persons God intended us to be. It depends on what we do with the pain. If we offer it back to God, He will use it to do great things in us and through us, because suffering is fertile. It can grow new life.

So it is with the personal witness you're about to read. David Morrison — as his writing vividly shows — is no stranger to the pain, doubt, self-destructive behavior, and alienation that mark so many of the men and women who struggle with homosexuality in their daily lives. This is the story of his journey from an active gay subculture to new life in Jesus Christ. This is his diary of discovering the Catholic faith. It's a real, flesh-and-blood conversion story, the kind with restless echoes of Augustine; the kind that will stay in the memory a long time. But a word of caution: Anyone looking for a casual spiritual boost, or a quick read for his or her spare time, would do well to close this book now. Compelling, it is. Moving, it is. Comfortable, it is not.

The importance of this work, though, is larger than David Morrison's personal conversion. That's just Act One. What Morrison accomplishes in the final two-thirds of his book is something extraordinary. He takes the raw material of his experience, and building on it, he offers one of the best explanations and defenses of Catholic sexual ethics in years. He not only accepts what the Church teaches. He understands it with his heart . . . as perhaps only someone who's paid dearly to find the truth, can. Equally important, he has the gift of sharing it persuasively with the reader, not as a burden or a duty, but as a joy and a freedom.

Not everyone will welcome this book. While the author

clearly respects members of groups like Dignity and its Episcopal Church cousin, Integrity, he disagrees strongly with these organizations' goals. He does not believe the truth is served by revising the Christian faith to approve or accommodate homosexual activity. On the contrary, he argues that homosexual activity is not just morally wrong but destructive, because it leads the person away from God and the authentic human good. Yet at the same time, he writes with great compassion for those trying to make sense of their homosexuality.

He also questions the pastoral approach of some Christian groups: for example, those which argue that with enough faith and proper therapy, most homosexuals can assume fullfilling heterosexual lives. Morrison believes that while some homosexually inclined men and women have the ability to reorient themselves to heterosexual lives, others probably do not. But God's love for *all* His children, no matter what their particular burdens, never fails. And the meaning of human sexuality and the Christian call to chastity apply to everyone with equal force and equal love: married and unmarried, "gay" and "straight."

Scripture tells us to speak the truth in love (Ephesians 4:15). David Morrison has done so. This is a book marked by balance, intelligence, and respect for everyone touched by the issue of homosexuality. In the process, he and Our Sunday Visitor have made an invaluable contribution to the discussion of one of the central moral controversies of our time.

✠ CHARLES J. CHAPUT, O.F.M. CAP.
ARCHBISHOP OF DENVER

CHAPTER ONE

Why this book?

Outside of perhaps the emotional debates over abortion and euthanasia, few more divisive issues tear at the fabric of American culture and politics as those surrounding same-sex attraction and sexual activity. In families and communities, offices and boardrooms, Americans are being asked to reconsider how they view sexuality, sexual expression, tolerance, and compassion. When does "tolerating" something slip into approving of it? Have holidays in your house become battlegrounds where family members who demand acceptance of both themselves and their sleeping arrangements fight other family members concerned with falling moral standards? Can you love others and not approve of everything about the way they live their life? If you think you must approve, and what they are doing is genuinely harmful, are you really being compassionate towards them? What can society demand that a person accept as a condition of participating in public life? To paraphrase a chant which I used to yell at rallies from time to time, if people living with same-sex attraction are "here and queer" what should getting "used to it" mean?

Questions proliferate in the public realm. Should men and women in actively homosexual relationships be allowed to teach school or adopt children? Should teenagers who may experience same-sex attraction be "affirmed" in an identity based upon that attraction? How about relationships? Should society consider all relationships where "love" is present equally good? What is the nature of marriage? What is sex for, anyhow? What is the nature of love?

Questions such as these crowd local and national headlines almost daily, but they also make personal and family news as well. Using a conservative estimate, approximately three million people in the United States live with a predominant sexual and emotional attraction to a member of their own sex. Multiply that by a reasonable number of parents, siblings, and spouses and there may be as many as 12 million Americans whose interest in the societal debate over same-sex attraction could be described as more than academic. That means 12 million people for whom every charge and counter-charge, every misunderstanding, miscommunication, mischaracterization, and slur can strike right at the heart of who they consider themselves to be or the kind of life one of their loved ones is trying to build. No wonder questions of same-sex attraction, gay or lesbian rights, and same-sex marriage or adoption have the explosive emotional force they do.

I hope this book, while addressing many of these questions, will not contribute further to any of this issue's combustion. To borrow somewhat liberally from Shakespeare, I write neither to praise same-sex attraction nor to condemn it. Those who have opened this book hoping to find denunciations of "evil" gay rights activists will go away disappointed. So will those readers who wish to see opponents of a same-sex agenda vilified. Rather, what I hope this book does will be to point a third way — a path God has been gracious enough to show me in my life, by which one may live with same-sex attraction while refusing to be defined by it or act upon it. In short, for individuals who live with varying degrees of same-sex attraction, as well as their families, friends, pastors, and colleagues, I hope this book offers some light at the end of what may be a very dark tunnel.

The depth of this tunnel's darkness feels as though it has only deepened with the passage of more time. I must reiterate, since many of this chapter's facts are rather unpleasant, that I do not report them to stigmatize, bully, or otherwise slam homo-sexually active men or women. The sheer number of windows in my house would dictate a lot of caution were I inclined to throw stones. But one of the key lessons life has taught me concerns the primacy we, as human beings, must accord the truth. Whether welcome or disdained, convenient, troublesome, or indifferent, truth must be respected and sought. If we do not seek it, we shall never really understand who we are or where, exactly, we stand.

Dead canaries

Since the late 1960s, men and women who have engaged in same-sex activity, either part-time or predominantly, have been the canaries in the sexual revolution's coal mine. As long as what passed as "love" remained widely understood as "free," society seemed to be opening up, at least in places like New York and San Francisco, for people whose experience of attraction and sexual desire had been denied and kept under wraps for many years. But as soon as the air in the mine began to go bad, the canaries were the first to die. Consider what author and activist Eric Rofes says in *Reviving the Tribe* about what the years 1981 through 1995 would mean for many men who were sexually active with other men:

> By 1995, half of the men you've loved, hugged,
> talked, danced, cruised and had sex with will be
> dead or dying. You will feel like a time-traveling
> dinosaur before you reach middle age. The clubs
> you've inhabited will be gone, the music will be
> trashed and disappear, the history will evaporate
> into a vacuum. You will rip cards out of your
> Rolodex like pages from a calendar. You will ex-

perience so much death that you will forget who
died and who is still alive. You will run into men
on the street who you thought were long dead.
You will send out Christmas cards each year and
receive a half dozen back stamped "deceased."

Although not everyone has experienced this degree of loss,
and despite the significant emotional and spiritual renaissance
that a number of men report after testing positive for the Human
Immunodeficiency Virus (HIV), the overall effect of AIDS on
much of the self-identified "gay" community was one of deep
loss. The AIDS memorial quilt, with its thousands of handmade,
grave-sized blocks, became a unifying symbol for a community
that struggled to come to grips with an experience few, if any,
expected. The nights Rofes described as giving him "a persistent,
low level, sense of doom" and Randy Shilts, in his landmark book
And the Band Played On pictured as a potent mix of desire and
potential disease, flickered with the signs of approaching disaster, but few were able to read them. Too many actively homosexual men and lesbian women had burned too many bridges to
allow themselves the luxury of time to take stock in what they
were doing or where, individually and collectively, they were
going. Identities forged in opposition to a society that had not
understood became, in this terrible hour, not unlike armor that
protects on the battlefield but drowns its occupant when the ship
goes down. When researchers from the Federal Government's Cen-
ters for Disease Control (CDC) and related organizations told
leaders of San Francisco's actively homosexual community that
the community should consider closing the bathhouses where HIV
was being spread most rapidly, the activists booed the researchers off the stage. The love that feared to speak its name less than
one hundred years before had found its full-throated voice, and it
would take more than a whisper of illness to silence it. Until, that
is, actively homosexual men began to die, followed soon after by
the others whose activities or circumstances made them vulnerable
to infection. Then, and only then, did the self-identified gay community pause to question itself about the way it lived and loved.

And, to be sure, the community had, and still has in my opinion, much to question. How wise is it to base an identity on sexual desire? What role does the sexual part of one's psyche have on the rest? Does "liberation" mean freedom to be dominated by one's desires, or is taking authority over desire the path to authentic freedom? One of the points Shilts makes in his book, which many have chosen to overlook because of its political incorrectness, is that the actively homosexual community he witnessed was ripe for some sort of infection even before HIV. The virus associated most closely with AIDS was only the latest in a line of aggressive and opportunistic disease vectors to take advantage of a community whose primary sexual expression left individuals easy to infect. In building an identity on sexual desire, early gay activists took their bodies for granted and misunderstood the roles and purposes of sex and freedom. Consider Rofes reminiscing in *Reviving the Tribe* about the role of a "a gay men's VD clinic" in forging a sense of identity among actively homosexual men in the 1970s:

> Simply walking into Boston's Fenway Community Health Center, Chicago's Howard Brown Memorial Clinic, or Los Angeles' Gay Community Services Center a "gay men's VD clinic" represented a major step toward self-identity and personal power. I recall looking around the waiting room at the Fenway at several dozen men of different ages, classes, and ethnicities and feeling solidarity and pride. Despite the risks of those years, each of us had seized the moment and claimed status as sexually active gay men.

While I would not want to extrapolate Rofes's experience to all contemporary men who acted upon, or even merely experienced, same-sex attraction, Rofes is a significant voice for the revival of an actively sexual culture among self-identified gay men, and his perspective, both from memory and research, must be examined and interrogated. How healthy is it, emotionally, physically, or psychologically, to adopt an identity which bases itself on an activity which appears prone to transmit disease as a part of its very nature? Yet this question appears never to have been asked in a broad or systemic way even, as one Rofes's interviewee notes, it was possible to document "two dozen specific sexually transmitted diseases" running among San Francisco men active with same-sex partners in the heady days of the gay rights movement.

A survey of the relevant medical literature reveals how deep and wide-ranging are the non-HIV related emotional and physical problems of homosexually active men. In the course of writing *Straight and Narrow? Compassion and Clarity in the Homosexuality Debate*, Author Thomas E. Schmidt surveyed more than two hundred scholarly, secular, medical, and social scientific publications that had offered research on some aspect of emotional, physical, or psychological health among homosexually active men. All of the journals consulted were either neutral on the subject of homosexuality or took an openly "affirming" position on the subject. As of 1995, here is the poignant way Schmidt summarizes his research findings:

> Suppose you were to move into a large house in San Francisco with a group of ten randomly selected homosexual men in their mid-thirties. According to the most recent research from scientific sources, whose authors are without exception either neutral or positive in their assessment of homosexual behavior, and with the use of lower numbers where the statistics differ, the relational and physical health of the group would look like this.
>
> Four of the ten men are currently in relationships, but only one of those is faithful to his partner and he will not be within a year. Four have never had a relationship that lasted more than a year and only one has had a relationship that lasted more than three years. Six are having sex regu-

larly with strangers, and the group averages almost two partners per person per month. Three of them occasionally take part in orgies. One is a sadomasochist. One prefers boys to men.

Three of the men are currently alcoholics, five have a history of alcohol abuse and four have a history of drug abuse. Three currently smoke cigarettes; five regularly use at least one illegal drug and three are multiple drug users. Four have a history of acute depression, three have seriously contemplated suicide and two have attempted suicide. Eight have a history of sexually transmitted diseases, eight currently carry infectious pathogens and three currently suffer from digestive or urinary ailments caused by these pathogens.

Again, the point of this chapter is not to throw stones at men who experience same-sex attraction or even those who act upon that temptation. In fact, it should be noted that Schmidt himself, in later paragraphs, makes it clear that it is same-sex sexual activity, rather than the mere experience of desire, that carries with it these costs. Further, I recognize that this statistical summary does not include all homosexually active men. I myself have known male couples that beat the odds on the average length of time in relationship, though none that remained monogamous throughout. Instead, the point is to make clear that the darkness that afflicts the homosexually active community is not merely a figment of imagination or of anti-homosexual propaganda but is instead a very real shadow with a very real associated price. Actively homosexual men and women who have been lucky enough to duck the darkness are overwhelmingly the exceptions, not the rule. If you are a homosexually active man or woman who has lived your life without any of these surveyed problems, count yourself lucky. The vast majority who have gone before you have not been as fortunate.

But this book seeks to do more than simply cry in the public square about a situation that, some argue, actively homosexual men (and some women too) bring on themselves. Rather, this book wishes to offer hope, even if it seems no stronger than the old gas streetlights, to beat back the deepening gloom from the lives of hundreds of thousands, if not millions, of men and women around the world.

Nihilism: the changing nature of darkness

In early spring of 1996, on my way to San Francisco to address a conference on chastity and homosexuality, I read in the *Washington Post* that noted gay activist and author Andrew Sullivan, the former editor of a prominent journal of opinion called *The New Republic,* had publicly come forward to reveal his HIV status. Sullivan was HIV positive. I recall sitting on the five-hour flight from Washington to San Francisco in a state of minor shock and grief. Sullivan and I were not great friends. Mutual acquaintances had introduced us at a couple of stuffy parties, but our sharply held and contradicting opinions kept our conversation politely at arms length. Yet, Sullivan and I shared enough commonality that I found myself tracking his career, reading some of his pieces and books with a mixture of appreciation and indignation. He and I both lived with same-sex attraction, both wrote, both cared passionately about the issues and problems of the day, both had been or were currently activists. In fact, I identified in some of Sullivan's "conservatively gay" positions many of my own assertions that I had only recently abandoned for a more orthodox Catholic approach. Most especially it was our common Catholicism from which I drew a link. We both lived lives as Catholics with same-sex attraction and had experienced, I was sure, that odd sense of ambivalent longing common to our position. Both of us experienced, I knew, the feeling of having a foot in two apparently sharply diverging communities. We each, I suspected, felt compelled, by both religious longings and sexual drives that neither one of us completely understood, to join communities whose goals were almost entirely at odds and yet whose roles in our lives felt completely essential. And now he had HIV, and I sat in a plane on the way to San Francisco to give a talk on chastity in a parish church within a few miles of the still heavily gay Castro District.

The news about Sulllvan weighed on my address. Although I had not written it with this situation in mind, I found several of my talk's themes resonating with my grief until, finally, I mentioned it directly. How sad, how tragic, I said, that one as young, intelligent, creative, and filled with promise should have been sidetracked into something as dark and, then particularly, hopeless as HIV. After all, AIDS and I were no strangers. Helping other friends live with the disease until they died had yanked away any inclination I might have felt to cover the disease in cotton-candy sentimentality. HIV is a potent, relentless agent in the human body. It attacks cells the body so needs that most people never even know of their existence until they stop working. Once these cells are destroyed, the body awaits invasion from armies of other pathogens like Rome open before the barbarians. Fungi, cancers, other sorts of viruses, parasites, and even other forms of degenerative diseases all have their day until, finally, the patient can no longer sustain both himself and the invaders and so dies. Absent a medical miracle, I said, this is what awaits Andrew Sullivan.

After I completed my talk, a young man, a gay activist who had been so upset with my lecture that he had walked out, approached and challenged what I said about Sullivan. After he introduced himself as Wayne he asked if I hadn't been "a little bit" too pessimistic about Sullivan's prognosis? Yes, I agreed, the shock of hearing the news might have left my thoughts a little bit too dark about it, although, I added, it was probably better to be too clear-eyed about AIDS than to not see clearly enough. Then, apparently emboldened by a lack of argument, he posed a question that staggered me. He asked whether I wasn't also being a little judgmental about AIDS. At first I despaired, imagining that he had left so early that he had missed crucial parts of my discussion. "No," I began, "I don't blame people living with AIDS for . . ."

"No, no," he said, "maybe he doesn't look at AIDS like you do. Maybe having HIV was his choice."

21

"I beg your pardon?" I said, certain I had misheard or misunderstood.

"What if he decided that living to age 50 or 60 or 70 without sex wasn't worth it?" Wayne asked. "What if having HIV is his choice? Aren't you being judgmental about HIV?"

Two days later, as the continent-hopping jetliner sped me toward home, I returned to Wayne's question. I hadn't had an answer for him there, and the intervening two days had been too busy for me to really think about it. The question left me feeling helpless and angry — as though somehow the years spent holding hands, encouraging eating, moving bedpans, and fixing meals for so many dying men had somehow been reduced to little more than a statement of whim. Could life, which I thought so important and worth fighting for, really be considered as something less important than sex? Did Wayne's question mean sex's importance as a basis for identity had reached too high a plateau or that life's importance as a context for everything else had diminished too much? And how many other actively homosexual men felt as Wayne alleged Sullivan might have felt?

Sadly, all too many. I soon discovered that while HIV gave rise to a community that seemed to pull together in the face of disaster, the virus and its diseases fostered in many individuals a powerful nihilism. The fruit of this nihilism runs a gamut from what I have come to call the "sex-at-any-cost" movement among some activists to the numbers of young, self-identified gay men who tell opinion pollsters that they never expect to see their fortieth birthday. An unwillingness to live life without sex or to restrict sexual contact to behavior dictated in so-called "safer sex" campaigns appears to underlie much contemporary gay nihilism. Given the choice of no sex or severely restricted sexual expression and risking even life itself, many sexually active men seem to be choosing risk.

Two attitudes have consistently turned up in my conversations (mostly done by e-mail) with men who confess to choosing sex at the risk of HIV. The first is the almost acidic nihilism that reflects surveys of young men who self-identify as gay and who state, rather blithely, that they do not expect to live to age forty. But the second may surprise, and I believe it represents reaffirmation of truth about sexual activity against the lies that our so-called sexual revolution has promulgated. Essentially, many of the homosexually active men I have interviewed, or have seen interviewed elsewhere, report seeking sex in general and, in particular sex without condoms, because they seek the connection, the deeper meaning and even "communion" they say sexual intimacy represents in their lives. In short, far from being something casual, light, easily manipulated, or cast off (the subject of safe sex "campaigns" for example), many homosexually active men think they have found even in same-sex relations something similar to the profound intimacy the Church teaches is one of sexual expression's chief aspects. We cannot accept the nihilism, these men seem to be saying, of a life reduced to condoms and masturbation even if practicing safer sex may extend our lives. We will seek a communion of sexual activity in order, we hope, to experience meaning, even if it means taking risks.

It has been an odd feeling as a former gay activist and now (at least striving to be) orthodox Catholic to read articles where Catholic couples and sexually active gay men can almost swap passages of dialogue. In one, Catholic couples returning to a deeper and more active faith describe their decisions to eschew contraception and, in another, actively homosexual men give reasons for why they have stopped using condoms. Both groups, at least on the emotional and physical level, expressed many of the same sentiments about the feeling of intimacy sexual expression brings to their lives, the shared closeness they experience during sex which condoms or other contraceptives help destroy.

This, of course, is not to imply an equality of value or even of approach. The willingness to open their lives to the possible realities of parenthood give the Catholic couples a depth of sexual communion that same-sex or otherwise intentionally infertile couples cannot share. Yet in these men's recognition of their need for intimacy, a spark of truth about the power and purpose of sex flickers. This spark, properly fed and fanned, might blaze into a fire large enough to draw thousands of men and women into an understanding of themselves and of their lives which does not rely on sexual attraction for identity or accept sexual activity as a price for intimacy.

This, then, is the reason for this book: To give witness to the truth about same-sex attraction and activity both as they are expressed in theology and philosophy and as I have found them in my life and observed them in the lives of friends. By drawing from an understanding about human nature that is defined in both dogma and daily life, I hope to reveal a humanity that goes deeper than mere sexual inclination. There is so much more to life than sex. Our stage as human beings is so much larger if we would but open our eyes to see it.

At its deepest level, this book is not about same-sex attraction *per se* but about Catholicism and the relationship with Himself into which Jesus Christ calls every Catholic. His is the light that cannot be hid, the city that shines on the hill and the hope that will not die — and He is open to everybody. I hope this book will help lay to rest the debate about whether that hope is closed to any individual or group of people because they live with sexual attractions or desires for members of their own sex. There is a better way of life both in this world and for the world to come. It is open to all, to quote the psalmist, who today hear God's voice and "harden not" their hearts.

CHAPTER TWO

Conversion

Lately at speaking engagements I have heard myself introduced as an adult convert to Christianity, a fact that is partially correct but not the entire story. My first real contact with Jesus Christ came in Mrs. Ivy's Sunday School class at the Metropolitan Baptist Church that still stands, as of this writing at least, on Sixth Street near East Capitol in Northeast Washington, D.C. Mrs. Ivy wore long skirts, black shoes, and her gray-white hair pulled back in a bun. I remember she smelled of rose water and goodness and something we kids thought was the aroma of cookies. In my memory, her pale china blue eyes focus on her charges and brightly snap as we come into the room. If I am feeling down or a bit discouraged about something, and I'm in a quiet place, my shoulders recall her embrace — Mrs. Ivy believed fiercely in hugs — and my cheek her almost bruising kiss and my ears her comforting voice, as fragile and lovely as a dried flower. We kids all loved her, of course. Simply because she loved us and routinely, Sunday in and Sunday out, she poured herself out for us so that we, no matter what our circumstances at home, might catch at least the tiniest glimpse of Jesus Christ. Mrs. Ivy made believing easy. If God could make Mrs. Ivy, my primitive theology ran, He was OK by me. When Mrs. Ivy (or later, as her arthritis grew worse, one of the other teachers) pounded out "Jesus Loves Me" on the sagging piano in the corner as we sang along I knew, just as certainly as there were stars in the sky, that it was true. Jesus *did* love me and all the other kids like me. All of us, whether red, yellow, black, or white, were really precious in his sight. I became a believer.

But, sadly, my faith did not last. Although both my parents were from North Louisiana, just to the right of the Bible Belt's buckle, neither one had brought their faith north with them — if they had ever had much. It wasn't that they opposed Christianity. Both, my mother in particular, honored Christianity's ethical code of how to treat other people. Rather, active Christianity clearly belonged to that part of their lives they sought to leave behind, along with tortured race relations, small-town parochialism, and the peculiar angst of Southern liberals. It says volumes, for example, that while I looked forward all week to Mrs. Ivy's Sunday School and singing about Jesus, my parents saw the time as an opportunity for an interlude with each other, coffee, and the Sunday *Washington Post*. But the facts also demand charity. The small-town Protestantism of my parents' childhood is a world away from expressions of faith now familiar to me. I cannot say, if faced with a narrow faith with much obvious conflict, I would have persevered any better than they did. Thus my sister and I were reared ethically, but not particularly faithfully.

This lack in my education produced some interesting side effects. Even at a fairly young age I remember being interested in some of what I recognize now as serious philosophical questions, for example "what is good" and "why be a good person." I recall, even as a young boy of eight or nine years of age, my mother dragging me along to help her deliver Meals on Wheels, which a local Methodist church ran out of its kitchen. Once a week my mother and I would drive over to the church and pick up the food and then set out on the rounds. My mother would pull our big Jeep Cherokee over to the curbside and I would get out with the cold meal and the hot meal (fresh from a big warmer box in the back) and carry it up to the house. I used to hate going and would sometimes plead not to have to go. The old people we visited weren't like Mrs. Ivy. They sometimes smelled of urine, not flowers, and when they hugged me it wasn't like Mrs. Ivy's warm embrace but something grasping and scary. Once a woman held me so long and fiercely that I was afraid she had died holding me and I would have to scream for someone to come and cut me loose from her twisted and greedy fingers. Later, when I carried food and hugs to men living with HIV, I recalled squirming out of those other lonely hugs — I understood, and felt ashamed.

I struggled to place the Meals on Wheels chore into my rudimentary moral context. Once, after a particularly smelly and scary round of delivering food, I demanded my mother tell me why. Why was it so important that we do this for these people? We didn't even know them! But the only answer I can recall my mother giving was that this was "what good people do," an answer which, even then, failed to satisfy and which, not surprisingly, left me more primed for doing bad than good. Who were "good people"? Was I one? Why? And if I was, did I want to be? I could recognize the goodness in someone like Mrs. Ivy, but I mistook it for a quality of her *being* rather than a result of her *striving* after grace. And I was rapidly concluding that there were two types of people in the world — good and bad — and that membership in each group was probably immutable and may not be a matter of choice.

In this regard even the Baptists, currently so active in promoting notions like virtue and knowledge of right and wrong, let me down. By the time I walked out of Sunday School for the last time, at age thirteen or so, I knew lots about God (old guy on the Heavenly Throne who zapped people) and the commandments (mostly dry rules) but not much about Jesus. In retrospect I have often wondered about this. How could a church that placed such a high importance on personal conversion and an intimate knowledge of Christ have done such a poor job of fleshing out Jesus for

27

me? Were my ears stopped? Did I simply not want to hear? Or was the message simply presented in such a way as to be unrecognizable? I don't know. But I began to believe "good" and "evil" were permanent categories of persons. Later events were going to make a strong case for my being in the "evil" category.

No discussion of my early foundation of faith would be complete without touching on my parents, their relationship with one another, and their relationship with me. American popular culture is now mired in a tendency to blame the parents for the problems of the children, but I will not do that. I have no desire to trash my former nest. My parents did the best with me that they knew how. In many ways I was a particularly challenging child whom they were trying to rear at a time when rearing children safely and sanely was extremely difficult. The problems my decisions have brought me are my responsibility and belong to me. Yet early family life has a strong influence on later spiritual life. Early family experiences often form the basis of natural personality that the Holy Spirit may, or may not, later build upon with supernatural grace. In my case, my early childhood left me with two obstacles the Holy Spirit would later need to transform: a deep inner conviction of failure and a corresponding loneliness.

During the late 1960s and early 1970s I imagine my father held one of the top one hundred most powerful positions in the US government, if anyone were to keep such a list. He served as both senior administrative aide and senior legislative aide to United States Senator Allen Ellender. At that time and until his death in office in 1972, Ellender served as the senior representative of Louisiana's congressional delegation and the Senate's president *pro tempore*. In that position, many important pieces of legislation needed Ellender's approval or at least cooperation to advance, and my father advised him on much of that legislation. My father lived a public life, with a lot of meetings, late-nights, and formal dinners. He was absent much of the time and carried himself with an air of grave importance when he was at home.

At home my father tended to work off my grandfather's

model of fatherhood. He looms in my memory as aloof and demanding as my primitive theology told me God must be. Things I did well (good grades, for example) were merely taken as givens, while problems I had (difficulties learning math or a foreign language) I understood to be shameful failures. My first real conviction that I must be stupid came on my parents' small patio when my father sat down with flash cards to teach me the multiplication tables that had completely confounded me in school. Having to teach his "stupid" son this way, I could tell, frustrated him deeply, and I hated doing it. Actually, scenes like this one are rare in my memory of my father. Most of the time I recall him as indifferent. It's not that he neglected the more proprietary part of being a father — food always came to our table, a roof covered our heads, and clothes warmed our backs. Rather, he wasn't particularly interested in my life unless he needed to discipline me for some failure, which he did in the bathroom with a wide belt.

Meanwhile, I recall my mother making herself all too accessible. Where my father was aloof, my mother was cloying. I quickly understood that the family dynamic was she and I against my father. My sister, wiser than her years or simply preserved by the four-year gap in our ages, mostly sat out the conflict. When my mom complained about my father — which she did with increasing vehemence as the years passed — she came to me at least some of the time. Her complaints assumed an authority in defining my father that was probably not useful.

In addition to my sense of failure at home, I also experienced early social and athletic setbacks. My father, who inherited his family's stature (at 5'9" on tiptoe I am a tall Morrison), didn't have a particularly strong sports career in school and tended not to push sports at home. I can't recall one time when my father ever tossed a ball with me. Sports weren't his thing, and I didn't make them my thing either. But my mother became very interested in my athletic life when, at age seven or so, my parents sent me down a slim little lad to visit my paternal grandparents in Louisiana and got back a boy a good deal heavier. This inaugurated my ongoing battle with weight and real hatred for my body, especially as I perceived it in the eyes of my peers. To her credit my mother saw the danger at hand and tried to help remedy it. But the constant battle over weight and diet, control versus the consolation food provided, tended to be merely one more place for me to fail.

For a while my mother and I found a solution in swimming. I liked the water, had picked up the necessary skills early, and there was a swim club that used the local Boys' Club pool downtown. While I enjoyed the hours of practice and the exercise surely kept the weight at bay, it was clear I was not in the same league as most of the others on the team. The nightly locker room high jinks and exposure did little for my body image. I remember one memorable night when, to my horror, I found I had lost my swimsuit somewhere between my front door and the pool. Officially, this was no big deal. At that more innocent time men and boys swam naked in the pool fairly routinely and I remember my friend Gus Anderson telling me how lucky I had been to lose my suit. "It feels pretty cool to swim naked," he said, grinning, "sorta tingles." But there was no way I could swim naked in front of all the guys on the team, before whom I already felt shy, and strangers too! When the carpool arrived and dropped us at the door, I hung back in dread and, in a flash, bolted from the lobby to walk seven or so miles across town to home. I might have made it, too, had not a passing US Park Service police cruiser taken an interest in why a pudgy ten-year-old boy was walking across the Washington Monument grounds with a beach towel at night. The officers flashed me in their spotlight to get me to stop and then took me home. My parents later rebuked and hugged me, but I can't recall if I ever told them the real reason I ran away.

My failures with sports, weight, and body image set up the final major childhood failure. Unlike many living with same-sex attraction, I don't believe I was "born gay." In fact, I was rather painfully and hopelessly heterosexual when, in fourth or fifth grade, I gave some toy or trinket I had won a neighborhood fair or school event to a girl I liked named Nancy. Even then, as clueless about girls as only a fifth grade boy can be, I knew my gift would be controversial. Nancy was rumored to be an "easy kisser" and even a devotee of "petting." Most of the other girls hated her, and the guys were mostly contemptuous. There would not be a lot of social support for my affection. Yet I thought her blond hair more than made up for her alleged moral failings. We were coming up on the last quarter of the school year. There wasn't a lot of time left, so I gave her the gift and caused an immediate furor. Neither the other girls' opprobrium nor the guys' open jeering, though embarrassing, pained me the most. Rather, what is burned into my memory is the look on her pretty face and the toss of her golden head when she shoved the toy back with a sniff: "I don't want any gifts from you." It was a pattern that would happen through junior high with other girls as well until, finally, I just stopped trying.

In the end I blame none of these struggles completely for the way things turned out. I cannot simply say, "There, that's the important one," or, "There, that's why he wound up attracted to boys." I rather think that all these struggles and failures were part of a larger piece. They twined around each other, supporting one another like vines choking a tree. My failure to believe I could ever please my parents, especially my father, gradually became a deep-seated attitude that spread tentacles throughout my life. My failure to lose weight, succeed at sports, and genuinely like my appearance contributed to my feeling constantly ill-at-ease with other boys and an alien among my peers. My failures to interact well with girls on anything but an intellectual or scholarly level tended to become a self-fulfilling prophecy. Girls found me "nice" to know but inadequate material for romance, a pattern which has endured (and which I may subconsciously project) even to the present day. But in the end, it probably all comes down to mystery and providence. Men whose lives made me most curious when I was in college or my twenties had pasts that bore close parallels with mine and yet did not wind up with same-sex attraction. How were our experiences different? What preserved men whose high school peers royally slammed them for being "nerds" or who failed at sports or who couldn't get a date if Armageddon was next week, from being drawn to other boys as I had been drawn? Why wasn't Woody Allen marching in gay pride parades? Why wasn't Bill Gates shacking up with a guy? Why hadn't anyone invented the pink triangle pocket protector? God only knows.

I want to present a balanced picture of my early life. There were happy days, weeks, and even months when I was a child. I treasure many childhood experiences and attitudes I gathered from my parents. Both gave me a love of learning and the ability to learn. Both, I know, love me. My parents were not blind to my loneliness and isolation, but I believe they genuinely didn't know what to do about it. At one point, on the advice of at least one of my teachers and over my father's objection, they sent me to a counselor my school recommended. She was a big Jewish lady who wore flowered clothes a lot and smelled a bit like Mrs. Ivy. But I didn't trust her, and when she began to get close after four visits, I stopped going. I knew my counseling time with her was doomed when, during my final session, I told her that as "sort of a literary exercise," I invented friends to write letters to and actually wrote them. A wave of shame at admitting, in my then teen years, to having invented "imaginary friends" broke over me and I didn't want any of my other secrets, like how I felt about some of these imaginary friends, to come out. No, the problem ran both ways. If my parents didn't know how to help me, I also didn't know how to let myself be helped.

The matrix of failures and doubts left me isolated and longing. Throughout my high school years I never allowed my few adolescent friends to really get to know me, to see me as a I really was, or to know how I really felt. Which is not to say I didn't want to. Something about traveling the difficult passage from boyhood to manhood demands allegiances and alliances, the brotherhoods of shared experience. I was deeply envious of the characters in the books I read who had those relationships; the Sawyers and Finns, the brothers in the *Swiss Family Robinson,* the beach trio in *Summer of '42*, the orphan fraternity of *Oliver Twist*, the Hardy

Boys. How strongly I wanted that experience — someone with whom I could safely be myself, someone to whom I could be loyal and from whom I could expect loyalty, someone with whom I could share encouragement. But such a friendship seemed unattainable.

Not surprisingly, these longings were the context for my first conscious same-sex attraction. I remember having my usual fantasies about being really good friends with boys I knew, but this time with the added twist of seeing what they looked like with their shirts off or, if I knew that already, their pants too. Somehow, in my fantasy life, I changed. No longer overweight and lacking coordination, I became an almost totally other boy with my fantasy friends — a better, happier, more confident boy, sharing some of my mental attributes and my name of course, but that was all. Few of these early fantasies I recall were specifically sexual, although if I thought this way in bed I would get this funny ticklish feeling and what I eventually learned were erections. But I lacked the knowledge I needed if they were to include a specifically sexual element, until one summer day.

On that day, when I was perhaps eleven or twelve, I met one of the neighborhood boys, whom I trusted and tended to idolize, in a narrow alley that ran from the back of my parents' house to Second Street. I don't remember his name or exactly where he lived, but he hung out at the neighborhood basketball courts. I admired him a lot for his skill and the fact that he wouldn't throw us younger kids off the courts when he came to play. He must have been about sixteen or seventeen then, with skin the color of *café au lait* that he got from having a mom who was white and a Jamaican dad. He wore jeans and a tank top T-shirt. I can't remember what I was doing in the alley that afternoon, maybe running an errand for my mother or just getting out of the house. But it was clear what he was doing — smoking and probably drinking beer out of the bottle concealed in the brown paper bag at his side. He stopped me. "Hey," he said.

"Hey," I replied.

"What's up, little man?"

"Not much." (If it was running an errand for my mother, it clearly could not have been too important.)

"Stay here and hang with me a bit. Smoke?" He offered me one of the cigarettes out the pack, tapping it so that only one stuck out, but I just shook my head no.

"Thas cool," he said. "Probably bad for you anyway, stunt your growth." Then he kind of laughed to himself. I didn't say anything, just watched as he smoked the cigarette. The late afternoon air felt drowsy and warm. Then he said, "Hey, wanta hear a joke?"

"Sure," I said.

"What's big and gray and comes in gallons?" He asked with a kinda funny smile.

"What?"

"An elephant," he said and then burst out laughing.

My confused expression must have given me away because he pulled up short. "Don't you get it? Elephants? Big animals? Shoot big loads?" My persistent confusion stopped him momentarily. "You know what come is, right?" I shook my head no, my face burning with embarrassment. As often as I had overheard the term on the playground, I still didn't know what it meant.

"Weeellll," he said, standing up suddenly. "It looks to me like somebody needs an education. Do you want to know what come is?" he asked. I hesitated. Part of me longed to find out, but another part was pretty sure it was something mostly "bad" people knew about. Yet here he was, right in front of me, offering to teach me something I had nobody else to teach me. I found myself nodding yes. "Cool, little man, follow me," he said and headed down some steps to a part of the alley which ran lower than the other, between the basement wall of one building and the alley itself. I remember how cool the air was down there, even only six feet lower than the upper alley, and how the light filtered down in patches from between the buildings overhead. And how private and quiet it was. He stood about eight feet down the lower alley with his back to the alley wall. "Come here, little man," he whispered, "let's show you what there is to show," and he started unsnapping his jeans. I remember my face flaming and my stomach weirdly tossing. I didn't want to go see, but it was as though my legs and eyes had a mind all their own. I stepped closer as he finished unsnapping and unzipping and his jeans sagged down his strong thighs, the bulge of his arousal tenting his white underwear out. "Yeah, little man, bet you never seen a big one hard have you," and he laughed that low laugh again. His jeans were at his knees now and he put his hands at his underwear as I stepped right up on him. I remember I felt almost dizzy with excitement and dread. My own was very hard with what I had just recently learned was called a boner, but I had never seen any one else's, much less a boy's as big and strong as he was. He slid his underwear down to mid thigh while his reared up like a snake in scary movie and slapped against his belly. I stepped back almost involuntarily. "Whoa, little man, ain't never seen one like that before I bet." He was clearly proud of it and I, wide-eyed, red-faced, and trembling, clearly impressed as much as I was repulsed, shook my head no. Then he looked at me expectantly. "Well, come on," he said, "let's see what you got." I shook my head "no" emphatically. Only two years previously I had decided to walk across town in the dark rather than swim naked with peers who had a whole lot less than he did. There was no way I was going to let him see mine, which was a whole lot smaller even hard. "C'mon, let's see," he reached down and began sliding down my zipper. At that point embarrassment kicked in even more strongly than failed virtue, and I turned and ran from the alley as fast my eleven-year-old legs could carry me. To this day I can still hear his laughter echoing strangely off the lower alley walls.

As much as that incident scared and embarrassed me, I replayed it that evening and many future evenings in bed and it assumed more importance as I have grown older and more reflective. Before that day, I might have longed for closer male friends. I might even have, in a minor way, eroticized that desire. But after that day, so much I innocently (and ignorantly) imagined became all too physical, sexual, and real. Surely it's possible that some other event might have done the same thing. After all, I could not hide from the world forever. But in my life it was this event, for better or worse, that made my fantasy friends fantasy sexual partners as well.

My first bona-fide affair happened about two years later, at age thirteen or fourteen. Robbie and I met over an extended time at Boy Scout summer camp when we each attended one week with our troops and one week as part of a provisional or "Provo" troop. Provo troops form at Scout camps so those scouts who are at camp alone will still have a troop. I remember the tightness in my belly, the thrill, when Robbie walked over and said: "Hi, you want to bunk in my tent?" His offer surprised and delighted me, since I had spent most of the morning on the bus to the Provo site admiring him from a seat in the back. Although a year older, he was no taller than I, but he moved athletically where I was clumsy. His body was slim and mature where mine remained heavy and mostly hairless; his personality was confident and cocky where shyness crippled mine. I remember how handsome I thought his face, with the tongue of black hair he frequently had to push out of his eyes. Later, in our tent's quiet shadows after taps when he pulled down his sleeping bag to show me just how developed he was, there was no question but that I would do what he asked even as I foresaw the pit of guilt waiting next morning. His approval, even his nickname for me — "Spunky" — proved a seduction more powerful than almost any I can imagine.

In many ways the affair with Robbie, though it lasted but a week, set a pattern of same-sex attraction that would follow for years. A boy or youth I admired or found attractive, often but not always older, would include me in his life and this often meant having sex. The relationship would persist for some weeks or months until he grew tired of my hanging around or until my own guilty conscience broke off the relationship. It never occurred to me that such friendship could be mine without sex, nor that the strong feelings I experienced could be better directed elsewhere.

I gradually came to believe I was a "bad" person, and much of my behavior reflected that belief. To my parents' consternation, I went from being a mostly malleable and obedient child to being shifty and dishonest. Once at age thirteen I was almost arrested for shoplifting. Other times I narrowly escaped being arrested for possession of minor amounts of marijuana, whether the boy-of-the-month's or mine. Only the threat of being pulled from my dearly beloved high school which, at least academically, offered me so much in my life, made me clean up my act. Superficially, at least.

I passed the next milestone at age nineteen or twenty, when the years of adolescent loneliness, frustration, guilt, and self-hatred finally concluded in a serious, self-destructive depression. By that time my parents' contradictory relationship had finally torn their marriage apart and my father was unavailable to voice his long-standing opposition to counseling. The unmistakable crisis in my life forced me to open up as I realized, in the words of an old rock-and-roll song, freedom really *is* just a word for nothing left to lose.

Strangely, I cannot remember my first counselor's name, but I recall so much else about him. He wore his brown hair short and the color of his little John Lennon glasses sort of matched it. I can never recall him in anything but jeans and a thick sweater with a collar that almost cradled his lean, long, and inscrutable face. His voice, when he spoke at all, reminded me of the sound my feet made walking through dry leaves. During the first three ninety-minute sessions he didn't say anything except to ask, quietly in the first five minutes of the very first session, "So, how can I help you?" He was the first person I told about the same-sex attraction in my life. "I think I'm homosexual," I blurted at the beginning of the second session. There, I had said it. Silence. I looked up at him and he didn't say anything. His face registered neither approval nor disgust. Somewhere, deep in the building, I heard the furnace rumble to life. "Well," he said finally. "Go on."

My life's revolution started in that nondescript office, under the too-bright lamps, sitting on the edge of a tacky, uncomfortable chair. It began to dawn on me that no one cared if I lived with same-sex attraction. The huge, unbearable secret that I had carried, denied even to myself for many years, turned out to be no big deal when seen in the open. Now, years later, this is one of the only things upon which advocates for same-sex activity and I agree: life is far better outside the closet than in it. No, I am not suggesting that everyone needs to cry from the rooftops that they live with some degree of same-sex attraction, and heaven forbid that I should swell the ranks of personalities on the *Jerry Springer Show*. But the power the attraction holds over life drops sharply when we first admit its existence to ourselves and then to at least one other person whom we trust and know loves and supports us.

From age twenty or so my advancement into gay life and activism was swift and steady. Within a few months I visited my first gay bar, a country-western place called Equus, in my own Washington neighborhood of Capitol Hill. I remember how nervous I felt, walking round and round the bar's block daring myself to go in and then how disappointed I was when everyone inside was so . . . ordinary looking. A week later, I first went with a man I met there to his home to have sex. He was older and flattering and offered to buy me a completely new wardrobe if I would just move in, but I was still scared and never called him after that night.

I got involved with activism through socializing. When I started taking classes at the University of Maryland at College Park, I decided to give the Gay and Lesbian Student Union (GLSU) a try and got hooked rather quickly. There is something almost intoxicating about being in a gay or lesbian group after hiding the attraction for many years. The common bond made quick friends for a boy who had spent years keeping his peers a distance. Without as strong a need for food as a consolation, my weight began to drop and soon I had a very full dance card indeed. Much of that first year of college was energetic, gleeful — almost heady. When one of the Campus Christian groups advanced a motion before the student government to cut the GLSU's funding, I was quick to offer myself for the defense. The University's student newspaper, the *Diamondback*, offered half its op-ed page to the controversy. I would write on one side defending the GLSU's right to use funds gathered as part of the University's Student Activities fee and, for the other side, a Christian would make the cases for why we should be forbidden to do so. At the time Christian apologetics on this issue were particularly immature and badly done (they are only slowly getting better) so the contest had an almost foregone conclusion. I wrote from my recent, real-life experience of growing up with a same-sex attraction in isolation, loneliness, and fear and of the liberation I found as part of GLSU. The Christian wrote that homosexuality was a sin, an overturning of the moral order, and deserved to be condemned. When the measure came before the student government, student lawmakers voted it down overwhelmingly.

In much the same way that my previous affair with Robbie set the pattern for much of my adolescent sexual life, this early activism established a pattern that characterized my activist career. Most of my activist work involved writing, speaking, and organizing against Christians and what was presented as the Christian position on homosexuality. I succeeded many times in doing this because most people, including myself, didn't know (and still don't know) what constituted the Christian position on homosexuality. What we understood to be the Christian position was really little more than a caricature, an impression created in ignorance but perpetuated because it helped activists make political and social points.

After college my activist career continued on a volunteer basis as I put together what passed, in the 1980s, for a very gay life. After a period of routine promiscuity, I settled down with one partner for what I hoped would be a lifetime. I began to advance, slowly, in my career as a writer and editor. I bought property, vacationed in "gay-friendly" places, had mostly gay friends, and told my family about my sexual identity shift. When the time came, I began to donate my time and money to helping friends and strangers react to the catastrophe of HIV/AIDS. With a mixture of care giving and activism as ever more friends and acquaintances sickened and died, I threw myself even more into working for change.

Ironically, working as a gay activist helped disillusion me about so much of the actively homosexual life. As hard as I wanted to believe the rhetoric I wrote, gradually the reality of what I promoted kept seeping through. It was not merely that so many were ill or dying — that produced a rage at my helplessness more than anything else. Rather, so little of this gay life came to hold any meaning for me. Over and over again I found myself thinking — whether in bed or in the gay bookstore, at dinner with gay friends, or protesting some injustice — is this all? Is this really all there is to my life? Is the most important thing really being gay? And I chided myself for having so much and feeling so ungrateful.

In hindsight, which is almost always perfect, I recognize that the angst I felt then was an inevitable result of a life built upon the shifting sands of an overwhelmingly sexualized — and sexually active — identity. No one spoke of such things then, and few speak of them now, but the common sexual denominator by which the gay community chooses to define itself most often produces a culture that is numbingly boring, dangerously self-indulgent, and spiritually stunted. Or, in the words of Larry Kramer, prominent gay author, "we don't have a gay culture . . . [w]e have our sexuality and we have made a culture out of our sexuality and that culture has killed us." Marshall Kirk and Hunter Madsen echo Kramer in their book *After the Ball* and get down to the root boredom that reduces so much of the gay culture to emptiness:

> As one gains experience, vanilla sex with one partner becomes familiar, tame, and boring and loses its capacity to arouse. At first, the increasingly jaded gay man seeks novelty in partners, rather than practices and becomes massively promiscuous; eventually all bodies become boring and only new practices will thrill. Two major avenues diverge in this yellow wood, two nerves upon which to press: that of raunch and that of aggression.

Actually, Hunter and Madsen were only partially correct. Despair presents a third option. It was in despair, late in the fall of 1992, that I found myself drinking too much beer at a friend's last barbecue of the season. As the crowd broke up I stayed to help clear the table and kill the case, and I expressed more and more of the acidic feelings that were eating away at my life. Finally my friend, who has since died and who, as far as I knew had never darkened a church door before his death, turned to me with his hands in the dishwater up to the elbows and asked, "why don't you pray about it?" I remember I was both surprised and offended. "Pray," I huffed to myself, "nobody prays anymore!" But my friend's suggestion outlived the next morning's hangover and I found myself pondering the idea deeply.

The idea finally came to fruition about five or six months later, in late April or May, when I had the house to myself. Turning the shower off and pulling the curtain, I noticed how absolutely quiet the warm spring air had become. Even the birds, usually so busy on the balcony, had flown away or gone silent. As I pulled my towel around my waist after drying off, the thought popped in my head, almost audible, "You could pray now." Oh, that's ridiculous, I thought, nobody prays anymore. But the thought persisted. "Just do it as an experiment. Nobody will find out." I sighed, stalked into the master bedroom, and knelt in the only attitude I could imagine for prayer, the only one Mrs. Ivy had endorsed so long ago: by the bed, elbows on the covers, like a little child. I paused. Now what? I didn't remember any prayers! So I offered the only prayer I could imagine I could offer honestly. "Lord, I don't even know if you exist, but if you do, I sure need you in my life."

And He came. The wind stirred the curtain slightly from the open window and I became, suddenly, deeply aware of a presence in the room. His presence. It's not that I saw Jesus or heard Him, but like the way a change of pressure pops the eardrums or the atmosphere weighs more heavily before a rain, I knew He was there. He was Jesus, He was there, and He loved me. In *Go Tell It On the Mountain,* James Baldwin's young character describes the moment of his conversion as a falling out of his life and of a jerking, desperate ascent from hell to heaven. There, on the hot, dusty floor of a storefront church, Baldwin's character sees clearly for the first time where he has been and what he must do. I, on the carpeted bedroom floor, saw a similar vision. It's not that Jesus negated my sins. It's not that He declared them null and void as if I had never done them. Instead, like oil upon my troubled soul, He soothed and calmed me in the midst of my wrongdoing. Panting and crying in the bloody afterbirth of my own sins I understood, suddenly and irrevocably. In His eyes there are no "bad people" — only His children who have been deceived about who they are. From that moment everything about my life changed. Not immediately and not easily, but inexorably and firmly, like a plant growing up from the concrete. Change has come.

CHAPTER THREE

"Gay Christian"

I got up from my bedroom floor that morning, tired, red-eyed, and filled with more questions than answers. When Jesus told Nicodemus that people must be born of both water and the spirit to see the Kingdom of God, He didn't add much about life after that point. Most people come to Christ assisted by other people. Their parents baptize them as children and godparents help teach them the faith. A friend tells them about the Gospel or invites them to share worship services. They answer an altar call or accept an invitation to Sunday school. In most cases new Christians have other, more experienced Christians to midwife their conversion. By accident or God's design, I had no one. The friend who first planted the idea of prayer was not a Christian and I imagine he may have been surprised to hear what grew up from the seed so easily cast. I began my Christian life without a church, without Christian friends, without even a Bible, standing instead on the power of a deep experience where the God of the universe had heard a small, humble, and skeptical prayer and seen fit to draw near.

I didn't network to find my first church — after all, as none of my friends or family were Christian, whom would I ask? —

but instead turned to an instinctive practicality. I found it in the yellow pages, after scanning the boxes and lines for the mix of location and denomination that I hoped would most fit.

Mrs. Ivy notwithstanding, enough water had flown under the bridges of my life that I didn't expect to feel comfortable with the Southern Baptists again. But I had come to know Anglicans through the work of groups like Episcopal Care and Action on AIDS and found them, on the whole, to be sane, friendly, and open. At least their eyes didn't register shock and disgust when I told them I was gay. So I started looking for an Episcopal Church and on the Sunday after my experience on the bedroom floor. I found myself, feeling awkward in my good clothes, sitting at the back of Trinity Episcopal Church on Columbia Pike in Arlington, Virginia. While some things appeared similar to the Metropolitan Baptist sanctuary of my youth — a cavernous and shadowy hall in my memory — other elements confused me. On the one hand I recognized Trinity's very Low Church decorations, very Baptist, very little gold, no stained glass, very clean lines. A similar parade of pews, fewer in number than Metropolitan, marched from the back of the sanctuary to the front, but sitting in them felt harder than I remembered. The windows, free of any remotely Roman stain, let in the outside. Everyone sang from a red-backed book. Then a number of people got up and read from the Bible and then the pastor rose to preach. All this echoed in my memory. But an unfamiliar altar table also stood in the front of the sanctuary, and after the sermon I found something else here too, something new to me but that I also understood to be very old. After the sermon the pastor led the congregation in an assertion of why they had gotten out of bed so early on a Sunday morning, of why they were here. After an older man handed me his book open to the right page, I began taking part, linked in some powerful way with everyone else in the room. *We believe in one God, the Father, the Almighty, maker of heaven and earth, of all that is, seen and unseen* . . . and I began to believe I might have found a place to stay.

My early experience with the Bible did not go as smoothly. My first Bible had a red, faux-leather cover, thin pages I could see through, and Jesus' words in red as translated by the body of "scholars" responsible for the *New Revised Standard Version*. I can't remember exactly why I chose that one. It may have been on special sale at Virginia Seminary's bookstore where I bought almost all my early Christian books. (Seminarians from Virginia Seminary had ridden horses to the early Trinity Chapel when it was still merely a chapel on the ground of the Lee family's Arlington estate, and there was still a close connection between parish and school.)

I brought the book home, curious about it. I knew that what I understood as the Christian position on homosexuality stemmed in a large part from the text of this book and I felt an odd disquiet about it. Was it possible that Christians were right? Did God, the God who had so recently shared with me such an enormously loving presence, really condemn my sex and love life? I wondered what God had to say about it all and I decided to try an experiment that I read about somewhere. Kneeling beside my bed when I was alone at home I put the Bible on the covers and prayed, "Jesus, I really want to see what you have to say about this; please show me." Then, truly at random, I opened the Bible to Genesis, chapter nineteen, the story of the Destruction of Sodom and Gomorra. Heart sinking and racing at the same time I read the account and swiftly shut the book. Conviction loomed. I had prayed and God had answered. Now what was I going to do?

Not surprisingly, I wasn't the first person living with same-sex attraction to have confronted Christianity's historic teaching on that subject and asked that question. Although I didn't see it right then, I stood on the edge of great crowd of clerics, theologians, gay and lesbian activists, and others who have spent a significant part of their lives working to reconcile Christianity and same-sex sexual activity, and I found them soon enough.

My first contact came via an internet service. Online services, then in their relative infancy, have long held a special attraction for people living with same-sex attraction, providing the necessary mix of anonymity and connection to people separated by many miles. Even today, as many as half of the public "chat" rooms or forums available through some popular internet services are devoted to same-sex themes. It was in one of these that I first came across so-called "gay theology."

A woman, I think named Torry, first explained the rudiments of gay theology. Torry told me she was "out of the closet" as a lesbian, and a minister of a small church on the West Coast which was part of an "evangelical" organization of gay and lesbian Christians called T.E.N. (The Evangelical Network). Torry, whose background was evangelical and charismatic Protestantism, had lost her place in previous churches after confessing her wish to act upon same-sex attraction. I remember her attitude on the phone was humorous, loving, and patient. She told me not only that the Bible had nothing to say about homosexuality as we understood it, but that even the scriptural condemnation of same-sex activity was "hopelessly culturally conditioned." She took her primary Scripture references from St. Paul's letter to the Romans, its eighth chapter, first "There is therefore now no condemnation for those who are in Christ Jesus" (8:1), and then "Who shall separate us from the love of Christ? Shall tribulation, or distress, or persecution, or famine, or nakedness, or peril, or sword?" (8:35). No amount of persecution or confusion from Christians who didn't understand could pull me from Jesus, Torry said. I recall that her words fell on willing but disquieted ears. It wasn't just concern about what people might say that bothered me. I wanted to do the right thing. In later phone conversations with her, I tried to explain, for the first time ever, what had happened when I had asked God for help and He had sent me Jesus. Torry listened and, in a few minutes, I could hear her sniffle a little bit. Jesus had touched me, she said, and it was important I not turn my back on the way He had made me (Torry believed that God created people gay or lesbian). But, she said, it was better I not listen to her (or anyone else about this). T.E.N. published a workbook designed to help believers "work through" Scripture's "killer passages" allegedly dealing with homosexuality, and she would send me one.

It's important to note my state of mind at this time. It's not that I felt hopelessly in love with active homosexuality. Actually, by the time of my conversion I had fallen away from many of the more public and sexual same-sex activities (attending bars, cruising, vacationing in "gay friendly" places). I recall even thinking to myself that if I lost those things as a cost of following Christ … well, no great loss. But I was also involved in a relationship of seven or eight years at that point, a relationship that, while it had a lot of codependency in it, nonetheless was very important to me. The possibility of losing this relationship, the fear of what might happen, provided much of the energy for my initial push into so-called "gay theology."

The workbook arrived. Appearing to have been photocopied rather than printed, the half- inch-thick volume took a more skeptical than dogmatic approach to the Scripture in question. I can't recall the book ever saying outright that the Scriptures condoned homosexuality, but working through the workbook significantly clouded the interpretation that traditional Christianity has most often used — that Scripture condemns active homosexuality.

For example, Torry (or the workbook) pointed out that the idea of homosexuality (or a predominant sexual and emotional attraction to one's own sex) had not occurred to anyone when Scripture was written, and thus Scripture should not be used to condemn it out of hand. I turned to the workbook's discussion of Genesis 19, the chapter which had so convicted me just weeks earlier. The workbook pointed out that the rest of the Bible condemns Sodom and Gomorrah not for homosexuality but for greed and unwillingness to live by the covenant God has delivered. Further, the crucial sense of the Hebrew word *yadha* (to know) as sexual intercourse, upon which the anti-homosexual exegesis hangs, only occurs ten other times in the rest of Scripture. Rather than homosexuality, most of the rest of Scripture equates Sodom with far more universal human failings. In addition to making the name Sodom almost a code for spiritual infidelity, the prophet Ezekiel specifically laid the city's charges before her. "Behold," the prophet said, "this was the guilt of your sister Sodom: she and her daughters had pride, surfeit of food, and prosperous ease, but did not aid the poor and needy" (Ezekiel 16:49). Since, the workbook asked, Christian tradition demands Scripture first interpret itself in light of other Scripture, is it proper to contend that Genesis nineteen primarily concerns homosexuality? Instead, the workbook suggested that Sodom's real crimes were inhospitality (a tradition with a good deal more meaning in the Near East of that time than in ours) and homosexual rape akin to prison rape. In this regard the workbook seemed to be on as thin an ice as the traditional position, as neither one of these appeared elsewhere in Scripture either. But then the workbook asked that I compare the Genesis nineteen story with a similar tale in Judges.

The two passages are remarkably similar. In the Sodom story of Genesis nineteen, two angels encounter Lot sitting in the gates of the city and he invites them to his house, over their initial objections that they will remain that night in the street. During the night "the men of [Sodom], both young and old, all the people to the last man, surrounded the house" and demanded Lot's visitors be put out of his house so that they could be raped. Lot, appalled that his neighbors would act this way, offers the crowd the sexual use of his daughters, something that shocks twenty-first century audiences as much as the demand of the city's residents concerning the men. The crowd refuses and demands the visitors again and, at that point, the angels reveal their angelic power by striking the crowd blind, giving Lot and his family time enough to flee the city before the judgment of heaven overturns the city.

The passage in Judges, chapter nineteen, is longer but very similar. A traveler making his way home with a female companion (a concubine) stops for the night in the town of Gibeah, which was in the part of Israel belonging to the tribe of Benjamin. Similarly to the angels, the visitor has no place to stay and one of the men of the town opens his home to him. Just as in the Sodom story, "the men of the town, base fellows, beset the house round about, beating on the door" (19:22) and demanding that the visitor be turned over to them for sexual abuse. The man, like Lot, offers the crowd his own daughter and the visitor's concubine but the crowd refuses. Finally, in desperation, the man puts out his concubine and the crowd rapes and kills her. But aside from the gruesome ending, the story differs from the Sodom tale in that God does not overthrow Gibeah. Instead, the incident sparks a long war between Benjamin and the other tribes of Israel.

The comparison of the two passages, whose language and events appeared so similar, really made me pause. How likely would it have been, I thought, for God to have rained fire and brimstone on Sodom for the attempted rape of the strangers (the traditional position) and yet apparently done nothing about the incident in Judges? Further, there was the whole matter of the innocents in Sodom. How credible was it to suppose that all the men, much less women and children, were *all* actively pursuing homosexual sex? *Lord of the Flies'* metaphor notwithstanding, I thought of the toddlers and other small children I had known in my life. How likely was it that they were all corrupted and deserving death? And if they were not, what did their deaths say about God? I walked away from the passage considerably more confused than when I began examining it. I had been so sure of what God seemed to have been saying. Could I have been so far off the mark?

Similar passages, when put through Torry's workbook, also lost much of their punch. When viewed on their face the prohibitions in Leviticus, chapters eighteen and twenty, appear to be fairly cut and dried. "You shall not lie with a male as with a woman; it is an abomination," declares the eighteenth chapter, verse twenty-two. The twentieth chapter, verse thirteen, adds that "if a man lies with a male as with a woman, both of them have committed an abomination; they shall be put to death, their blood is upon them." Yet the workbook demanded that I look closely at the context for these chapters, which occur as part of so-called Holiness Code by which God asked the Hebrew nation to separate itself from its neighbors' idolatry and other practices. Viewed in this context, didn't it seem likely that what this chapter originally condemned was not so much homosexual behavior between consenting adults but ritual or temple prostitution as practiced as part of idolatrous rituals?

And so it went. Paul, writing in the first chapter of his famous letter to the Church in Rome, seemed to condemn homo-sexuality as a symptom of an idolatrous culture and mindset, but wasn't it more likely that he was harking back to the Holiness Code? In his letter to the Church in Corinth and his subsequent letter to Timothy, he uses two words that would seem to condemn homo-sexuals and keep them from inheriting the Kingdom of God. But when it is examined, can we really claim to know that *arsenokotai,* a compound word made from the words for intercourse (*kotai*) and man (*arseno*), really meant male-intercourse? I can still recall Torry's scorn of the traditional position on this point. "Good grief," she exploded into the phone, "two thousand years from now some-one might come across our English term 'ladykiller.' Now will they interpret that to mean someone who kills ladies or a lady who kills? Neither one is the right meaning in our cultural context but they are the only possibilities that can be drawn from that word."

By the end of the workbook I had, more or less, signed on to the "Gay Christian" position, although I still had doubts. The shadow of the Cross fell across my heart and I had found it more chilling than reassuring. If this compromise was what was needed to keep peace between the Body of Christ and myself, then so be it. I could only hope that Christ's heart would be big enough for all of us.

Of course, what I lacked at this point was knowledge of the depth of discipleship and the broader context in other Scripture, in my own life, and in the life of the Church, for these passages. The Church's position (and my own) on the proper expression of marital sexuality, on chastity in and out of marriage, and on the immorality of same-sex sexual acts does not rest only upon the teachings of Scripture; they also draw upon the teachings and example of tradition, the evidence of natural law, and the mystery of what true discipleship concerns. Viewed alone, in an isolated way (which is how many Christian apologists on both sides of the question have traditionally approached them), it is possible to argue that these passages of Scripture lack an ability to completely address the question of same-sex sexual activity. I think such a case amounts to a special pleading in exegesis, and doing so reminds me of the old expression that "a text without a context is a pretext." Yet such a case is the one advanced by gay theology and one which, for a while, I accepted as a workable compromise.

But the gay Christian position carried an additional lure, beyond my own relatively naïve and narrow self-interest. As a part of the gay community for more than seven years at that point, I had heard many stories of cruelty, loss, and sorrow that my friends had suffered at the hands of people claiming to be Christ's followers. Some acquaintances and friends had been the subjects of sermons in their churches while they sat in the pews. In one terrifically horrid case, the preacher had pointed at my friend from the pulpit (my friend was age thirteen at the time) when he got to the part of the sermon about the hell awaiting homosexuals. Pastors had told others, beaten by their peers, only that they needed to "straighten up" if they wanted to insure that such things did not happen again. Other pastors and priests, though they had been well-liked, were dismissed once their congregations discovered the reality of their same-sex attraction. Christians could not seem to acknowledge their double standard concerning sexual sins. Sexual misdeeds on the part of heterosexual males, including even large sins like adultery, multiple marriage, fornication, and pornography appeared to get a wink and nod from Christians even as the same things done by gays brought rivers of condemnation. Just as I had long ago begun to oppose Christians politically, so now too I began to oppose much of what seem to pass for Christian pastoral policy on this issue as well.

During this time friends asked why I bothered with Christianity at all. Although he respected me too much to say so, I think my partner spent much of this period when I was discovering Christianity hoping it was a phase. Other friends were more direct, demanding at one point that I "come to my senses" or accusing me, as one did, of "joining the enemy." Before all of these, almost with Christ before Pilate as my example, I remained determined, and I quietly kept learning more about Christ. As much as I may have compromised on gay theology, as oddly out of place as I felt at both Christian *and* gay events, Christ's touch on me on my bedroom floor remained locked in my memory. All loose ends aside, deep in my heart I knew Christ was the answer to so many of mine and my friends' enduring problems. So many with whom I shared a social circle then had lives which were certainly "gay," but very little of how they lived brought genuine satisfaction or seemed to make them really happy. The worm that gnaws at so much of what this world treasures, about which Jesus tried to warn us, remained as hungry as ever.

My developing friendship and communion with the Christians I met at my parish served, crucially, as almost the only brake on my slide into a solidly gay Christianity. I simply couldn't figure them out. Why should we be friends? We had so little in common! Most of them had spouses, lawns, pets, kids — in the words of one of John Cheever's characters, "the whole catastrophe." So many barriers appeared to loom between us. In addition to their living situations, most of them were older than I, some were of other races, many or most had been Christians for a long time, and many were from stable family and youth backgrounds. Further, I had no doubts that most of them were very conservative. As part of its "low" Anglican tradition, Trinity Parish retained an almost evangelical character. Sure, I noticed that none of the people I met made anti-gay comments (even though I was not obviously gay) and I noticed that most were not overly political — but I felt sure they voted Republican (actually the political breakdown turned out to be about fifty-fifty).

But when I was honest with myself about it, I had to admit Trinity's evangelism attracted me. I liked that Trinity parishioners knew Jesus and why they came to worship and what they were about. I liked that the rector, a Michigan-born man named Nicholas Lubelfeld who had been educated in England, did not fear to talk about sin. I liked that Trinity kept up a tract rack in the back of the Church and that the tracts dealt with both "practical" questions like alcoholism, good parenting, and better marriages as well as "theological" matters like "The Episcopal Church: Trinitarian or Unitarian?" But I was still an activist, and knew I wouldn't want to stay in the closet. There was only one thing I could do. I had to come out to the rector. I made a mid-week appointment to talk to Nicholas.

When I think back on it now, my fear of that interview almost makes me laugh. About a week in advance of the meeting I called a friend of Episcopal Care and Action on AIDS to ask about Trinity and Nicholas in particular. Without revealing anything proprietary or private, what could she tell me about them both? Yes, she said, Trinity was one of Episcopal Care's supporting parishes in Northern Virginia, although she didn't know much about Nicholas. "I think his reputation is mostly conservative but a thinking man," she said. "He hasn't been to many supporters' meetings but I don't think he has ever stood in the way of our trying to raise funds." My hopes for the meeting rose.

Nicholas welcomed me into his marvelous office on, I think, a Wednesday afternoon, after lunch. I had warned him that this might be a somewhat lengthy meeting and he had done me the service of clearing most of his afternoon schedule. While I sat jumpy as a cat on the large couch, he tilted his head back in the big chair and listened to a condensed version of my life to that point. I told him about my family and my upbringing, about my discovering same-sex attraction at a relatively early age, about the University and my friendships there, about my having a partner of many years' duration, about my anxiety that the Gospel message make it further into the gay community. Through it all Nicholas sat listening, nodding sometimes, occasionally writing something down to jog his memory later. Ever polite, he saved his questions until after I had finished and then had only three or four. Was I sexually active with my partner now? Did I love my partner and, most surprisingly for me at that time . . . what did I need from him?

His question pulled me up short. I hadn't come into the meeting with an agenda for requests and I remember I stammered my answer. "Umm, well, I don't know. I guess I just wanted you to know you had a gay activist in your congregation," I said. He nodded and then leaned forward, his serious eyes looking right at me — I have remembered what he said ever since because it had such an enormous impact on my life. "David, if you need me to affirm what you do in bed, I can't, because I think that's sin. But if you need me to affirm you as a brother in Christ I can do that. Anyone who confesses Christ is welcome here." I thought about it. Did my sex life need "affirmation?" No, not really. Certainly I could be open-minded enough to recognize that there were two positions on the issue, and besides, it was clear that Nicholas didn't hate me and he might be open to changing his mind. So I got up and offered my hand. "That sounds workable to me," I said, and then sucked in my breath as Nicholas rose and embraced me with one of his strong and bearish hugs.

Thus began one of the most remarkable periods of my life so far, the year that I — a homosexually-active, openly-gay, and fairly aggressive political activist — spent with an evangelically-minded Anglican congregation and liked it. As the year began I planned to worship Christ with the Trinitarians and, perhaps, educate them out of any "backward" ideas they may have had. By the end of that year, my backward and wrongheaded ideas were the ones that had changed, as the same God who had called them called me into an ever-deepening communion with Himself.

CHAPTER FOUR

"Christian Gay"

Ironically, but not surprisingly, other so-called gay Christians played an important role in undermining my faith in gay Christianity. It wasn't so much that they were "bad" or unfriendly people, rather it was that in so many ways they resembled the world of actively homosexual non-Christians. My relationships with Torry and other gay Christians began and remained friendly, but gradually I felt a tinge of frustration. If Christianity in the gay church looked so much like life outside the gay church, I thought, why bother?

I made a good effort, over a number of months, at joining in. Many Catholics and Anglicans in the United States (and some places overseas) will recognize the Catholic group Dignity and its Episcopalian counterpart, Integrity. Headquartered in Washington D.C., Dignity is a national organization in the United States with ties to similar groups overseas. The group claims, not unreasonably, about seventy-five chapters in the United States, though many of these, at least in my experience, were very small. Essentially, Dignity exists in opposition to the Roman Catholic Church's teachings on homosexuality in particular and sexuality in general. Dignity's statement of purpose declares the group exists in part to "work for the development of sexual theology leading to the reform of its teachings and practices regarding human sexuality, and for the acceptance of gay, lesbian, bisexual and transgendered peoples as full and equal members of the one Christ." In practical terms that means Dignity promulgates all the teachings of gay theology that I learned from Torry and T.E.N. *and* challenges the natural law about sexual expression and the meaning of sex that also underpins the Church's teachings on this issue (and which I will discuss later). Thus, for example, in the online version of the brochure *Catholicism, Homosexuality and Dignity,* the group opines:

> Besides appealing to Scripture and Tradition (constant Church teaching), the Catholic approach to morality also relies heavily on human reasoning. The argument from natural law is a prime example. Other instances are the study of the human sciences or attention to people's personal experiences. But arguments from natural law are inconclusive, for the nature of human sexuality is debated. Procreation is certainly one aspect of sexuality. Yet the Catholic Church allows marriage between known sterile couples and sex between couples beyond childbearing age. Moreover, Catholic teaching has recently emphasized the unitive aspect of sex — loving, caring, interpersonal sharing. Is the biological or the personal the key aspect of sex among human beings?

This I swiftly recognized was the heart of the matter. While I hadn't done much thinking on the question, I was willing to accept at least what appeared written on paper. But how Dignity's paper theology played out in real life left me with deep misgivings.

All the Dignity worship services I attended, while welcoming me as a non-Catholic, lacked, ironically, the dignity that I had come to expect and appreciate in worship. I didn't come to church to hug or be hugged, to cruise or be cruised. I didn't come to church as a prelude to seeing the same people with whom I shared Mass at the bars a few short hours later. I came to Church seeking an opportunity to deepen the connection with the God who loved me no matter what. I came for love, but all too often I got a grope instead. Frequently, I also got an apology printed in the service leaflet for the "sexist elements" in the Nicene Creed.

I tried Integrity for a while too. Founded in 1974, Integrity has been called "Dignity Lite," but that's not particularly fair or accurate. Just as the Episcopal Church in the United States lags behind the Roman Catholic Church in size, so, naturally, Integrity's size lags behind Dignity's. But Integrity has made very good use of the Episcopal Church USA's open democratic structure and historic liberalism to push its agenda. Even in the early '90s it was evident to other activists and myself that it would only be a matter of time before the ECUSA would openly celebrate same-sex marriages (or "unions") and come down firmly on the side of gay rights. I found in Integrity services many of the same problems I had found in Dignity and, if it were a possible, an even greater elevation of the politically correct over the spiritually centered.

But worship style and political pushiness only symbolized the deeper problems I had with their communal life: the lack of focus, the lack of what I came to realize is called "discipleship," and the unremitting sameness of it all. In short, being a Dignity Catholic or an Integrity Anglican didn't seem to mean much when it came to how one lived life, particularly in the bedroom. I lost track of the numbers of Dignity members I met who had long reserved a spot in the "serial monogamy" parade. "Serial monogamy" came into fashion as ever-greater numbers of credible researchers linked the expanding HIV epidemic with promiscuity. Instead of having four sexual partners in a week, for example, serial monogamy suggested having four in a month, or even two months, and thus keep oneself safer from the AIDS virus. I could see how that might help slow the spread of HIV, but I wasn't at all sure how it stood up as a standard for Christian behavior. I recall the case of a deacon, an ordained man, who was HIV positive but who had not allowed either his ordination or HIV status to interfere with his pursuit of sexual partners. He did allow that since discovering his HIV he didn't "bottom" (passively participate in anal sex) as much as he used to.

I discovered that in 1989 a committee of Dignity members, the Task Force on Sexual Ethics, presented a document for the general membership's approval that was meant to reflect the organization's guidelines on what was or was not moral sexually. It reflected the membership's general confusion on the topic. I discovered that the document, *Sexual Ethics: Experience, Growth and Challenge*, came from a "task force" whose ideological commitment ran counter to the notion of the Church instructing its members in the faith. Instead, it held that instruction ran in the other direction, declaring that "[t]he operative principle [in the document's creation] was that the Church must be instructed by the lived experience of its members." This "lived experience" included many of the sexual couplings possible, and the document listed some:

> Most of us almost instinctively reject sexual activity that is selfish or manipulative, that harms or exploits. Some prefer to reserve sexual lovemaking for one person in the context of a lifelong commitment, and many regard lifelong fidelity in a monogamous relationship as the ideal to strive for. Other couples have remained faithful to one another while allowing for some sexual expression outside their relationship, and some attempt completely open relationships. Others of us are sexually active as singles, either because we choose to be single, or because we have not yet found a companion.

In short, virtually anything goes, and the more I got to know of Dignity members, the more I began to realize that a church led by such an ethic would truly be a pit into which the blind had led the blind.

The other deep problem I had with both groups concerned their numbing sameness and relatively narrow vision. Standing one day in a crowd of gay men and a few lesbian women at a Dignity Mass, I realized in an almost visceral way how deeply identical we all were. Despite our disparate histories and our somewhat varying backgrounds, we remained almost overwhelmingly white, middle class, and ideologically dedicated to the notion that whatever we did in bed must be OK. I suddenly understood part of what made Trinity so attractive to me: *I wasn't like everyone else*. I had friends there who were different colors, different nationalities, from vastly different backgrounds, and of many ages. Trinity was a place that offered the full Christian experience: babies were baptized, youth confirmed, the dead buried, couples married, strangers welcomed and, above all, the Gospel preached. No singular selfishness in these people's lives had brought them together in that place, nor any single worldly interest. They came to Trinity because Christ had called them. At Trinity, Christ, not any ideology or particular interest, ruled. Over time I stopped attending Dignity and Integrity events.

The way Nicholas, his family, and other Trinity parishioners treated me also undermined my commitment to gay theology and made it easier to leave the Dignity/Integrity orbit. While it is true that I left Nicholas's office after the interview with few ground rules, I did have a couple. First, Nicholas expected that responsible Christian adults would take a role in helping to make the parish a better place, and I soon found myself serving the Parish as Director of Adult Education. Second, Nicholas didn't want me to hide the fact of my same-sex attraction from the parish. While he didn't advocate my passing out flyers about it on the steps after church on Sunday, he also didn't want me to take any pains to hide the facts of my life. "Controversy we can confront and address as a parish," he said, "but secrets can really destroy a community."

So, I didn't keep any. I maintained a simple rule on self-revelation. Until I found I would have to lie to cover up the fact — changing my partner's name in conversation to a woman's for example — the matter remained moot. Once it became clear I would have to lie, I told the other party. My revelation surprised most, if not all, of them.

No one, during my entire time at Trinity, agreed with me on the issues surrounding same-sex attraction and activity. But I also never met anyone who "hated" me because of my sexual identity or found our disagreement so disturbing that we could not be friends. Despite our disputes, I was still invited regularly to Bible studies, prayer groups, Baptisms, dinners, brunches, picnics, and other activities. I found that far from being the "black sheep" in Trinity's fold, our little flock had a number of people with pasts which would make my stereotyped stuffy Christians (if any such existed outside of my own mind) blush. I met Anne, a woman whose tattoos mutely testified to her life of alcohol and other abuse before she came to Christ. Gerald, a dignified older Englishman, whose days had been those of a typical merchant mariner, had women in many ports before Jesus called him to "follow me." Susan told me of how, in prayer, Christ had comforted and reassured her that she would one day see her child, aborted when Susan was seventeen. Alan told me of his struggles with misunderstanding and discrimination due to the serious epilepsy which, eventually, contributed to his death. I discovered that the old maxim was true. The Church of Jesus Christ existed far more as a hospital for sinners than as a hotel for saints. All of us, each one in our unique and horrid way, had contributed to the reason Jesus strangled to death on His Cross.

I cannot emphasize too strongly the need among Christians to cultivate this attitude of memory and humility. St. Paul wrote it best in his letter to the Church in Corinth:

> For consider your call, brethren; not many of you
> were wise according to worldly standards, . . .

not many were of noble birth; but God chose what is foolish in the world to shame the wise, God chose what is weak in the world to shame the strong, God chose what is low and despised in the world, even things that are not, to bring to nothing things that are, so that no human being might boast in the presence of God (1 Corinthians 1:26-29).

I wonder sometimes if some Christians really read that passage carefully and listen to it. God chooses the *despised* things of the world, the lowly things, the things that are not, the things of our society and culture that little children on school playgrounds cast into insults, so that none may boast before Him. Some do perhaps, but most don't. We hold our sins before our eyes. We know who we are. Yet many Christians do boast. We boast every time we allow our shock at someone's else's sins to show, every time we act surprised at how someone else's depravity has leapt the shallow wall of their heart and made it into action. Some people are innocent. Some of the things I write about in this book may shock and surprise those who have led more sheltered lives. But if these things shock, it must be because they are unfamiliar, not because "good people" don't act this way. Christians must remember that we were not chosen because we were good. God did not want us because we were worthy. In one very real sense God did not choose at all but allowed us to choose. Each one of us, by getting to a point in our lives where we ceased struggling and let God love us (which is what He has wanted to do anyway), chose for God. In the question of our salvation, God is the suitor and we, no matter our human gender, the much-sought-and-treasured beloved.

That understanding of God and his role in my life was one of the fruits of the third element which undercut my belief in gay theology — my Baptism and the study time that preceded it.

When I came to Trinity I came believing that at some point in my previous Christian life I must have been baptized. I had attended a Southern Baptist Sunday school for almost a decade. I had been precocious, eager, strong-willed, and believed in Jesus. Surely, sometime in that distant past that smelled, still, of Mrs. Ivy, chalk, starched shirts, and cookies, I had been found worthy of, or demanded, Baptism. But when Nicholas asked one day for the exact date so the records of the parish could be kept, I found I didn't remember it.

"Find out for me, please," Nicholas asked. "It's no big deal but it helps us keep the files straight."

Dutifully, later that week, I called the Baptist Church and explained that I needed my exact date of Baptism. Could they help me find it? The secretary, whose voice sounded as round and sweet as a glazed doughnut, replied that yes, sugar, she would check. What year would that be? A detailed search over thirty minutes, with drawers sliding open and shut, large books thumping open on desks, and thick sheets flipping brought back only her disturbed voice. "I'm sorry, sugar, but I just can't find any record anywhere. Are you sure it wasn't in some other church?"

Nicholas took the news with uncharacteristic breeziness in the sober and penitent week of Ash Wednesday. "Fine," he said. "We will baptize you at Easter. No more communion for you."

That Lent, my first really, did a great deal to focus my mind about the issues that had plagued me for so long. Although Nicholas could have, and perhaps should have, given me a lesson on Christian basics before Baptism, an upswing in both our busy schedules prevented anything so practical. Fortunately as it turned out, I was left much on my own that Lent and once again, under my own initiative, took up the topic of the Bible and sex. In many ways I imagined the topic would be "old hat." After all, I had only recently finished T.E.N.'s workbook. Yet this time I sought not, as I had before, to merely discredit so-called "proof texts," but instead set out to look more deeply into what the Bible said about the entirety of sex. What, in the mind of God as best I could discern it, was sex for?

This broadening of the discussion proved instrumental in significantly widening my thinking about sex and sexual expression. Over and over again in Scripture, God's witness is to a fully-human sexuality, a sexuality which includes sex drive and tenderness, orgasms and eggs, passion and possible parenthood. In short, fertility matters! It was not that sexual intimacy should be reduced to a method of fertility, but that fertility cannot be simply discarded from the sexual act as irrelevant or meaningless.

I recall being so surprised that God's witness to this truth extended even into the realms of sexual sins and errors. The moment when the prophet Nathan confronts King David over his adultery rings with an abiding tenderness and understanding, even as David's observation of Bathsheba at her bath carried an almost palpable desire:

> There were two men in a certain town, one rich and the other poor. The rich man had very many flocks and herds; but the poor man had nothing but one little ewe lamb which he had bought. And he brought it up, and it grew up with him and his children; it used to eat of his [food], and drink from his cup, and lie in his bosom, and it was like a daughter to him. Now there came a traveler to the rich man, and he was unwilling to take one of his own flock or herd to prepare for the wayfarer who had come to him, but he took the poor man's lamb and prepared it for the man who had come to him (2 Samuel 12:1-4).

Even setting aside for a moment the part of the passage that troubled me — the notion of a woman being compared, even in parable, to a domestic animal — I remember being struck by the deliberate tenderness Nathan uses to describe the relationship. The "lamb" is no mere sheep like others but one with whom the man in the parable had shared his cup, had allowed in the house with himself and his children, had slept with in his arms. It "was like a daughter to him," Nathan said, and thus illustrated in a devastating way how wrong David had been to break the bond between Uriah and his wife. It was for this breaking of the bond between a man and woman, even more than sending Uriah deliberately to die in battle, that Nathan convicts David.

Other Scripture passages from that study stand out in my memory. Jacob's love for Rachel, so deep that he would toil fourteen years in his uncle's service to marry her, touched me. The deeply passionate poetry of the Song of Songs impressed and surprised me with the depth of its expression. The fact that Jesus chose to first reveal His first miracle not in a healing or other work of forgiveness and power but as a work of generosity at the Cana wedding made me wonder if, in other circumstances, He would have married. I noted the way Jesus used a wedding and marriage to describe the Kingdom of God. "The kingdom of heaven may be likened to a king who gave a wedding feast for his son," Jesus says (*NAB* Matthew 22:2). Be ready, He warns, lest the Kingdom catch you unprepared like the foolish virgins who had not kept their lamps ready for the wedding feast. If you would seek the Kingdom of God, He said, do so humbly, taking the lowest seat at the wedding table.

I had to conclude too that Scripture loves children, fertility, and births. To Nicodemus Jesus explains the miracle of coming to the Kingdom in terms of second birth. He repeatedly calls the disciples to let the children through the crowds who come to see him, and warns us often that unless we become as little children we will never see the Kingdom of God. And when God uses a miracle to set His seal on some activity or promise, He uses fertility at particularly key times. Isaac got his name because Sarah, his mother, laughed when she heard that God would bring her a child when she was ninety years old to seal Abraham's promise that he would one day father a great multitude. Years later one of this multitude was a virgin girl named Mary who asked the angel Gabriel how she could bear a child while still remaining virgin. Gabriel pointed to Elizabeth's conception of John the Baptist, late in life, to prove that "nothing is impossible with God" (Luke 1:37).

Gradually, with each of these pulling and tugging me along, I approached Easter and the day of my Baptism. Through it all Nicholas had been restrained and, I thought, somewhat distant. Each communion he stood, robed as usual but more somber somehow as I approached. With my arms crossed over my chest as though dead, I came not to receive the Body and Blood but instead, in the manner of catechumens of old, to receive the dry manna of his blessing — a few words which had to carry me during those long weeks as I waited a seeming eternity to be reborn. Finally, on the last Sunday of Lent, when we stood chatting briefly on the Church steps and long after the last of the altar guild had gone away, Nicholas turned to me, his face suddenly very serious.

"You know you are a great challenge to me David, " he said. I paused, holding my tongue. " I have described your case, without naming you, to other pastors with whom I work and the opinion is divided over whether I should baptize you without demanding you at least *try* to lead a more . . . regular Christian life." I held my breath. "But I have thought long about it and prayed and it seems to me that your heart is on Christ no matter where the rest of you may be. So if you promise me that, when I baptize you, you will lay your whole self, sexuality and all, on the altar of God — to be open to His will — I will baptize you at Easter." In the tense silence after he spoke I remember my ears ringing as over and over again a voice in my head pealed out "choose!" and "decide!" Everything I had been living up to this point seemed to hinge on this moment. Did I, could I, trust Christ enough? Did I know I was right? What if I was wrong? In the end, really, did any of it matter? My blood sang when Jesus called. Nothing else mattered. "I will, I promise," I whispered and Nicholas, grinning suddenly, clapped me on the shoulder. "Good man!"

After that, the actual day of my Baptism was a bit anti-climactic. Embarrassed and suddenly shy in front of everyone, I bent my head. Splish, splash over my hair and down my back in the name of the Father, the Son, and the Holy Spirit and it was done: I was Christ's forever. But in reality it had only just begun, and I walked away from the altar and the crowd that afternoon ripe for the changes Christ would work in my life and willing, at last, to take up my cross.

CHAPTER FIVE

The cost of discipleship

The weight of my cross began to make itself felt very soon after my Baptism. During my earlier life as a gay Christian I had agreed to help a friend, Chris, establish a small monthly newsletter/magazine called *Malchus*. Malchus, in the Gospel of St. John, was the high priest's slave who lost his ear to St. Peter's sword when the crowd arrived to arrest Jesus. Further, St. Luke's Gospel records that, though Malchus is not named, Jesus healed his ear before being bound and taken away. These two relatively obscure Scripture texts gave us the background metaphor for *Malchus*'s name. St. Peter, representing the Church, routinely attacked and wounded people because of their same-sex attraction, the metaphor went, but Jesus healed us of that attack. Of course, the metaphor's flip side named our journal after a servant of the high priest, a man arguably one of the Gospel's wicked characters, but we rarely discussed that part.

Chris founded *Malchus*, with the help of other same-sex-attracted Christian friends, in order to edify and encourage other gay and lesbian Christians who were often isolated, especially when living away from large cities, and to spread the Gospel among gays and lesbians generally. Both those goals I could support. But, eventually, the same problems I had found with other gay and lesbian Christians began to rear their head with *Malchus* too. *Malchus*'s editorial line, increasingly, began to be more about justifying same-sex activity than about Jesus, and when other *Malchus* editors and volunteers began exploring the area's more "diverse" forms of same-sex sexuality, I felt my time with the journal drawing to a close. Gradually my articles, which reflected many of my examinations of the very foundations of gay theology, fell increasingly out-of-step with the rest of *Malchus*'s content. Soon my conscience demanded a change, and one of the journal's fall issues contained my final article in the publication:

At a Parting of the Ways

It is with a mixture of emotions; sorrow and relief, uncertainty and confidence, that I contribute this last article to an issue of *Malchus*. On September first of this year I resigned my responsibility as *Malchus*'s Assistant Editor as well as any further role as a contributing author.

Most of our readers, I imagine, must already have inklings as to how and why *Malchus* and I have had to go our separate ways. A careful reader of what has been our steadily improving effort cannot have helped but notice that my articles have become increasingly out of step with those of other contributors on some pretty profound areas. This, to a certain extent, is to be expected and even encouraged, however some topics, such as sexual identity and obedience, rest very close to the heart of what *Malchus* is all about and thus call for a degree of at least minimal agreement.

At their deepest, my disagreements with *Malchus* run right to the heart of what I believe it means to be a Christian in the latter part of the twentieth century. Not, please note, what it means to be a homosexually oriented Christian, or a white Christian, or a male Christian, but a Christian. Over hours and months of reflection and prayer I have come to understand my relationship with Christ and His Church to be far more about what He would have me do than what I would have me do. This, I have observed, runs sharply counter to the surrounding philosophy — the ballpark if you will — in which *Malchus* operates. Unlike many others who write for *Malchus* I find my battle, as a Christian, to be more one of bending my own selfish will to the Moral Law than of trying to bend, twist, reshape, or recast that Moral Law to endorse my will. I have come, for better or worse, to feel *Malchus* endorses a course of life that is willfully sinful; in as far as it supports a demand among some that God change to meet their actions and desires rather than change those actions and seek purification of those desires out of love of God.

It has been my observation that one cannot embark upon a path of sexual misconduct and sin without finding the other aspects of one's being, body, soul and spirit, eventually to be also corrupted. While homosexually active I accepted with only minimum regard, assumptions regarding Scripture, the nature of sacrifice and the nature of what Christ demanded from me. These assumptions do not bear up under closer scrutiny and intellectual honesty demands I abandon them in favor of those closer to the Truth. This is why I can no longer assent, willingly, to have my name upon a publication which is founded upon premises which I have to regard, at best, as sin-induced error or, at worst, as a sinister attack upon souls.

Finally, I want to make it clear that I have nothing but fond, if regretful, feelings about Chris and everyone I have met in connection with *Malchus*. Chris, in particular, has managed contributors' conflicting creeds and cultural divisions with an aplomb that ought to merit him a post in the Diplomatic Corps. The Bosnian conflict, indeed, likely merits as delicate a touch. I am truly sorry that we could not agree more. Maybe, some day, we shall.

My resignation from *Malchus* marked a watershed, and I recall those months after my Baptism like the hours before a thunderstorm. I could almost feel the weight of change in the air, and the shape of things to come towered like clouds in the distance. But as yet the clouds withheld the first lightning. Everything awaited a spark.

That spark arrived one day in the early spring after I had resigned from *Malchus*. While seeking shelter from a bleak rainy and snowy day in an area mall, I found myself attracted to one of the large, chain bookstores that had begun to spring up around the area. Large signs reading "Inventory Reduction Sale" decorated the front of this one and I approached the tottering tables of titles like a prospector panning for gold. Perhaps I would find something useful amidst the pile of exotic cookbooks, coffee table doorstops, and guides to the perplexed. A small, green paperback caught my eye. *The Cost of Discipleship*, the gold letters announced, by Dietrich Bonhoeffer. Interested, I picked it up and opened to the first page. "Cheap grace," Bonhoeffer wrote, "is the deadly enemy of our Church. We are fighting today for costly grace." I read it again, reached into my pocket and began to pray I had at least enough left over from the day's shopping to buy this book. If I borrowed from the penny tray in front of the cash register I would just have enough. I bought the book, took it home, and read it through in three days. Then I read it through again and began to seek out everything on Bonhoeffer that I could find.

Dietrich Bonhoeffer, along with his twin sister Sabine, was born in 1906 in Breslau, Germany. A precocious child in an intellectually astute family, Bonhoeffer had many possible career paths open to him but instead felt called to the ministry as a Lutheran pastor. He completed his doctoral studies in 1927, at age 21, and began teaching at the University of Berlin in 1930. He traveled fairly widely for his time, served as pastor in a couple of congregations, and was very active in the fledging international movement toward building an ecumenical Christianity. But, no matter how all that impressed me, it was his life of activism and eventual martyrdom that set the seal of authenticity on what he wrote in the *Cost of Discipleship* and other works.

When Hitler's National Socialism began to gain ascendancy in Germany in the 1930s, many Christians' reactions were sluggish or worse: but not Bonhoeffer's. As the National Socialist machine began to assimilate and control more and more of German life, extending even to the churches, Bonhoeffer resisted. With others he helped found the Confessing Church, a body whose leaders elevated Jesus Christ, not Hitler, as the ultimate authority over how Christians lived their lives. Bonhoeffer spoke out against the rise of Nazi-inspired theology. When the seminaries became totally corrupted with it, Bonhoeffer founded another, whose seminarians belonged to the Confessing Church. Bonhoeffer was involved in the movement to hide Jews from the Holocaust and to resist Hitler at every step until, caught in the round up after a failed assassination attempt, he was hanged at Flossenberg concentration camp in 1945.

Bonhoeffer's writing changed my theological life and thinking in so many ways. Like rain falling on drought-stricken land, certainly, but also as something a good deal more violent.

Bonhoeffer confronted me. His martyred voice, long dead, rang with conviction and demanded that I open my eyes. Holding Christ's crucifixion immediately before my face, he grabbed my attention and said, "Look at this, look! And tell me how you live your life."

Consider, just as an example, how Bonhoeffer addresses the question of "cheap grace:"

> Cheap grace means grace sold on the market like cheapjacks' wares. The sacraments, the forgiveness of sins, and the consolations of religion are thrown away at cut prices. Grace is represented as the Church's inexhaustible treasury, from which she showers blessings with generous hands, without asking questions or fixing limits. Grace without price, grace without cost! The essence of grace, we suppose, is that the account has been paid in advance; and, because it has been paid, everything can be had for nothing. . . .

By contrast costly grace is "the treasure hidden in the field, for the sake of it a man will gladly go and sell all his goods. It is the kingly rule of Christ, for whose sake a man will pluck out his eye which causes him to stumble. . . . Such grace is costly because it calls us to follow and it is grace because it calls us to follow *Jesus Christ*."

Ouch! Ouch! Bonhoeffer shredded my thin sheet of gay theology. Not at the level of the picky quarrel over what this word might have meant in Greek or that word in Hebrew, but deeper, at the level of Jesus Christ, the very origin and meaning of the conversation. Bonhoeffer's arrival in my intellectual and faith life was akin to St. Thomas Aquinas's mystical moments before the Cross, after which, he declared as so much "straw" everything he had written to that date. Confronted with Christ, Bonhoeffer's work made clear that a man or woman has but two possible choices: I will follow and serve or I will not. Nothing else, if discussed honestly, is possible.

Notes I scribbled down as I read Bonhoeffer for first time reveal the impact his work began to have, particularly affecting my thinking on topics like authority, commitment, and suffering love.

Bonhoeffer noted that Christ's authority in the life of the Christian is, and must be, total. The call to discipleship in Christ is at once a call to individuality and obedience, he said. Delving deeply into the text of Levi's call, Bonhoeffer observed that Levi's response was both immediate and total: "After this he went out, and saw a tax collector, named Levi, sitting at the tax office; and he said to him, 'Follow me.' And he left everything, and rose and followed him" (Matthew 9:9).

When Jesus found Levi sitting at his tax collecting and said, "Come, follow me," Levi got up and followed Him, without debate, without compromise, without even making plans for someone to take care of his business while he tramped the countryside with this itinerant rabbi. Bonhoeffer considered this obedience was, in a sense, inevitable on the basis of Jesus' identity.

Because Jesus walked among men as the Christ, in Bonhoeffer's view His was the authority to demand obedience to His word. In the life of a Christian, as Bonhoeffer understood it, Jesus summons disciples to follow Him not as a teacher or a pattern of the good life, but as Christ, the Son of God.

In Bonhoeffer's view, Levi's conversion encapsulates the essential element of all conversions; a recognition, ultimately, of Jesus' person as the Son of God and obedience to Him in that context. Levi's conversion episode is short in part because the point is Christ and not Levi. Bonhoeffer points out that when it comes to our discipleship to Christ, obedience is the only road forward. Bonhoeffer also observed that Jesus' call makes men and women individuals:

> Through the call of Jesus men become individuals. Willy-nilly, they are compelled to decide and that decision can only be made by themselves. It is no choice of their own that makes them individuals; it is Christ who makes them individuals by calling them. Every man is called separately and follows alone. But men are frightened of soli-

tude, and they try to protect themselves from it in the society of their fellow men and in their material environment. . . . At the very moment of their call men find that they have already broken with all the natural ties of life. This is not their own doing, but his who calls them. For Christ has delivered them from the immediacy with the world, and brought them into immediacy with himself. We cannot follow Christ unless we are willing to accept and affirm that breach as a *fait accompli.*

Both these ideas, the authority of Christ and ultimately individual response, underlie Bonhoeffer's life-changing observation *that only the person who believes is obedient and only the person who is obedient believes.* When I called and asked Jesus to come into my life, I was akin to the rich young man standing before Him in the road asking, Rabbi, what must I do to inherit eternal life? I had no desire for Jesus the Person, whether human or divine. I didn't even really comprehend His mere possibility. I had a practical problem of despair and desperation and, in my shortsightedness, sought God as a practical answer. But Scripture records of that incident that when He saw that the rich young man was not going to cease asking, *Jesus loved him* and told him what he really didn't want to hear: Go, sell all you own and give it to the poor . . . and follow me.

Likewise Jesus had responded to my cry and, in turn, had called me to follow Him. But, to my deep, bone-shaking horror, I realized that, like the rich young man, I had turned my back and begun to walk away. The only difference between our actions was that the young man was both honest and decisive, deciding right then that the cost of discipleship was too high and that he needed to be on his way. I, on the other hand, weak-willed and listless, had hovered on the outskirts of the crowd, postponing my decision even as I appeared to step forward and make it.

Bonhoeffer's point is absolutely crucial. Faith is not abstract. Faith is not a classroom ideal, or a theory, or something we use to comfort ourselves. Faith necessitates action, an act of the will to do or not do something. It's a paradox, almost like the riddle of the chicken and the egg. If one does not have faith, how can one obey? But unless one obeys, how can one be said to have faith? It is part of the power of God that such riddles vanish in the presence of the One whose very nature is the answer. As a shivering child at the end of the dock, I could have claimed a great deal of faith that the man waiting in the cold lake six feet down would catch me in the water and save me from drowning. But my claims remained mere conjecture until, with real faith, I stepped from the edge and dropped into his arms. All around me, since coming into contact with gay theology, I had been surrounded with a crowd of men and women at the edge of the dock, arguing, debating and, for some, finally denying the necessity to step into the cold. Bonhoeffer's meditations on the reality of Christ, His authority and call, had brought me right to the edge of the tin platform and left me, cold toes forward, shivering, near naked, to decide what to do. Bonhoeffer again:

> The first step places the disciple in the situation where faith is possible. If he refuses to follow and stays behind he does not learn how to believe. He who is called must go out of his situation in which he cannot believe, in the situation in which, first and foremost, faith is possible. But this step is not the first stage of a career. Its sole justification is that it brings the disciple into fellowship with Jesus which will be victorious. So long as Levi sits at the receipt of custom and Peter at his nets, they could both pursue their trade honestly and dutifully, and the both might enjoy religious experiences, old and new. But if they want to believe in God, the only way is to follow His incarnate Son.

Bonhoeffer's second major attitude-changing theme concerned commitment. "When Jesus Christ calls a man," Bonhoeffer wrote, "he calls him to come and die." The Christian's battle, which I had so long supposed to be distant and theoretical and which others in my life considered to be about social sins — "homophobia" and sexism for example — Bonhoeffer's writing brought nearer, more intimate and personal. Bonhoeffer's point is that Christians meet the Cross not at the end of their life with Christ but right at the beginning. Christ helps them confront the Cross over and over again as part of their ever-deepening relationship with Him. As soon as Christ calls a person, Bonhoeffer wrote, he or she can discern the shape of the Cross. Turning to Christ, by definition, means dying to self, and the death does not mean merely elevating Christ to be viewed as one value among many. This death to self means coming to a place where the disciple wants only what Christ wants and the old self-will does not exist any longer at all. This resonated deeply with me. I remembered how I had shut the Bible so firmly when I had asked God what He thought of active homosexuality and had gotten an apparently adamant and negative answer. I had seen the shape of the Cross in my life, as Bonhoeffer said I would, and had turned my back on it. Could I take it up now?

Bonhoeffer's last major theme — at least the last one that changed my thinking — concerned how Christians need to see love. For the Christian, Bonhoeffer noted, love means suffering. It's not that Christians should want to suffer for its own sake, but rather that Christians must want to really love their fellows just as Christ loved them. That, by necessity, means suffering with them and for them. Love, it began to dawn on me, meant doing the *right* thing that is not always the merely *comfortable* thing. In fact it is often is the complete opposite of the comfortable thing. Gradually I began to take stock of my relationships with people I claimed to love in my life. Did I really love them, and what did that mean? "As Christ bears our burdens," Bonhoeffer wrote, "so we ought to bear the burdens of our fellow-men."

This love principle really became significant when I considered my relationship with my partner, a relationship I so feared losing that merely thinking about it almost paralyzed me. For so many years, as far as gay relationships could go, it had been good. My partner had come to mean so much more to my life than a mere bedmate. Yet my meditations on the nature of sex had gradually convinced me that God meant sex for so much more than mere pleasure or even the building up of companionship. Now Bonhoeffer began convicting me of the way I persisted in treating someone — a way which, I had come to realize, radically underrated his humanity. I began looking repeatedly down at the water under the dock and the Man who promised to catch me. Could I jump? Would I?

It's probably important to note my state of mind during this time. Ever since my Baptism some months before, I had felt almost as though I was a character in someone else's play about my life. Very big ideas, well-articulated and forcefully presented, had changed my thinking and even my identity. Same-sex attraction, which I had once considered my most important defining element, had come to fall, if not completely away, at least very far down my list of priorities, replaced instead by the knowledge of myself as a part of something, Someone, so much bigger.

Confronted with the truth, I knew I had to choose. Love, Christ, and real faith demanded that I cease treating my partner, or anyone else, as an object for sexual evaluation or pleasure. God meant human beings to be so much more than that. Chastity, I came to see, made up a significant part of my Cross and Christ had called me to myself. On a Saturday afternoon I had lunch with one actively gay friend who found me distracted and distant. Late Saturday night I wrote a last note to Torry and a few others explaining, as best I could, why I had chosen as I had. On Sunday morning, the following day, I went to my partner of so many years and said, "I love you. Could we please not do this [have sex] any more?"

After my decision for chastity, much of the rest of my life, like life after Baptism, seemed anti-climactic. My decision, made unilaterally, shocked my partner and began a yearlong conversation about the roots and foundations of our relationship. If we weren't sleeping together any longer, our discussion began, then what was I to him and he to me? Did he want to leave me? Did I want to leave him? In the end, in a graced moment, we concluded that we experienced so much of life together that our relationship meant far more than merely what happened in the bedroom. For better or worse, for then and now, we remained and remain very close friends, akin to brothers, and I feel grateful for his presence in my life.

My decision for chastity soon led me into the Catholic Faith. My reasons for this decision are, in part, the reasons for this book, but it is appropriate to briefly discuss them to round out this chapter.

Catholicism came fairly quickly after chastity because, in so many ways, the Catholic Church is the only Christian body in the United States which addresses questions of sexual morality not merely from the perspective of actions but also from the deeper questions of the nature of men, women, and love. During the months after my Baptism, Nicholas had come to the difficult decision to move on from Trinity, and I had decided to do so also. My search for another Anglican parish in the Washington, D.C., or Northern Virginia area opened my eyes. Several had so little support for any sort of chastity for people living with same-sex attraction that they hosted Integrity and Dignity "socials" for actively homosexual men and allowed "same-sex unions" to be performed. One rector, upon hearing of my search to live a life I understood to be more obedient to Christ, asked me, somewhat incredulously, "Why?" One rector of an Anglican Church in my old D.C. neighborhood turned out to be on the record as an atheist. I discovered that the other side of the Anglican house, while smaller, was not necessarily better. One Anglican associate rector I encountered, who at least kept an open mind about the difference between temptation and activity, told me that he firmly believed that men and women living with same-sex attraction should seek, as a matter of obedience, to change their predominant "orientation" to heterosexual. I began to feel a bit like a stranger in a strange land.

But if Anglicans thought that what I wanted to do was weird, Catholics, or at least some Catholics, thought it worth doing. They directed me to a little-known but tremendous Catholic organization called Courage. Courage, which I will discuss in greater length later, exists to help support Catholic men and women living with same-sex attraction in living a chaste life. Courage is not about orientation change and does not require a commitment to orientation change as a condition of membership — but Courage *is* about supporting Catholics (and others, should they choose) living with same-sex attraction in their battle to live as better Catholics. If I was considered weird in Courage groups, at least it would not be because I thought living chastely a value worth pursuing.

But my interest in the Catholic Church gradually grew beyond the narrow parameters formed by issues surrounding same-sex attraction. I had gradually come to be impressed by the historicity and scope of the Roman Catholic Faith. Even though I was not yet a member, I began to perceive and understand G.K. Chesterton's observation that the Roman Catholic Church is so much bigger when seen from the inside than the outside. At a point in my life when I began to seek examples of holiness and leadership, saints really, the number of the "great cloud of witnesses" who were Catholic began to introduce me to Catholic truths about Christ and human beings.

Finally, what I would understand later to be the incarnational nature of my faith began to grow in importance. When I had been barred from communion while I awaited Baptism I had been forced to realize how important communion has become to me — not merely the communion worship service (which I loved) but communion itself, the consumption of that little wafer and sip of wine. I certainly didn't have any notion of the Real Presence, even in theory. Indeed, I think I would have been shocked had I known it. But when I took communion I began to grow in awareness that this was something deeply special that Christ had gone significantly out of his way to share. Likewise, I started noticing the way certain churches, particularly the older Catholic and "higher" Anglican ones, tended to speak to the whole of me. I had never really considered how rooted in the intellect Trinity's faith (to which I am very grateful) had been. Clearly these other churches, even those whose doctrine and leadership seemed so clearly "off the wall," had initiated a different conversation than the one whose topics and language had more to do with the mind than the body, more to do with intellectual faith than incarnate spirituality. The architecture of a place like Washington, D.C.'s, National Cathedral made my spirit soar. The altars in old Catholic and Anglican parishes that captured choirs of saints singing to heaven made me want to sing too. The statues, the stained glass, the holy water, the colors and smells, everything spoke of holiness and richness at the same time.

I came to understand how much the Catholic Church existed to serve people, particularly poor and helpless people, whose actions in the churches touched me deeply. I recall the day that I decided to take the step and ask for instruction in the Catholic Faith through Catholic University's Rite of Christian Initiation for Adults (RCIA) program. On that cold winter afternoon I stalked through the cutting wind toward my car, which I parked almost in the very shadow of the Basilica of the National Shrine of the Immaculate Conception. It dawned on me that I had never been inside. Here I had asked for instruction in Catholicism but had never visited one of its major shrines in the city! I shoved my books into the car and climbed the stairs to the door. It was almost a disaster. Every Protestant and iconoclastic objection to Catholicism seemed distilled into this one massive stone building with the gold dome. Yes, it was open and yes, there were people worshipping and not merely visiting there. But the statues! The candles! The images of Mary everywhere! Clearly this was idolatry, wasn't it? Lord, what have I gotten myself into? What is it you want?

Confused, I wandered into the chapel of Our Lady of Suffering. Here a Cross, crowned with a wreath of thorns, hangs above a smaller than life-sized version of Michelangelo's Pieta, and in the shadow of its quiet austerity I knelt to pray for clarity. A small rustle of cloth and plastic made me open my eyes. In the small corridor between the seats at my right an old Hispanic woman slowly set down a small army of plastic grocery bags and walked down the corridor to the base of the statue and Cross. She was short — even the smaller than life-sized statue loomed over her. Apparently unaware of my rude fascination, she slowly and gradually touched her fingers to her lips and then to each of the wounds in Christ's body, draped over the lap of His Mother, that she could reach. Then she knelt, not on a kneeler at the seats but right there, on the cold stone steps, and prayed briefly. Then she got up, slowly walked back to her burden of bundles, gathered them carefully, and almost staggered out under their weight, her devotions complete. None of Protestant Christianity I had experienced, I realized, could approach the love this woman's actions embodied.

I loved it that Catholic churches were open so much during the day and that people like this woman worshipped there. I liked it that Catholics, unlike so many Christians I had previously met, did not appear to compartmentalize their faith — or if they did, the compartmentalization was not as evident. I loved it that some Catholic churches, within walking distance of my downtown office, offered Mass and devotions throughout the day. No matter what time of the day it seemed, if you walked into a Catholic church you would find something going on. Mass, a prayer service, or at least the waves of the faithful poor, rippling around the bases of the saints and slipping onto their knees into the pews for rosaries or quiet prayer.

But as sweet as all this was, and at times it was so wonderful I felt giddy, it was still not enough to overcome what I believed to be my objections to the Catholic Church. It took a whole weekend in a quiet place with Alan Shreck's *Catholic and Christian* to educate me about what the Catholic Church really teaches. I recall coming off that particular weekend openly wondering, "if that's what the Catholic Church believes, why aren't we all Catholic?" The reasons for the so-called historical schisms failed to impress me. Where, after all, was the truth? And if, as it seemed, the fullest measure of the truth rested in the historical Church of Christ, then that is where I needed to be. The Roman Catholic Church received me into her Militant ranks the following Easter, where I have been, struggling, dropping my cross and picking it up again, ever since.

CHAPTER SIX

The question of healing

If I had written this book a mere two years ago, the "auto-biographical" portion would have ended with chapter five. Gradually, as I have described, I have come to understand how powerfully God has worked to create me, how my sexuality includes fertility, and how discipleship means fully taking up my cross to follow Christ. A big part of that cross, as I understood it, would be an ongoing homosexual inclination and a resulting commitment to lifelong chastity. But God, to paraphrase popular advice columnist Ann Landers, controls what happens while we are making other plans.

The healing question

Few issues attached to the question of same-sex attraction have a greater emotional impact than the question of changing, diminishing, or even eliminating the degree of same-sex attraction in someone's life, with a resulting increase in heterosexual attraction. A number of significant factors have contributed to this subject's emotional volatility.

Historically, many gay and lesbian activists have believed that medical science generally and mental health professionals in particular bear a crucial part of the responsibility for how society has, in their view, misunderstood same-sex attraction and homosexual identity and mistreated people living with a high degree of both.

Second, gay and lesbian activists base part of their demand for widespread political, legal, and social acceptance of same-sex sexual activity on the argument that the underlying attraction is unchanging and unchangeable. Viewed in such a light, their argument questions how fair it is to ask people who live with same-sex attraction to do the impossible when, as they allege, society's attitudes are what need changing. Further, gay and lesbian activists point out that an understanding of same-sex attraction which is based on illness makes it easier for society to unfairly stigmatize or discriminate against people living with same-sex attraction. Activists also feel concerned that many people living with same-sex attraction will accept and internalize a definition based on illness and will suffer from the resulting internalization. Countering such feelings has been a major focus of the "gay pride" movement since the early 1970s.

Finally, many of the faith-based approaches to changing or diminishing same-sex attraction suffered in the early days from a high degree of naïveté and a corresponding lack of nuance and understanding. I recall encountering men and women who had tried a faith-based approach to diminishing or removing same-sex attraction, failed, and walked away with a highly-damaged spirituality. Some had been told they had failed because they hadn't "enough faith" and others because they hadn't "loved God enough." Stories like theirs only tended to confirm my bias against Christianity as a religion of rubes and snake-handlers. My skepticism about faith-based approaches to diminishing same-sex attraction persisted even after I had come to Christ and become a Catholic.

Today the topic is as contentious as it ever was, but the positions of different medical groups have changed, though they have not abandoned bias and politicized medicine. In 1973, after being heavily lobbied by gay and lesbian activists, the American Psychiatric Association (APA) membership voted to remove homosexuality from its Diagnostic and Statistical Manual of Mental Disorders which serves as something of a guidebook to recognized mental ailments. Homosexuality, *per se*, the APA said in 1973 and has significantly repeated, should not be viewed as mental or emotional illness. In 1975, the American Psychological Association passed a resolution affirming that action. Homosexuality, the psychiatrists say today in a briefing paper:

> was thought to be a mental illness in the past because mental health professionals and society had biased information about homosexuality since most studies only involved lesbians and gay men in therapy. [W]hen researchers examined data about gay people who were not in therapy, the idea that homosexuality was a mental illness was found to be untrue.

Thus spake the professionals, and many supposed that settled the matter. Same-sex attraction alone does not make you ill, or mentally or emotionally disordered. Homosexuality as an issue, therefore, had been addressed.

Except. The reality of homosexual practice and what began to pass as "gaily-proud" lives around the country also began to be felt. Actively homosexual men and women from across the United States and Europe, even in such gay-accepting and supportive places as New York, San Francisco, and Amsterdam, continued to experience the list of pathologies and sorrows Thomas Schmidt documented in *Straight and Narrow* (see chapter one). Some therapists began to see men and women living with a high degree of same-sex attraction who were unhappy with the kind of life this tended to bring. These therapists began to suspect that same-sex attraction could possibly be lessened or even eliminated therapeutically. In spite of opposition from the APA, which maintains that "scientific evidence does not show that conversion therapy works and that it can do more harm than good," these therapists have begun to treat men and women for same-sex attraction and to document their work. Writes one therapist in a paper presented before the National Association for the Reparative Therapy of Homosexuality (NARTH):

> The APA decision in 1973 which depathologized homosexuality was a political one. Even writers sympathetic to the gay affirmative position agree (Bayer, Mass, Lewes). Although both sides state that based on the merit of their argument, their side would have won the day, this discussion has never taken place.

> During the last three years I have become acutely aware that the gay affirmative therapists' point of view of homosexuality permeates the professional schools and, therefore, the opinions of the professionals who have graduated during the last ten to fifteen years. Having never been exposed to a dialogue between the two sides of the argument, nor to the documented results of therapy with men who sought to change their sexual orientation, these professionals tend to respond in an almost reflexive manner which causes me great concern (Paul Popper "Coming Out of the Closet: Why I Decided to Treat Homosexuals Who Want to Change Their Orientation," NARTH Conference, 1995).

Condemnation from gay and lesbian activists and the APA has been swift and fairly vitriolic. Not only must the people claiming a diminishing or change of same-sex attraction be dishonest, activists say, therapists attempting to help them are *ipso facto* unethical. Activists maintain that problems actively homosexual men and women experience do not have anything to do with same-sex attraction or homosexual behavior but are the fault of societal prejudice and bias. The APA also maintains that therapy aimed at diminishing same-sex attraction cannot rely solely on measuring something objectively identifiable, like behavior, but must instead seek to measure the whole range of human response attached to the issue. "Changing one's sexual orientation is not simply a matter of changing one's sexual behavior," the organization maintains. "It would require altering one's emotional, romantic and sexual feelings and restructuring one's self-concept and social identity" (APA "Statement on Homosexuality," July, 1994).

Concurrently, faith-based approaches to the question of changing same-sex attraction have gradually matured, developing a deeper understanding of the issue as they have grown. Many now recognize that there is a significant element of grace in addressing such deeply-embedded parts of the psyche as sexual identity and persistent same-sex attraction. Many have also come to understand that the issue revolves around both inclinations and actions, and that ministry in this area cannot be rushed. For example, men who leave lives of same-sex activity for lives of heterosexual sex outside of marriage are not necessarily any better off spiritually, physically, or emotionally. Nor is a young man or woman who abandons same-sex activity necessarily better off by jumping rapidly into marriage. Even if issues of same-sex attraction have been addressed, organizations are beginning to realize that marriage is itself a complicated, demanding vocation, one which demands care, precision, and time. It is not necessarily open to everyone, no matter what his or her sexual attractions. The faith-based movement that seeks to help men and women diminish or eliminate same-sex attraction from their lives has come to understand that while God still retains the prerogative to move mightily, the issues surrounding same-sex attraction are deep, complicated, and often painful to confront.

While the dispute's configuration has changed quite a bit, the practical fallout is somewhat similar. People living with same-sex attraction *still* dispute with medical professionals about the content of their lives, but this time from a different perspective. Although no longer seeking medical approval of what is, essentially, an identity built around the bedroom, these men and women still face a politicized and dogmatic APA — this time backed by an activist establishment. Understandably, many of these men and women feel invalidated for reporting a truth in their lives that contradicts what can only be described as a secular dogma. Most of the men and women I have met who have experienced a diminishing of same-sex attraction are reluctant to speak much about it — intimidated by the thought of going against a medical establishment which seeks more to label and stigmatize them than listen. But they are living out their lives with the changes they have experienced and they give thanks to God and to the people who have helped them.

My investigation and experience with this issue has led me to conclude that a more healthy, honest, and useful approach might include the following elements:

First, many people with same-sex attraction would probably be helped if the American Psychiatric Association took a more neutral and less dogmatic view of the question of diminishing same-sex attraction. The APA and gay and lesbian activists should admit that same-sex attraction and identity are not fixed in stone but, as has been long understood and was even reported in the widely attacked (though never on this point) Kinsey studies, are better understood as a continuum. Likewise, many people living with same-sex attraction would probably be helped if the APA and activists admitted that a person's place on this continuum is not necessarily fixed but can, and does, move over time. Such an admission was not terribly unusual among actively homosexual men when I was a gay activist and, in fact, occasionally cropped up to explain everything from the abandonment of marriages and long-standing heterosexual relationships to bisexuality.

Second, the APA's standards for what counts as "orientation change," in my opinion, are unrealistic and unnecessarily rigid. By way of comparison, consider a person who has been smoking cigarettes for decades. After many years, he or she gets counseling to stop. But the habit of cigarette smoking is deep-seated. Research has identified that it has a biological component and the best the a person can do is move from smoking two packs of cigarettes a day to smoking two cigarettes a month. Furthermore, even worse, if they see others smoking, the desire for a cigarette still persists. They can't legitimately be called "nonsmokers," but no one looking at this situation fairly would say that their life and health have not experienced change. Likewise, some people who work towards diminishing their same-sex attraction experience similar degrees of change, but under the activists' definition, the change in their lives would not be recognized. A more realistic, compassionate, and authentic way of looking at either therapy or faith-based counseling would reflect the reality that degrees of change along the continuum are every bit as valid as total shifts in both attraction and identity.

Third, people who have experienced a diminishing or removal of same-sex attraction from their identities, personalities, and lives do not deserve to be stigmatized or have their character impugned. Such attacks are particularly grievous, anti-intellectual, and mean-spirited. It implies an enormous unwillingness to confront reality as it is but to adopt a view of people's lives based primarily on bias. Same-sex attraction cannot diminish, the theory holds; therefore, people who have experienced it diminishing in their lives *must* be lying, deluded, or fraudulent.

Pre-judging the situation so strongly can even lead to individual gay-affirming practitioners doing damage to the very people they are ostensibly dedicated to helping. In early March 1997, I was seated in a Pittsburgh, Pennsylvania, hotel meeting hall with some 400 mostly same-sex-attracted men and women at a conference sponsored by New Ways Ministry. The keynote speaker, Dr. Richard Isay, an openly gay psychiatrist, told the audience that married people living with same-sex attraction are violating their natures and, essentially, are ill for choosing to remain married. After the program I noticed one of the men at my table looked particularly disturbed, and I approached him in the lobby afterward to ask what was wrong. "Carl" indicated he felt very troubled and conflicted by Isay's speech. He was married, he said, and the father of two little girls whom he loved very much. The thought of leaving them "makes me want to cry," he said, adding that he had come to the conference to better understand his underlying same-sex attraction rather than have it justified, much less to be called sick for his fidelity to his marital vows. Carl, like so many others, found his own individual experience of same-sex attraction subsumed in someone else's agenda regarding the *issue* of same-sex attraction. I firmly hope that gradually everyone, no matter what side of the question they happen to be on, will remember the individuals involved first when discussing same-sex attraction and the policies, laws, and procedures meant to address it.

In the end, as long as same-sex-attracted men and women continue act upon their attractions, many will likely continue to seek help from both faith-based ministries and therapists. Their deep-seated dissatisfaction with actively homosexual lives cannot simply be blamed upon an openly hostile or otherwise disapproving culture. The problems associated with active homosexuality have far more to do with same-sex activity than with the context surrounding it. Whether the actively homosexual community wishes to acknowledge it or not, the experiences of many living with same-sex attraction resemble those described in the following letter and citations.

> I was in the gay lifestyle for eight months. I was liberated inside because I had self-acceptance, but I did not have peace in the outside environment. I thought that gay people were the same as the heterosexual people I knew. . . . They weren't. I didn't like the club scene at all. Through a couple of people I met, I learned quite a bit about the gay world. I learned that there was very little loyalty, and it seemed that most of the people at these clubs especially the one in _____, were very immature, like sixteen-year-old girls at a high school dance. Everyone knew everyone else's business. Gay men seem to be extremely

materialistic, very concerned about their outward appearance, and with the few that I met, they had no depth to them. Even more important to me was the fact that there was very little concern for the risk of contracting HIV. People have oral sex with little worry of the disease. I started to feel that maybe I was crazy for being so concerned. I don't believe that anymore. After the first four months in this lifestyle, I met a guy that seemed to be what I was looking for. He was masculine and seemed to have a brain in his head. I talked to him on the phone a couple times and we finally got together. There are so many things I could go into detail about, but I will leave that for another letter. He was great at first. Infatuation always feels good. I was so happy with this twenty-two year old that I felt that we should move in together so he could go to school up north, being that he lived in _____.
Well, after the first month of our relationship he started to show other sides of himself that I particularly didn't like. He had mood swings, he always was asking me to get him things from his bedroom, kitchen, or car like I was a servant. He was very sarcastic in his humor, and was very into material things as well. I basically tried to accept all of the things I didn't like about him, instead of talking to him about them, but he couldn't talk about serious topics without feeling awkward. I was realizing that this man was nothing like me. I think deep down it was because I was a Christian since the seventh grade, and now being twenty-five, most of the qualities that God has blessed my personality with are imbedded deeply. After another two months of inner conflict trying to feel love for this man, I realized I did not trust his character because he

had very little. He had been reluctant to get an HIV test even though he knew how paranoid I was of the disease, and I had asked him so many times to do so. The lack of trust just kept growing. I couldn't take it anymore and I broke it off. I had told myself that after this relationship I was not going to dive back into the lifestyle. In a short period of time in the gay lifestyle I witnessed a great deal of Godlessness, and a group of people that I had at first felt a part of, I was now at odds with. Now I face my major problem. I am a very sensitive person. I have very deep feelings, having an artist's personality. This guy was the first person I was ever intimate with. We had sex. We bonded ourselves together. It was very powerful. Only now do I understand why God doesn't want us to have sex randomly with people we are not bound to by marriage. The emotional attachment sex causes, can cloud your mind and make you act out of pure emotion with no logic in your thoughts and motives. . . (from a private letter sent to the author).

These problems do not generally abate with the length of time in relationship, as documented by researchers, some of whom either support same-sex activity in others or partake of it themselves. An enduring relationship between gay men may look "relatively normal" to neighbors but is quite different from a monogamous marriage. Two actively gay social researchers, David McWhirter and Andrew Mattison, spent five years studying 156 male couples — 312 individuals — "in loving relationships lasting from one to thirty-seven years," and published the results in 1984 in their book *The Male Couple: How Relationships Develop*. At the beginning of these many partnerships, the pair found that many spoke about, thought about, or hoped for sexual fidelity. "My parents were faithful to each other, and I expected us to be the same" said one man, expressing the not-infrequent ideal. But such hopes, the authors document, are simply contrary to homo-sexual yearnings, and not a single couple reported sexual fidelity lasting longer than five years.

Marshall Kirk and Hunter Madsen admit to similar find-ings in their 1990 work *After the Ball*, lamenting the fact that:

> Relationships between gay men don't usually last very long. Yet most gay men are genuinely pre-occupied with their need to find a lover. In other words, everybody's looking, but nobody's find-ing. Among "permanent" gay partnerships, the wayward impulse is inevitable . . .

> Yes, that wayward impulse is as inevitable in man-to-man affairs as in man-to-woman, only, for gays, it starts itching faster. It's a disastrous as-pect of human nature that, sooner or later, no matter how fortunate we may be, the bird that we glimpse in the pubic bush starts to look more ap-pealing than the bird that we hold in our hand. And no matter how happy a gay man may be with his lover, he's likely, eventually, to go [looking for someone else].

One experience of healing

Unlike many who have lived with same-sex attraction, I had not been terribly concerned with how it might have come about. Sure, like others, I felt curious about the phenomenon and con-cocted my own theory about how it might have come to pass, but I do not recall being as obsessed with the question as was Edmund White, who declared that "surely something so ubiquitous re-quires an explanation."

But while I never felt much of an urge to plumb my depths for answers, the fact that I had never *chosen* to feel the way I did about other boys and men remained the only dogma of my own beginnings upon which I remained as firm as granite. Later, as the hours of education, reading, prayer, and reflection brought to light the artifacts of my own history, I came to recognize certain key experiences which probably had an impact on my developing a same-sex attraction. And if I am honest I must admit that had I the chance I would have changed those experiences if I could. But on the whole, even with the parts of my life that seemed catastrophic, I did not believe I would have opted to change my lot significantly.

I was not alone in my reluctance. One of my longest and most interesting conversations with same-sex-attracted male friends, when I was still a gay activist, took place one night as we enjoyed a bottle of wine amid the wreckage of a good meal. "What," I asked, "if someone brought a box with a button on it into the room right now and set it in the middle of this table. Push the button on this box and you will be straight, heterosexual, as attracted to pretty women then as you are to cute men now. Would you push the button?" Conversation about the question lasted long into the night, but in the end no one opted for the change. It's not that the homosexually active life so enamored us — all had been around gay ghetto blocks far too often — but rather that all of us realized we preferred to live lives with the devils we knew than to open the door to unfamiliar and unrecognized demons.

So you can imagine my surprise, and even consternation, when a mere five years later I realized I felt so attracted to a woman with whom I worked that I wanted to ask her out on a date. Although at the time I found attraction to Katherine disconcerting and even a little alarming, in retrospect it shouldn't have been too surprising; Katherine had so many of the characteristics which I have come to find appealing in a woman. Experience with life's complications had deepened her faith in Christ; sharp intuitive intelligence graced her with a curious and determined mind, and years living in New York had left her open to many different types of people. Most oddly for me, however, her hair and figure attracted me as well.

My buddy Paul, a Catholic family man, stood firmly on the side of romance. "Go for it, Dave. Man, you ought to ask her out if you like her. Every guy hates asking — just get up the courage and do it." Days of indecision and urging passed. Finally, after much prayer and with butterflies filling my belly, I set out for her office. On my way I ran into another coworker who knew Katherine well and I pulled her quickly into an empty office. "Don't ask any questions right now. Just tell me — is Katherine seeing anybody like, seriously?"

"Yeah, I think so . . . she's got a boyfriend, why?"

"A serious one?"

"Yeah, pretty serious I guess. Why," she asked, a smile sliding over her face. "Does *David* have a girlfriend?"

"No! Don't be ridiculous," I said adding, "just a misunderstanding, I guess." And I went back to my office. "See," I said to Paul later, "obviously I was just mistaken. No budding straight boy here!"

Obviously I had been wrong, I thought. If my being attracted to Katherine had been from God, she would have been available to at least go out on *one* date. Something else must have been going on. Like Dickens's Scrooge on Christmas Eve, I was all too ready to blame the phenomenon of attraction to Katherine on a "a bit of bad mustard" or other external factor. Katherine and I would remain close friends and that was all. Whatever odd feelings I had when she stood close, laughed, pulled back her hair, or shot me a smart-ass comment I chalked up to some other phenomenon. No new tricks, I thought to myself, would intrude on *this* old dog's life. And, sure enough, the passage of time seemed to ratify my decision not to ask her out. Her close boyfriend proposed marriage and Katherine accepted. They set a date which eventually drew closer and closer until, finally, her last day at work before the wedding arrived and I looked up to find her with two cups of coffee outside my cubicle.

"May I come in?"

"Sure, of course, please sit," I said, pointing to the one free chair in my otherwise terminally cluttered office. We talked of obvious, comforting things, the sort of small talk I could offer when she seemed nervous and uncertain. Suddenly I found myself suppressing an almost overwhelming desire to hug her, to somehow ease her mind and make her feel whatever approached would be fine. Instead I heard myself blurting suddenly, "Katherine, I think you are the prettiest, most intelligent, compassionate, gentle woman here, and if there were anyone in my life that I would ever want to marry, it would be you." Then, as I had been standing, I had to sit down. "There must be something in the coffee," I mumbled into my cup. Then I looked up. She had gotten out of her seat and stood looking at me quietly as I blushed furiously. Then she walked over to me, kissed me on the cheek, and left the cubicle. Two days later she married and I was left with the unavoidable realization that something significant and new had begun to take root in my life — whether I wanted it to or not.

I had little idea of what I really wanted to do from that point forward. A couple of my friends at the time were seeking orientation change through therapy but I doubted I had either the emotional or financial resources needed for that route. Besides, everyone else I knew who had experienced a diminishing of same-sex attraction had fervently sought that result. I, by contrast, felt tepid and even indifferent to the idea. The concept in my own life had dropped, more or less, from the sky.

Unsure of what to do, I bided my time, noticing at first with alarm and then with greater appreciation that other women — again those with characteristics much like Katherine's — occasionally caught my eye. While I certainly did not delude myself by imagining all my attraction to men had vanished (a cute guy shirtless on a hot summer day still caught my eye as well) I had to admit to a greater bisexuality in attraction if not identity.

Even though I continued to be mostly unconscious of the changes God was working in me — and certainly remained innocent of starting them — I began to make changes in my life that deepened my realization of, and identification with, heterosexuality.

First, I became a friend with Mike, the most remarkable man I have ever met. Although writing about him here may embarrass him terribly, no real appreciation for the way that same-sex attraction has fallen away from my life would be possible without mentioning his friendship. Essentially, Mike's role in my life has been to accept, affirm, and encourage my identity as a man, particularly as a Catholic man. This is not something he has done self-consciously, in my opinion, because we have not discussed it. Rather it flows from his regard and concern for me as a human being. Essentially, Mike has had the grace to see me in ways many others, for example my family or even myself, have never seen me or even imagined seeing me. Since Mike is an active man who loves sports and is also a patient teacher and a Catholic, much of the challenge of our friendship has revolved around sports and faith. Over the course of knowing him I have done things that appeared so unlikely, that ran almost outrageously against the grain of my former identity, that my faith in Mike's faith in me provided the only way I could continue. So many of my conversations with Mike have ended with the his phrase, simultaneously desired and feared, "David, I know you can do this. Trust me."

Mountain biking, rock climbing, soccer both with older adults and college-age students, trail races, one-hundred-plus-mile bicycle rides, backpacking trips in subfreezing weather, and participation in demolition derbies have all been a part of my friendship with Mike and have all contributed, in part, to my moving away from an identity based in same-sex attraction. Of course it would be simplistic and even a little silly to attribute such a major shift in attraction and identity to sports. I know that there have been more than a few sports stars whose identity, in large part, appears based on same-sex attraction. But in my life it has been largely the world of physical challenge and limitation that has played a central role in hobbling how I understood myself as a man. Now, thanks in part to Mike's encouragement and faith in my ability, those limitations have largely fallen away and with them much of my same-sex attraction. No longer is my primary identity one of being homosexual or even fundamentally same-sex attracted.

Second, in order to save money on gas, time, and wear and tear on my automobile, I began living with Mike and his brother's young Catholic family. Andrew (Mike's brother) and his wife Regina needed a renter to help with the monthly expenses, and I needed a place to stay rather than make the long drive home every night. Living with Mike, Andrew, Regina, and their two children, Caleb and Rose, brought home to me the real joy of a loving, functional, and strong family life. What an eye-opening experience it was for me to live with a family where parents genuinely loved their children and did not fear to let them know! How wonderful I felt to share rosaries with them at night; not at first because I was such a rosary devotee, but because I treasured the peaceful glimpses into how mothers loved their children. Even more important, I began to understand and really see how fatherhood could be something very different from what I had seen in my own life. Every night Andrew blessed Regina and the children. Every night the whole family shared an intimacy and total acceptance that I, whose experience of family life had been so different, found completely beautiful and endearing. Gradually, in a very deep place in my heart, a lot of my misconceptions about family life, as well as my wounded memories, began to fall away.

These two phenomena, my experience of living in a Catholic family setting at least part of the time and my friendship with Mike, I would later discover fit into a pattern particularly common to men who experience degrees of diminishing same-sex attraction. Doctor Gerard Van den Aardweg, a Dutch psychotherapist, has been helping men and women diminish same-sex attraction from his Amsterdam practice since 1963, and in 1997 published *The Battle for Normality: A Guide for (Self-) Therapy for Homosexuality*, a book I heard him discuss while attending a Catholic conference. Van den Aardweg's work interested me in part because it seemed a synthesis of what other therapists in the field had already done. Reparative therapy, like many other therapies, tends to be as controversial and competitive among its practitioners as it appears to the lay public. Members adhere fairly firmly to different theories and sometimes heatedly denounce others. Van den Aardweg's position, by contrast, appeared less interested in claiming credit for theories than in really helping the person needing assistance, drawing liberally from other researchers and in the field. Van den Aardweg's approach also appealed to me because unlike everyone else, he validated my almost instinctive distrust of therapy and therapists. Van den Aardweg writes in *The Battle For Normality:*

> If I make a correct estimate, "psychotherapy" has had its best years. The twentieth century has been the age of psychology and psychotherapy. Great expectations were aroused, which promised new great discoveries in the human mind and new methods of behavior modification and curing mental problems and diseases. It turned out otherwise, however. Most "discoveries," like many ideas from the Freudian and Neo-Freudian schools, proved illusory — even if they still find tenacious adherents. Psychotherapy fared no better. . . . "Psychotherapy," if it is sound, can offer valuable points of insight about the origins and structure of troublesome emotions and sexual habits, but not discoveries that will cause a change overnight. For instance, no psychotherapy can provide a sudden liberation, as is pretended by certain "schools," for blocking repressed memories and emotions. There are no shortcuts through ingeniously devised learning techniques based on alleged new insights in the laws of learning, either. What is required is much common sense and quiet, daily perseverance.

Van den Aardweg's skepticism about psychotherapy doesn't throw out the baby with the bath water, however. In his spare, almost brutally-firm style, he expresses his confidence in the "common sense" insights and elements that men and women can learn from the collective experience of psychotherapy. He includes a method that lay people can apply to diminish same-sex attraction, describing an approach which, by coincidence, included some elements already present in my life. Consider how he describes the lay person who might be able to serve as "therapist" for those seeking to diminish same-sex attraction in their life. Again in *The Battle for Normality*:

> So for many who want to change but cannot find a professional helper, the "therapist" must be a person with a good dose of common sense and normal psychological insights, one who knows how to observe and has good experience in guiding people. He should possess a good intelligence and be effective in establishing rapport. Above all he must have a balanced, normal personality and sound morals. . . . I would advise the homosexually afflicted person to ask someone he senses has enough of the above qualities to guide him. Let the willing amateur therapist see himself as a helping older friend, a father, not having any scientific pretensions, but one who soberly uses his brains and normal human wisdom.

That description, in many ways, fits Mike to a "T," and as I read Van den Aardweg's book I realized how, without even realizing it, I had been working to ease same-sex attraction in my life. Merely tearing down so many of my preconceptions about myself and what I could and could not do, combined with being Mike's friend, had put me on the right road. It says volumes, for example, that after Mike agreed to read the book and take on this role in my life, his behavior toward me didn't shift noticeably. It already embodied so many of the things Van den Aardweg said I needed.

Van den Aardweg's suggestions acted so powerfully in my life because, in so many ways, they merely targeted ancient wisdom on a contemporary problem. Thinkers and leaders from Socrates to the apostles, desert fathers, and saints have long urged their followers and contemporaries to live lives of self-knowledge and examination, and such examination provides the first step of Van den Aardweg's suggested program. Using specific, probing questionnaires which, I admit, led me to confront difficult memories, Van den Aardweg helped me arm myself with the self-knowledge and understanding that assisted me in confronting deep-seated attitudes and preconceptions. Mike assisted with liberal doses of good humor, encouragement, reassurance, and love. Gradually, slowly, like a seedling pushing its way from dry earth, I have come to a heterosexual identity that, while certainly not yet perfectly formed or mature, has been at least able to stand life's vicissitudes so far.

As powerfully as Van den Aardweg's program has been in my life, I hesitate to recommend it broadly for everyone and in every circumstance. English is not Van den Aardweg's first language. That and a deep conviction about his observations and experiences makes his writing blunt and his insights sometimes difficult to hear. "Reading the book went a lot faster," a friend of mine wrote me about *The Battle for Normality*, "after I stopped throwing it against the wall every ten pages." In addition, like all battles against a deep-seated behavior, anyone undertaking this work has to be especially graced or have tremendous desire to bring it to term. Only after experiencing this healing did I under understand the passage from John's fifth chapter:

> Now there is in Jerusalem by the Sheep Gate a pool, in Hebrew called Beth-zatha, which has five porticoes. In these lay a multitude of invalids, blind, lame, paralyzed. One man was there, who had been ill for thirty-eight years. When Jesus saw him and knew that he had been lying there a long time, he said to him, "Do you want to be healed?"(5:2-6).

Healing means change and growth. Change and growth are good, but also painful. It's not simply that looking closely and honestly at ourselves reveals our warts and pimples, it's that the new way of living often offers greater lasting joy but less passing happiness. Although I am embarrassed to admit it, honesty demands I confess that many times in this process I have turned to

God in anger and weariness, announcing that, at least right then, I had come as far as I could ever imagine going. But after some rest, prayer, and often the sacrament of reconciliation, I have picked up the battle and gone on. As the lyrical team Simon and Garfunkle once wrote about a boxer in one of my favorite songs, "I am leaving, I am leaving, but the fighter still remains."

Originally, I did not plan to include this chapter in this book. The experience of healing in my own life has been so close to my center, so personal, that I had a very strong argument for keeping it to myself. Also, the whole question of healing is so volatile and polarized that saying anything at all about it, particularly anything personal, can only invite trouble. I write this with the knowledge that whatever I have written here about my own healing will be seized upon and misunderstood. Some will say, "See, it is possible, so why hasn't it happened in my life, or the life of one of my loved ones?" Others will say, "Ah, poor sod, he's obviously deluded or maybe even a liar. There can be no healing. He should have simply settled down and accepted his homosexuality." Neither group, supporters or detractors, will be happy with what I have said.

Even as I have written this chapter, controversy has shaken the midsummer quiet. A number of Christian groups, some directly involved in healing ministry and others not, stepped forward with a series of full-page advertisements in major American newspapers about the issue of healing. The ads featured, either individually or as groups, people whose experiences have been much like mine even as each case differed in the particulars. The reaction from both the gay and lesbian rights establishment and their entrenched interests in the APA has been as predictable as it has been sad. The ads were examples of "hate," they said, and do not represent any concern for the individual at all, representing instead an overwhelming and overweening political interest. Writing in the *New York Times* about the advertisements, Andrew Sullivan said:

> The campaign is clearly a desperate gambit to change the terms of the debate about homosexu-

ality, a debate the religious right has been steadily, inexorably losing for two decades. The leaders of the far right realize that unless they can redefine homosexuality as a pathological illness, it is only a matter of time before the logic of civil rights protections embraces a group of people they find threatening.

Yet Sullivan, who is himself infected with HIV, might have pondered the matter a little bit more deeply before he wrote those sentences. If the "religious right" has been steadily losing the societal debate over homosexual practice, who has been the winner — actively homosexual men and women, vast numbers of whom still suffer and die from HIV and suffer alcoholism and other addictions? Has a society that has turned a complicit eye on waves of sexual excess, both of the heterosexual and same-sex varieties, really been better for people living with same-sex attraction? Sullivan admits that "[w]e have our problems — gay men in particular — but the problems are recognizably human problems: of love, commitment, sexuality, and intimacy." But in his dogmatic view such problems cannot be rooted in homosexuality itself, and thus led him to title his column "They've Changed, So They Say."

I have written what has happened because it is true and because someone needs to step forward and testify to the reality of God's power in an individual life. I can't say why I have experienced the healing I have. I don't know why others have not. I can't say I believe that dramatically diminishing same-sex attraction is possible in every life or can be mandated by anyone other than the people actually living with the attraction. But I must testify that despite the complicated web of wounds both real and imagined, deep longings and insincerity, doubts, failures, and desires, Christ stepped forward with the knowledge, resources, and the wise and loving friends I needed to break free. For this I am deeply grateful.

In the end the bottom line is that diminishing same-sex attraction in at least some people is possible. Now the debate both in the Church and the broader society must revolve around the question of whether it is more compassionate to declare some people's identities to be fixed or to listen when they indicate that yes, they want to try to be healed.

CHAPTER SEVEN

A Grand Canyon wide

"No Money, No Honey, and a Boss." A South Bronx interpretation of the three vows of religious life, poverty, chastity, and
obedience.

The Church's teachings confront an eroticized world

Although few people comprehend the depth of the divide, a
tremendous chasm separates the orthodox Catholic view of men
and women living with same-sex attraction from that of most of
secular society as well as from that of dissident Catholics and even
some other Christian churches. The bottom of the canyon floor
reaches to the question of who human beings really are, and the
dispute cuts a jagged gash upward from this foundation across such
central topics as the meaning of sex and sexuality, the nature of
love, and the eternal fate of human beings. A dispute of such great
scope calls for a good deal more ink than can be spilled in two
chapters of a broader book. Yet it is essential that men and women
living with same-sex attraction, as well as their friends, families,
and ministers, comprehend at least the rough outline of the debate.

From the Garden forward

Very early in my career as a gay activist, when I first began having fun bamboozling Christians, I made one of my opponents at the University of Maryland so upset that he wound up blurting out Jerry Falwell's throw-away line, "God made Adam and Eve, not Adam and Steve." Of course I leaped on the line and the assertion, treating it with little respect because, at least it seemed to me, it had been thrown out with little respect. Yet years later, when I began deeply pondering the role of same-sex attraction in my life and faith, I understood that that unfortunate little rhyme rested on a much deeper position than my opponent at the time had been able to articulate or that I had been willing to admit.

A very high, and indeed holy, view of human beings underpins all of the Catholic Church's teachings on sexuality and sexual expression. God created human beings, in the eyes of the Church at least, to be far removed from the evolutionists' "hairless apes" of the last century. Human beings are persons in the universe, which is to say we possess self-awareness, free will, and a soul with an eternal destiny. Humans, along with the angels, are the only creatures in the universe able to act completely as both subjects and objects of actions. Animals and other creatures of the natural world live lives tied primarily to instinct or to a relatively constricted reasoning ability dictated in part by instinct. This does not imply human beings have a universal right to act irresponsibly toward animals, but points out that while a chimp might learn to get termites out of a termite mound with a piece of grass, it appears doubtful that he worries about whether he looks ridiculous while doing so. The level of self-awareness that allows human beings to both be concerned with how they may appear while doing something, as well as *why* they do it, appears at this stage at least to belong exclusively to us. The *Catechism of the Catholic Church* (CCC) notes:

> Being in the image of God the human individual
> possesses the dignity of a person, who is not just

something, but someone. He is capable of self-knowledge, of self-possession and of freely giving himself and entering into communion with other persons. And he is called by grace to a covenant with his Creator, to offer him a response of faith and love that no other creature can give in his stead (357).

This freedom, this dignity of being some*one* and not merely some*thing*, covers human beings' entire creation, though individual human beings are free to lose at least some of their freedom through overpowering attachments to other human beings or even other things. To paraphrase a noted American evangelist, an idol is anything we cannot let go of which is less than ourselves. By that standard, many of us are idolaters, having subjected ourselves to money, sex, alcohol, other narcotics, or pleasure. In many ways an addict is an addict is an addict, but not all addictions are equal and some are more socially acceptable than others. But whether our addictions are of the type that raise our neighbor's rage or envy is really immaterial. Freedom lost is freedom lost. Our loss of freedom to these things does not argue that we never had it or, as so many participants of twelve-step programs know, we cannot get it back.

Human freedom in this regard extends to sexuality too. Human beings are singular among creatures in that we can express ourselves sexually without necessarily tying that expression to reproduction. Very few other creatures do this. Most use their sexual organs only at very specified times when reproduction is most likely, and many, much to the chagrin of zoos and planned breeding programs, will not try to reproduce at all if all the other factors — environment, food, etc. — are not perfect. Human beings alone have the freedom to make love and not merely have sex.

Now this is not anything terribly new. Many people, if not most, learned the basics of human reproduction in high school or college biology and we have whole industries of entertainment, advertising, medicine, technology, and manufacturing whose profits depend on widening the gap between sexual expression and parenthood. Yet in its rush to celebrate, indeed obsess upon, one aspect of sex and repress the other, contemporary culture has overlooked a central part of the mystery of human sexuality. In short, we have blinded ourselves to the fullness of sexuality and sexual expression God intended.

The missing link

A few years ago an Australian director and film company produced a truly bad movie, a kind of visual tour through many sexual stereotypes where "natural love" was meant to contrast, seduce, and finally overcome the traditional Christian morality, which the film portrayed as stilted, joyless, and repressed. In *Sirens*, three supermodels cavort naked on a beautiful tropical isle as live-in lovers (the Sirens) to an artist who paints voluptuous versions of classic works. An Anglican diocese has unwittingly agreed to show some of these paintings by sponsoring a show of the artist's works. Upon hearing of the content of the pictures, the bishop has dispatched one of his trusted ministers, with his relatively new wife, to the island to persuade the artist to withdraw some of the more scandalous and blasphemous pictures. During the course of their visit both the Sirens and the Adonis-like mute handyman gradually seduce the minister's wife, who then, in turn, seduces her husband into the atmosphere. The results, the movie wants to claim, are a marriage made stronger by infidelity and generally more open and "human" minds all around.

The movie was really quite silly and only merits mention at all because of the conversation which took place afterward between myself, a Catholic friend named Ray, and a secularly-minded Jewish friend of his named Dan. As we drove home, everyone deplored the film's aesthetics and imagery, which felt about as subtle as a jackhammer on a Sunday morning, but the conversation soon was hung up because Ray and I were convinced that the film was morally offensive and Dan was unable to understand our concern. This led to a fairly deep discussion of the meaning of sexuality and our attitude toward it, which culminated in Dan's frustrated exclamation: "But your view of sex is so, so . . . sacred!" Exactly. The secular world has forgotten what the Church never has. God intends that sex between two human persons, the subjects of their actions, who are themselves free to choose good or evil, is and should be sacred.

Through the years I have become convinced that human sexual expression belongs in the realm of the sacred for many reasons, but for the purpose of this book I will focus on three primary ones.

First, human sexuality and sexual expression involves the whole of the God-created person. Eyes of love and faith see not only the body of the natural world but also the humanity and spirit that are not necessarily evident. Second, a sense of the sacred must rule human sexual expression because human fertility is a part of sexuality and human fertility allows human beings, through their sexual union, to become co-creators with God of another eternally destined human being. Third, the human sexual act, faithfully done in the context of marriage, represents in microcosm Christ's relationship with each of us and foreshadows heaven.

I find it ironic that we have lost the sense of the sacred in sexual expression right at the point where, as a culture, we turn more to the discussion of self-esteem. After all, which is the higher view of human sexuality? Christianity's, in which human beings as free men and women give themselves to each other out of their own free will in a lifetime embrace, or the world's, in which human coupling appears to have more to do with being captive to emotion and desire than to free choice? Human sexual expression needs to be recognized as sacred (and thus tending to lift up self-esteem) because it involves the whole of the human person. God declared everything about the people He created to be good, and that characterization persists even through our own Fall and corresponding misuse of that goodness. Talk about a root of self-esteem!

Psychiatrists have a well-established principle called the psychosomatic union, or the psychosomatic unity. It's sort of a scientific refutation, although I am sure many psychiatrists would feel uncomfortable hearing it characterized this way, of some of the ancient heresy of Gnosticism's central tenets. Essentially, gnostics believed in a very dualist creation, which can be boiled down to the slogan "spirit (or soul) good, matter (or body) evil." Human bodies in the gnostic view tended not to be *part* of human beings, but instead to be something human beings use or wear, almost like cars or suits of clothes. Gnostics saw human bodies not as integral to the human person but external, separate, and thus to a large extent irrelevant. Acts done with the body, in the gnostic view, tended not to be viewed as moral or immoral because the body did not merit evaluation in a moral sense. But the Church's view, confirmed by the scientific understanding of the psychosomatic union of body and soul, refutes that premise with the reality that human beings are greater than the sum of their parts. Human souls, or *psyches,* and human bodies, or *somas,* do not exist as separate independent entities but instead interrelate. What is done in our bodies is reflected in our souls and the attitude of our soul impacts our bodies. We are multidimensional creatures with a foot in each of the spiritual or material worlds, not ghosts trapped in biological machines or spirits driving human bodies. Thus, the stress in our souls we experience because of a bad situation at work often plays out in our bodies with a number of physical complaints like high blood pressure and other illnesses.

Naturally, this means a good deal when it comes to sex and how we view our sexuality. Far from the current secular view that tends to downplay the importance of sexual acts, seeing them merely as something we *do*, sexual expression really comes very close to exposing *who we are.* The intimacy, communication, trust, and pleasure of sex, as well as the vulnerability of exposure and deep emotional bonding — whether between a married man and woman or mere one-night stand — impacts the soul more than the body. The flat, lonely, morning-after pain known all too well by so many is the inevitable result of a heart and soul given in sex, but offered in vain. The *Catechism* notes that the sexuality by which man and woman give themselves to one another through acts "proper and exclusive" to spouses is not just biology but involves the "innermost being of the human person," and is "an integral part of the love by which a man and woman commit themselves totally to one another until death" [FC 11] (2361).

The sacred should mark human sexual expression as well because God created human sexuality with fertility, and fertility is the power to co-create, with God, another human being who will consist not only of a body but of an eternal soul as well. This is a key aspect of sexual expression that our overly-selfish culture misunderstands and disregards. God did not create sexuality *only* to give pleasure or even to solely edify the couple's love for another, but to give human beings a glimpse, through a crack in immortality, at what creation is like. Creation, true creation, where something is made from absolute nothing, willed into existence, rightly belongs only to God. He was the One who has called us into existence or, as I like to speculate, *sang* us into existence. (Noted Christian writer C.S. Lewis has observed that heaven knows two types of sound, music and silence.) But God has given human beings a tiny share in that joy by allowing human love to spill over into procreation.

Our culture easily forgets procreation's role in sexual expression these days. Procreation incarnates parental love in children, and, as many secularists ask, who wants more kids? Children require sacrifice, maturity, patience, and tremendous energy. Children change your life and make you an adult forever, somebody else's mom or dad. How much easier it is to simply focus on the pleasurable aspects of sexuality, the playboy lifestyle. It's not surprising, as noted author and Boston College Professor Peter Kreeft has observed, that we speak of the play*boy* mentality and not the play*man*. Our created fertility makes human sexual expression sacred because it is the gateway by which sex moves beyond the mingling of souls and entwining of limbs into the intermingling of lives and destinies. When a man and woman open themselves sexually to one another, they also open the door to a possible continuing relationship as perhaps unwilling parents if unmarried or as willing parents with a deepening relationship if married. This is the hard reality which grounds romantic speculations. "Love" can be claimed by many and even acted upon physically, but marriage and fertility put love to a test with the annoying habits, snotty noses, wet diapers, and the other stuff of real life. Fertility matures the transitory, romantic passion of courtship and early marriage ripens into parenthood's harder, self-sacrificing love.

But above all else, the mystery of Christ's incarnation sets the seal of sacredness on human sexual, marital, and familial relationships. How often in the rush of Christmas shopping and parties do we forget that Christ arrived among us as a *baby*; that long before He shed blood and water from His side for the world's salvation He first lay in the blood and water of human birth. Throughout the Church's history, this has been a difficult teaching. Denying it has served as the starting point for many heresies, a few of which persist to this day. Can we dare ask, to paraphrase the skepticism of many early heretics, whether God needed to be wiped of the blood of a woman? That He appeared for nine months in a female womb? Yes, we must reply, He did. Heretics, from Arius to John Spong, stumble on this teaching. Arius taught the Christ wasn't really, truly God and Spong suggests that a passing Roman soldier, not the angel Gabriel, bears responsibility for Jesus' conception. Yet, analyzed closely and with charity, their arguments have to do more with a diminished view of femininity, masculinity, sexuality, humanity, and children than they do with decrying an unreasoning dislike of sex on the part of the Church. Our culture's problems with marriage, sexual expression, parenthood, and family stem not from the Church today making too much of sex, but from the secular mind's (even among churchmen) making too little of it.

Finally, human sexual expression must be seen as sacred because, in lifting marriage to a sacrament, Christ elevated the institution from the bonds of a merely legal contract to that of a specific channel of God's grace. Sacraments, as the Church says in part, "are efficacious signs of grace, instituted by Christ and entrusted to the Church, by which divine life is dispensed to us. The visible rites by which the sacraments are celebrated signify and make present the graces proper to each sacrament" (CCC 1131).

This can be seen most clearly in the way the Church understands Christ's repeated use of marriage as a metaphor for the Kingdom of God, the "hard" teaching He delivered on divorce, and the repeated way God speaks to Israel about fidelity as a sign of committed love. Beginning with the public miracle at the Cana wedding, Christ taught consistently that weddings and marriage were a suitable metaphor for the relationship between God and the people He loves. Changing water to wine at the wedding at Cana was a visible sign of the teaching Christ would deliver consistently over the course of His ministry and which Paul, the other apostles, and the early Church Fathers would build upon. Marriage, the Church insisted from the beginning, is meant to be a bodily, earthly sacrament of the relationship with God that culminates in heaven. In contrast with the Old Testament teaching on marriage, which tended to see the relationship more as a contract than a covenant, subject to divorce "for hardness of heart," Christ and the Church hearkened back to the Old Testament prophet's understanding. The *Catechism* notes:

> Sacred Scripture begins with the creation of man and woman in the image and likeness of God and concludes with a vision of "the wedding-feast of the Lamb" [*Rev* 19:7, 9; cf. *Gen* 1:26-27]. Scripture speaks throughout of marriage and its "mystery," its institution and the meaning God has given it, its origin and its end, its various realizations throughout the history of salvation, the difficulties arising from sin and its renewal "in the Lord" in the New Covenant of Christ and the Church [*1Cor* 7:39; cf. *Eph* 5:31-32] (1602).

So, I can hear some readers muttering, all this may be lovely and might even be true, but what does this mean practically? What does it mean on the street? What impact, if more people followed it, might the Church's understanding of the sacredness of human sexual expression have on the way human beings should relate to one another?

First, the reality of the Church's teachings on sex needs to be seen as the reflection of reality it is rather than as arbitrarily assigned rules. The Church's teachings on sexual morality are much more akin to Newton's laws, which primarily describe objective reality, than to national mores from which a government might make law. Just as physicists have no power to simply reverse the law of gravity, the Church has no power to simply change moral reality. One thousand bishops meeting for one thousand years could declare each year that premarital sex, divorce, masturbation, pornography, adultery, or same-sex acts are acceptable and even praiseworthy. But their thousands of declarations would not change the natures of those acts and would not stop human beings from paying a physical, emotional, and spiritual price for them.

Second, if more people accepted the sacred nature of the sexual act, there would likely be a social, cultural, and economic counterrevolution in the United States and across the developed world. Consider, briefly, how we have switched the values of the sacred and economic orders. In many situations sex has been reduced to being little more than a means of exchange, a tool of the advertising industry, an inducement to buy or sell, a recreation. I recall my first day in Amsterdam when, even as non-Christian and a fairly active immoralist, I felt a little shocked and perplexed by full frontal nudity on huge billboards advertising toothpaste. Did the advertisers really mean the message to be "use our brand and look better naked?" Sex on talk shows gets better ratings, sexual talk at parties has become more common, and Hollywood makes a movie that purports to say that everyone has a monetary price for which they would commit adultery. Pornography, both "soft" and "hard" core, has become a multi-billion dollar industry. And the more we have filmed, televised, pictured, traded, bought, sold, used, and abused sexuality, the more we have forgotten what God meant it to be — something holy in and of itself. All that would change, I believe, if more people came to a deeper understanding of the depth of meaning underlying human sexuality.

As our regard for sexuality has diminished, our regard for money has increased. Money is the very stuff of the marketplace and by definition a means of exchange, yet in many ways we have made its accumulation an end in and of itself. Quaker writer, philosopher, and commentator Richard Foster perceptively charts the different ways money has a spiritual power. Money becomes an idol so easily in our lives, offering the illusion of comfort, control, and, above all, power. The amount of money we have or don't have becomes something "private," "set-apart," and even almost sacred. Think back— at what age did your parents remonstrate with you for asking someone, if you ever did, how much money they made or whether they were rich? Such questions, I was told at an early age, were not "polite." Yet the topic of how much money we make or don't make ought not to be something we regard with either pride or humiliation but should be treated as something simply factual and belonging "to the street." Consider the irony that people will trade over their cocktails the most detailed gossip and conversation about sexual practices and issues, and yet will think it rude if in "polite society" someone asks the specifics of our savings or salary. Or consider an even deeper irony. As we strive in so many ways, by means of devices, drugs, and even abortion, to render sex infertile (unable to reproduce), we simultaneously seek advice, inventions, and schemes to make our money fertile (able to reproduce through a preferably high interest rate). Dante cast those who seek to make sexual expression deliberately infertile and people who lent money at interest close to one another in his poetic inferno. They each, in their own way, made war against the natural order, the first by rending infertile that in which God entrusted fertility and the second by making fertile that which is really sterile. It's not that money in and of itself is "dirty," nor is sexual expression. But both have a power to significantly alter the way we think and feel about each of them, and both can lead us to view each of them wrongly.

Of course this is but a small sketch of the richness of the Church's teaching on creation, human sexuality, and sexual expression. Nothing can really compare with reading some of the Church's key documents, or the *Catechism* itself, to get a fuller view of how beautifully the Catholic Church views human sexuality.

CHAPTER EIGHT

Go tell it on the mountain

I remember being surprised, when I purchased my first copy of the new *Catechism of the Catholic Church*, at how concisely — critics might complain, too briefly — the Church spoke to such a broad and, in my mind at least, important topic as same-sex attraction or homosexuality. "The subject didn't even merit an individual section," I huffed to myself as I flipped through the pages. The teaching on same-sex attraction appears as a subset of the Church's teaching on chastity, which itself serves as a subset of the teaching on sexual morality. "Buried!" I fumed to myself. At least it had a spot in the index!

But later, as I began to become more familiar with both the teaching and myself, I began to appreciate more deeply the logic behind both the teaching and where it appears. The message of the Church is that people living with same-sex attraction, like everyone else, are more than the sum of our temptations, and that she calls us to be saints. The *Catechism* sums up the Church's teaching in three relatively short, dry, technical and, frankly, some-what dull paragraphs. But behind the dull phraseology stands a unique and powerful liberating vision of people living with same-sex attraction. Here is the entire entry:

> Homosexuality refers to relations between men or between women who experience an exclusive or predominant sexual attraction toward persons of the same sex. It has taken a great variety of forms through the centuries and in different cultures. Its psychological genesis remains largely unexplained. Basing itself on Sacred Scripture, which presents homosexual acts as acts of grave depravity, tradition has always declared that "homosexual acts are intrinsically disordered" [CDF, *Persona humana* 8]. They are contrary to the natural law. They close the sexual act to the gift of life. They do not proceed from a genuine affective and sexual complementarity. Under no circumstances can they be approved (CCC 2357).

> The number of men and women who have deep-seated homosexual tendencies is not negligible. They do not choose their homosexual condition; for most of them it is a trial. They must be accepted with respect, compassion, and sensitivity. Every sign of unjust discrimination in their regard should be avoided. These persons are called to fulfill God's will in their lives and, if they are Christians, to unite to the sacrifice of the Lord's Cross the difficulties they may encounter from their condition (CCC 2358).

> Homosexual persons are called to chastity. By the virtues of self-mastery that teach them inner freedom, at times by the support of disinterested friendship, by prayer and sacramental grace, they can and should gradually and reso-

lutely approach Christian perfection (CCC 2359).

The difference between being and doing

The Church's teaching on same-sex attraction and activity rests on a central pillar. While Scripture, tradition, the nature of the human person, creation, and the full meaning of sexuality all testify to the immorality of homosexual acts, those acts' objective immorality does not slop over onto the person who is tempted to those acts. "Under no circumstances" may same-sex acts be approved, the *Catechism* reads, but people living with same-sex attraction "can and should gradually and resolutely approach Christian perfection."

I will discuss the importance of this central teaching in a moment, but several inferences drawn from these paragraphs deserve some additional comment.

First, the teaching recognizes the worth, value, and eternal destiny of every human person. Many men and women living with same-sex attraction have been victimized. Peers, their own Christian communities, or even their own family members have often made boys and girls, men and women who experience same-sex attraction feel alienated, dirty, ashamed of having the feelings they have. Most have no more control over those feelings than they control the movements of the moon in the night sky. But not here, not from Mother Church, who looks at people living with same-sex attraction and says, "They must be accepted with respect, compassion, and sensitivity" (CCC 2358).

Second, the teaching speaks to the reality of sex. Based on the Church's understanding of sex as having dual and sacred purposes (see chapter seven) the teaching, briefly, lays out the Church's objections to same-sex activity. "They are contrary to the natural law. They close the sexual act to the gift of life. They do not proceed from a genuine affective and sexual complementarity. Under no circumstances can they be approved" (CCC 2357).

Same-sex acts are contrary to the natural law because the natural law reflects the world and human beings as God created them. Natural law differs from regulatory or so-called positive law in that it speaks less to how things should be than to how they are, less to guide behavior than to point out cause and effect. In other words, natural law prohibits same-sex activity because same-sex activity does not include the full purpose of sex as it actually exists in flesh-and-blood reality. Natural law's objections to same-sex activity are not so much a matter of opinions as of molecules and cells, less a matter for bishops or legislators to debate than for anatomists to describe. Natural law speaks to the immorality, *per se*, of something like anal sex because anal sex does not employ the biology of the active or passive partner to the purposes for which it is clearly prepared. Anal sex is immoral in natural law terms, not because it violates mere opinions or human laws but because it violates natural biological boundaries, which arise from human nature itself. Participants in anal sex should not be surprised if their activity carries with it great risks of natural ills.

The teaching's observation that same-sex acts are contrary to natural law flows into the following observation: those same-sex acts are closed to the transmission of life. This on its face is obvious, but deserves comment because it is still occasionally misunderstood, and because, when I have pressed the point in discussions with people of opposing views, I sometimes confront the contention that "open to life" can mean more than procreation.

The Church does not teach that conception *must* occur for sexual expression to be moral, only that those sexual acts must remain *open* to conception of a new human being. In other words, in the Church's view, when a husband and wife make love they should be there completely to one another. They should withhold nothing of themselves from each other, not their fertility, not their personality, not their loneliness or desire. The ability to procreate is part of the human person, both in body and spirit. The Church maintains that we cannot morally disregard it or will it away simply because we have decided that it is inconvenient. Both husband and wife come to bed with all their different identities intact, that of husband or wife, lover, father or mother already as well as potential father and mother again or for the first time. All of them need to be represented, even if age or natural infertility precludes or renders unlikely that conception will occur. Sexual acts must be open to conception because all of the different roles that hinge on conception are part of the man's and woman's reality in their very creation as men and women. Being open to conception means being aware that the dimensions of the human personality reach into the bedroom too. Taking one another to bed does not simply flatten us from our three dimensional persons into two-dimensional cartoons — although we often act as though that were the case. (How many hearts have been torn when men and women awoke to discover the cartoon partner beside them actually has depth, personality, needs, wants, dreams, and fears and could not be reduced to a means for self-gratification?) By coming together fully, completely, with one another, both husband and wife provide the best safeguards they can against the danger that they begin to take one another for granted or to objectify one another.

Some argue that the Church's "open to life" requirement should not be so "narrowly" defined as procreation. "What about art," they ask; "what about music, philanthropy, discovery, wonder, aren't those experiences and products open to life too?"

Yes, they give greater joy and meaning to life, but no, they cannot be seen in the same realm as procreation. The assertion that such things are, also "life-giving" argues for a certain equivalence. A single human life, with its eternal destiny and even in its most shallow and degraded form, is still worth more than the sum of the greatest artistic works of history's greatest artists. There can be no equivalency of value. If I had a choice between saving the life of a filthy, diseased drug addict on the street outside the Metropolitan Museum of Art or of running inside to save priceless works of religious art in danger of burning, I would hope for the grace to save the addict. Same-sex couples who create great art can try to justify their sexual expression on the grounds that it opens their relationship to the creation of great art, but that cannot be seen as the same thing as being open to the procreation of a single human life.

Trying to justify sexual expression by tying it to anything

other than life moves the conversation again from the body — that stubborn construction of flesh and bone that refuses to obey our wishes and simply disappear. There may *be* a link between sexual expression and the creation of great art. Authors, poets, painters, playwrights, and musicians, dancers, and directors may believe they do their really outstanding and inspired work after making love to their wives or husbands. But the creation of that work is not why the fullness of their sexual expression carries with it a God-given fertility. The biological reality of ecstasy and ejaculation, receptivity and ovulation, remains oriented toward the (pro)creation of human beings — God's truly miraculous and eternal works of art.

The Church's teaching on the transmission of life is part of the meaning of her next observation: those same-sex acts do not flow from an essential *complementarity*. Webster's most recent Dictionary offers as the second and third definitions of complementary, which is the root of complementarity, "serving to fill out or complete" and "mutually supplying each other's lack." The Church recognizes that men and women, in a very real sense, lack something in their personalities and persons that they can only get from the other. The attraction between men and women, unlike that documented among same-sex couples, is rooted strongly in the desire for and exploration of the other. By contrast, same-sex couples often find attractive one another's similarities, even to the point, noted in one interview in *The Male Couple*, of feeling as though they share each other's bodies and breath. In the attraction of man for woman and vice versa there is a desire for the other as other; in same-sex couples there is often the desire for the other as redundant. It should be noted, that, in the published literature at least, the desire for sameness among same-sex couples is often named as a cause of same-sex promiscuity. The novelty of sameness declines fairly rapidly among many same-sex couples. They suffer from the lack of complementarity that serves as part of heterosexual couples' emotional base.

Third, "[Same-sex attraction's] psychological genesis remains largely unexplained" (CCC 2357). Here the Church, in all humility, admits that the she doesn't know everything about the science of this topic. I expect more information will become available over time. Mental and other medical health professionals and researchers already have a good deal of information about how same-sex attraction might develop, at least in men, and that information will likely gradually keep coming to the surface whether gay and lesbian activists want it to or not. But, for now, the results, observations, and research are not conclusive — and may never be. The Church chooses to keep her silence about what is, at its roots, still a mystery. But this sentence has a subtext too. It foreshadows the teaching in the next paragraph of the *Catechism* that men and women living with same-sex attraction do not choose their condition and for most it is a trial. It should be stressed as well that while knowledge of same-sex attraction's genesis underpins and informs the Church's teaching on the morality of homosexual sex acts, it does not determine it.

Being and doing II or the defeat of determinism

The points made above are all important aspects and background to the Church's teaching. But not *the* most important. The crucial point is this: *same-sex acts or inclinations do not define or determine the personhood or identity of people living with same-sex attraction.* We are more than what we do or even what we are inclined to do. We have a reality far deeper than that, and our essential depth cannot be, *ipso facto*, tarred with brushes sometimes reeking with the confused, selfish, or even wicked desires we might experience. In the Church's view, when it comes to seeking to follow Christ, people living with same-sex attraction are every bit as loved, desired, called, chastened, encouraged, and blessed, as anyone else. My temptations no more determined or dictated my actions when I was sexually active with men than other people's temptations determine or define theirs. The specifics of my own temptations neither promote me for sainthood nor preclude me from sanctity.

I find this a very humanizing perspective in the midst of a discussion that is more often dehumanizing on all sides. At a time when groups of many different affiliations appear ever more intent on treating people living with same-sex attraction as icons of a broader "issue," the Roman Catholic Church looks at us first as individuals. Her vision mixes maturity and maternity, hope, and responsibility, worry, expectation, and prayer. She is the Irish grandmother cooking us Italian meatballs in an African kitchen while singing Polish folk songs. And she scolds as she hugs, and calls us to grow when we least want to and to reconcile our hearts in matters which, in their hour of horror, appear beyond even a breath of forgiveness. She is patient. She knows what she is about and that this work is not, ultimately, hers but God's. She lives to see us home.

It is her lack of determinism, her complete willingness to deal with each of us first as individuals, that lifts the Church's view of same-sex attraction head and shoulders above everyone else's, whether they be to her left or right theologically or philosophically. In that she is (as far as I know) unique. All of the other major participants in this discussion with whose positions I am familiar — whether conservative Christian, radically gay and lesbian activist, or completely secularist — share a willingness to speak primarily (if not exclusively) about same-sex attraction and activity first as an issue over which to fight. So few seem able to remember what Thomas Schmidt took pains to remember on the first page of *Straight and Narrow,* that there are real people attached to this discussion, real people with real hearts and real pain in those hearts. Only secondarily, if at all, will either side adopt the quieter tone and listening manner that befits discussions of things so close to hearts, minds, bodies, and spirits. Yet it is this latter tone which so badly needs to be used more often.

From some on the right wing, the tone is one of condemnation, traditional self-righteousness, anger, fear, and even that darker emotion which lies beyond anger and which I don't even feel comfortable naming, much less discussing at length. This approach to the discussion of same-sex attraction treats people living with this temptation as pariahs by choice, wicked sinners, depraved participants in unholy orgies. It presents the damage of same-sex activity less as the sorrows of a distressed humanity than as the righteous proof of diseased souls. Naturally their ranks include those who march outside gay events with signs that say things like "God hates Gays," but it has also included some conservative Christian groups that line up against gay and lesbian groups along the American cultural fault lines created around same-sex attraction. One such group, for example, assured visitors to its site on the World Wide Web that "[c]ompassion — not bigotry — impels [them] to support healing for homosexuals who want to change their orientation." Further, a few lines down, the organization reassures visitors that the staff "wage the war against the homosexual agenda and fight to maintain the traditional meaning of 'family.' " People who protect families and children and seek to stand for righteous lives, the message implies, are purely heterosexual.

Using words like "war" and "fight" and lumping of all people living with same-sex attraction into one group pursuing a "homosexual agenda" tends to alienate and stigmatize and tends further to disregard the real voices of individuals living with same-sex attraction. Such an approach is deeply deterministic. By lumping everyone together, freedom of individual action is not encouraged and actually seems to be undermined. What would one of these groups do when confronted with one of the many people living with same-sex attraction whose life didn't fit the pattern? Would such conservative Christian organizations accept the support of someone whose heart might be on Christ but whose wrist was less than completely firm?

Now I would not want to make too much of this. As time has passed more conservative Christian groups have come to better understand same-sex attraction; their attitudes and rhetoric have changed. There is more willingness to recognize people as individuals with their own opinions, thoughts, and desires and not as mere automatons seeking an "agenda." Also, organizations like the Family Research Council, Concerned Women for America, and other similar groups are primarily lobbying and political groups. Issues are the stuff of their life, they might say, and they should not be expected to worry overmuch about providing a pastoral approach. Except that in so many cases conservative Christians I have met have tended to default to those positions as their own, and tend not to think more deeply or clearly about a topic that makes them feel uncomfortable. If the predominant Christian public face towards people living with same-sex attraction is going to be primarily political, then tremendous pastoral opportunities and obligations go begging.

The left side of the spectrum, which tends to reinforce identities based on same-sex attraction, ironically also employs determinism and looks at people living with same-sex attraction primarily as issue-icons and not as individuals. When I read the vitriol dumped on people who seek to diminish their same-sex attraction; when people pursuing chastity have been called "self-hating homosexuals" and dismissed perfunctorily; when the Dignity chapter in Pittsburgh, Pennsylvania, feels the need to form a chastity support group for people within its ranks seeking to live counter to the predominant Dignity culture, I see a failure to look at people first as individuals.

But the greatest damage, in my opinion, comes from religious leaders of both sides who choose determinism and an "issue" approach over the pastoral and the personal. Pastors on the right who have defined same-sex sins as "especially sinful" and, more importantly, state that merely being tempted to such sins preclude one from heaven wreak grave damage on individual men and women seeking to make sense of their lives in the face of a predominant same-sex attraction. And pastors on the left who deny the spiritual and bodily gravity of same-sex sins do the members of their flock who live with same-sex attraction no favors either.

Boston College Philosopher Peter Kreeft has pointed out the world of difference between individual Christians trying, and failing, to live by the moral Christian norm and Christian pastors attempting to define sin away. The first belongs with human nature — the struggle human beings have to go through seeking heaven. The second has its origins, I speculate, in human foible and also something a good deal more sinister.

Consider for a moment Christ's parable of the Prodigal

Son. The younger son, who had demanded his share of his father's wealth early and traveled to a far country, awakens one morning with the pigs. He has squandered his wealth, and he realizes that his life is miserable. Even his father's hired hands live better than he does. He goes home — and discovers when he arrives that the Kingdom of God exceeds all his expectations. The young man in the parable is really quite fortunate. When he finally realizes how badly he lives, he is able to set out for home. He remembers the way. But thanks to many well-meaning Christian leaders, thousands of men and women living with same-sex attraction are worse off than the prodigal son. If same-sex acts are not sinful any longer, how does one repent? On the morning after your one-hundredth one-night-stand, when you come to understand how far from grace and goodness you have strayed, how do you come home? Overly conservative and deterministic pastors on the right might build towering walls around the Kingdom of God, but faithless deterministic pastors on the left threaten to burn the bridges and destroy the maps leading there. Indeed, there is something I have always found maddeningly dehumanizing in the left's often (but not always) unspoken assumption that men and women living with same-sex attraction will be unable to live chastely and that they should not even be asked to try. How dare they decide, unilaterally, that men and women living with same-sex attraction don't even deserve the option? Free will is a key element of what makes us human beings. To take it away is to dehumanize, making of us something akin to mere animals.

The Roman Catholic Church's position avoids either extreme, neither automatically classifying people with same-sex attraction as especially blessed or particularly damned. The Church looks at men and women living with same-sex attraction and points to Christ, just as she does with everyone else. Life as Christ's disciple is not easy for someone with same-sex attraction, but it is not easy for anyone else either.

In this context I came to understand the quiet, understated place in the *Catechism* the Church sets aside for its teaching on same-sex attraction. This particular cross is no bigger or heavier than any others — just different. It has a different heft, a different weight, and requires a different humility, but with God's help it can be carried just as well.

Controversial points in the Church's teaching

Some might say this an overly-benign interpretation of the Church's teaching. Aside from the Church's teaching on chastity (which I will explore more deeply in a few pages) hasn't the Church also labeled people? Hasn't the Church called people living with same-sex attraction "objectively disordered?" No. The Church has never, to my knowledge, called *people* living with same-sex attraction "objectively disordered." What the Church has said is that same sex attraction is *itself* an "objective disorder." I haven't been able to track down the origin of the allegation that the Church has called people objectively disordered, but I have been able to discover activists' reactions to a 1986 letter from the Vatican's Congregation for the Doctrine of the Faith (CDF) in which the term first appears. Here are the specific paragraphs from the CDF:

> In the discussion which followed the publication of the Declaration [a previous Vatican document which touched on the topic], however, an overly benign interpretation was given to the homosexual condition itself, some going so far as to call it neutral, or even good. Although the particular inclination of the homosexual person is not a sin, it is a more or less strong tendency ordered toward an intrinsic moral evil; and thus the inclination itself must be seen as an objective disorder. Therefore special concern and pastoral attention should be directed toward those who have this condition, lest they be led to believe that the living out of this orientation in homosexual activity is a morally acceptable option. It is not.

As far as I can tell, some people reading this document in 1986 had identities heavily invested in same-sex activity and temptation. When the CDF letter appeared describing same-sex attraction as "objective disorder," people heard the Vatican call *them* objectively disordered, which the Church did not do. The Church's position remained (and remains) that people are more than the sum of their temptations.

In order to understand the term "objective disorder" in terms of same-sex attraction, it helps to have some of the insights of Christian anthropology. In Christian terms, God created human beings to enjoy communion with each other and with God. This communion is a relationship into which human beings enter (or not) of their own free will, as I mentioned previously. That ability to choose freely is the main thing that differentiates human beings from other non- or sub-personal beings. Further, this choice is key because the happiness of real communion with God will be the happiness of human beings experiencing the fulfillment of our creation — coming to the deep experience of who and what we are as human beings — as gendered, fertile, people. Remember that our bodies count as part of our creation and we cannot simply refuse to include the body in our definition of self or what constitutes happiness. God did not create human sexual capability solely for personal pleasure or solipsism. It was created for genuine love and the possible creation of children. Therefore, inclinations or appetites in the human person must be evaluated in terms of whether they are capable of leading to actions which are in order with all parts of the human person (body, mind, and spirit) and which are ordered toward our communion with God. Homosexual acts fail on both counts. Now, it's important to state clearly that this does not mean that every heterosexual act is intrinsically ordered. Extramarital sex, adultery, and masturbation are all, more or less, disordered actions, although they grow out of a desire of man for woman and woman for man which, in and of itself, is ordered to human happiness and God.

Describing same-sex sexual activity as "objectively disordered" has never carried the impact for me that it has for other people. Gradually I have come to understand the term and its

127

definition better, particularly in the light of the Catholic family life I have experienced over almost the last two years. After I tasted and saw, up close, the great good of a healthy, functional, and faith-filled family, and when I considered what family life means for both immediate family members and the broader community, I understood that the creation of strong family life is one great object of sexual expression. Even the relatively good, actively gay life I had previously led simply cannot compare. I understand how God-given sexuality could fairly be described as objectively disordered when it becomes ordered toward any other object — whether same-sex or fetish or anything else. It becomes a drive disordered in its very objectives.

The letter in which this term appeared also took note of the rise of the organization called Dignity and other groups of Catholics who claimed to represent the Catholic position on same-sex attraction (and whose "ministry" I had experienced myself). Catholics living with same-sex attraction, and others, the CDF said, should be wary of such groups:

> Nevertheless, increasing numbers of people today, even within the Church, are bringing enormous pressure to bear on the Church to accept the homosexual condition as though it were not disordered and to condone homosexual activity. Those within the Church who argue in this fashion often have close ties with those with similar views outside it. These latter groups are guided by a vision opposed to the truth about the human person, which is fully disclosed in the mystery of Christ. They reflect, even if not entirely consciously, a materialistic ideology which denies the transcendent nature of the human person as well as the supernatural vocation of every individual. The Church's ministers must ensure that homosexual persons in their care will not be misled by this point of view, so profoundly opposed to the teaching of the Church. But the risk is great

and there are many who seek to create confusion regarding the Church's position, and then to use that confusion to their own advantage.

When I first read this paragraph it resonated deeply with me and actually helped me clarify what I had found disturbing about Dignity and similar organizations with whom I had become acquainted. In those events the focus was not as much on Christ as it was on same-sex ideology, lifestyle, and practice. Their goal had more to do with trying to force truth into an ideological mold than to conform ideology to the demands of truth. The CDF's concern led to the following:

> With this in mind, this Congregation wishes to ask the Bishops to be especially cautious of any programs which may seek to pressure the Church to change her teaching, even while claiming not to do so. A careful examination of their public statements and the activities they promote reveals a studied ambiguity by which they attempt to mislead the pastors and the faithful. For example, they may present the teaching of the Magisterium, but only as if it were an optional source for the formation of one's conscience. Its specific authority is not recognized. Some of these groups will use the word "Catholic" to describe either the organization or its intended members, yet they do not defend and promote the teaching of the Magisterium; indeed, they even openly attack it. While their members may claim a desire to conform their lives to the teaching of Jesus, in fact they abandon the teaching of his Church. This contradictory action should not have the support of the Bishops in any way. . . . All support should be withdrawn from any organizations which seek to undermine the teaching of the Church, which are ambiguous about it, or which neglect it en-

tirely. Such support, or even the semblance of such support, can be gravely misinterpreted. Special attention should be given to the practice of scheduling religious services and to the use of Church buildings by these groups, including the facilities of Catholic schools and colleges. To some, such permission to use Church property may seem only just and charitable; but in reality it is contradictory to the purpose for which these institutions were founded, it is misleading and often scandalous.

This was the crux of the matter. Not only was same-sex "inclination" declared to be an "objective disorder," but with this letter the Church withdrew from the Dignity and like-minded groups the authority to make themselves appear Catholic. There was a difference, the Church insisted, between being a group whose membership had a majority that called themselves Catholic and being a "Catholic group." The CDF thought it important to maintain the distinction because the teachings of the Church and groups such as Dignity differ so widely, even in their assumptions about the human person and other bedrock principles of the Faith.

At the time, in 1986, I thought the eviction from Catholic property was unfair, but I didn't take it too much to heart. After all, what was one more battle between gays and Christians? But now, after the deaths of so many friends and acquaintances, I understand more of the discipline's wisdom. Ideas have relevance beyond the realm of the intellect. They have bodily, spiritual, economic, and social consequences too.

Suppose there were two men living with same-sex attraction, on the island of Manhattan in 1986, the year the letter came out. One, struck to the quick by the letter, chooses to abandon a life of same-sex activity and to choose a life of fuller discipleship to Christ through the teachings of the Church, participation in the sacraments, etc. The other continues to accept Dignity's positions on same-sex activity, the human person, etc. Which do you suppose would have a greater chance of being alive today, given that the rate of HIV infection among men sexually active with other men on Manhattan during that time reached 50 percent? When human actions begin to mean the very difference between living and dying, both spiritually and physically, the distinctions between authentic Catholic teaching and teaching that might only appear authentic begin to be very important indeed.

Does the Church support discrimination?

Another allegation that emerged from the 1986 letter declared that the Church supports efforts to thwart gay and lesbian "civil rights" legislation. The relevant paragraphs (nine and ten) from the letter actually assert:

> The movement within the Church, which takes the form of pressure groups of various names and sizes, attempts to give the impression that it represents all homosexual persons who are Catholics. As a matter of fact, its membership is by and large restricted to those who either ignore the teaching of the Church or seek somehow to undermine it. It brings together under the aegis of Catholicism homosexual persons who have no intention of abandoning their homosexual behavior. One tactic used is to protest that any and all criticism of or reservations about homosexual people, their activity and lifestyle, are simply diverse forms of unjust discrimination.
>
> There is an effort in some countries to manipulate the Church by gaining the often well-intentioned support of her pastors with a view to changing civil-statutes and laws. This is done in order to conform to these pressure groups' concept that homosexuality is at least a completely

harmless, if not an entirely good, thing. Even when the practice of homosexuality may seriously threaten the lives and well-being of a large number of people, its advocates remain undeterred and refuse to consider the magnitude of the risks involved.

The Church can never be so callous. It is true that her clear position cannot be revised by pressure from civil legislation or the trend of the moment. But she is really concerned about the many who are not represented by the pro-homosexual movement and about those who may have been tempted to believe its deceitful propaganda. She is also aware that the view that homosexual activity is equivalent to, or as acceptable as, the sexual expression of conjugal love has a direct impact on society's understanding of the nature and rights of the family and puts them in jeopardy.

It is deplorable that homosexual persons have been and are the object of violent malice in speech or in action. Such treatment deserves condemnation from the Church's pastors wherever it occurs. It reveals a kind of disregard for others which endangers the most fundamental principles of a healthy society. The intrinsic dignity of each person must always be respected in word, in action and in law.

But the proper reaction to crimes committed against homosexual persons should not be to claim that the homosexual condition is not disordered. When such a claim is made and when homosexual activity is consequently condoned, or when civil legislation is introduced to protect behavior to which no one has any conceivable right, neither the Church nor society at large should be surprised when other distorted notions and practices gain ground, and irrational and violent reactions increase.

A close reading of these paragraphs indicates the Church does not support discrimination but rather will not be drawn (although some individual prelates have been) into attempts in the civil realm to enshrine same-sex activity in the protection of law. The Church is still deeply concerned about persons more than actions, including persons who struggle with same-sex attraction privately in their lives, and who have not chosen to make it a central focus of their identity. In short, the Church refuses the gay and lesbian activist argument that in order to love people with same-sex attraction She must love everything they might do — a position that resonates with many parents.

I have little doubt that some people whose identities are strongly rooted in same-sex attraction and identity may understand these paragraphs as discriminatory or even unjust. But as long as the root of the debate remains over whether same-sex activity is moral or immoral, proper or disordered, activists cannot expect the Church to abandon her pastoral role in the civil realm. The Church's role in civil society — whether on same-sex activity or abortion in the United States, the need for land-reform and economic justice in Central or Latin America or human freedom in the former Soviet Bloc — has never ended at her front door. As teacher and guide for the millions of Catholics who experience same-sex attraction but who have not chosen a path of disobedience, the Church has a responsibility to continue articulating the truth and objecting when voices in the public square try to promote ideas which are less than truthful.

One final note on these paragraphs. Occasionally the charge is raised that "the Church condones gay bashing!" based on the CDF's observation that a social backlash could conceivably follow attempts to normalize same-sex activity in civil society and law. The Church does not endorse gay bashing. A reading of the paragraph just a few short sentences above makes that clear. But in this paragraph the Church advises that merely changing civil legislation cannot and will not overturn the natural laws resident in human hearts and bodies. Simple civil law will not and cannot make active homosexuality "right," either objectively or in the hearts and minds of other, non-same-sex-attracted citizens. Instead, such laws are liable to produce ill effects, as columnist Camille Paglia, who herself self-identifies as lesbian, noted in the online journal *Salon*:

> For gays to demand that sincere Christians cease lobbying Washington about the increasing liberal drift of government policy shows colossal historical amnesia. For pity's sake, it was the flamboyant, thunderous activism of evangelical Protestant ministers in the 19th century that powered the abolitionist movement and led to the end of slavery in the United States. . . . So gays should quit bitching about Southern Baptists exercising their constitutional right to free speech about homosexuality, which is indeed condemned by the Bible, despite the tortuous casuistry of so many self-interested parties, including clerics. I have been warning and warning for years that the insulting disrespect shown by gay activists to religion — which has been going on for 20 years virtually unchecked on TV talk shows, with their biased liberal hosts — would produce a backlash over time.

The courage to be chaste

How then shall we live? If sexual expression has a dual purpose which cannot be ignored either morally or practically, if men and women are created in the image of God to be ends unto themselves and never means to ends, what is left of same-sex attraction and activity? The Catechism's third paragraph on homosexuality states of people living with same-sex attraction:

> These persons are called to fulfill God's will in their lives and, if they are Christians, to unite to the sacrifice of the Lord's Cross the difficulties they may encounter from their condition (2358). Homosexual persons are called to chastity. By the virtues of self-mastery that teach them inner freedom, at times by the support of disinterested friendship, by prayer and sacramental grace, they can and should gradually and resolutely approach Christian perfection (2359).

Ouch! Chastity? You must be joking! Aren't you? No, the Church isn't joking. Human persons and human sexual expression are too important for jokes, although it is difficult to imagine a more counter-cultural position for the Church to ask Christians to take in Millennial America. "Chastity," sniffed one attractive, intelligent woman at a party where the topic arose, "it sounds positively medieval to me!" During the course of a later conversation, she admitted that her series of lovers had left her more exhausted and unhappy than anything else and that she had already considered stopping dating, at least for a while.

Chastity, which resonates with the soul and is filled with both self-respect and common sense, has an image problem. Typical, in an admittedly B-grade way, is the treatment of the idea of chastity in the movie *Elvira, Mistress of the Dark*. A subplot of the limited-distribution movie (it made at least one reviewer's list of the ten worst movies of all time) pits the buxom, fun-loving, and cool Elvira against a coalition of stuffy city officials, parents, and conventional morality. The filmmakers' particular malice was reserved for Chastity Pariah, an evil woman whose energy in self-righteousness stems from her vast reserves of suppressed sexuality. This characterization fits in well with the popular perception that reserving sexual expression over the long term is somehow psychologically and even physically unhealthy and that people who do so "must have something wrong with them."

Part of chastity's public relations problem, particularly with the issue of same-sex attraction, stems from some confusion about basic ideas and from a mistaken belief that chastity is not "practical." Each of these needs to be addressed.

One of the most prevalent misunderstandings confuses chastity with the virtue of celibacy. Celibacy is a vowed or promised state of singleness for the sake of the Kingdom of God. To the extent that it is part of a broader vocation like priesthood or membership in a religious community, the Church understands it to carry a particular grace. Celibacy in this sense is not open to everyone, being in some ways akin to marriage. Just as in marriage sexual expression is reserved for particular purposes, in this case furthering the Kingdom of God or because one is not married, celibacy refers mainly to not having sex and thus has a relatively narrow focus on sexual acts themselves. Chastity is a broader concept and carries with it the undertone of a foundational virtue. It is possible to be celibate and yet not chaste, and chaste, yet not celibate.

By contrast, chastity is a virtue that the Church has always understood to be normative for Christian life. Whether married or unmarried, Christians are meant to live lives of ordered sexuality, refraining from sex outside marriage and leaving sexual expression open to the possibility of family in marriage. Seeking to live chastely has long been understood as one of the graces and expectations associated with living a Christian life, particularly after Baptism and confirmation. In that sense chastity is for everybody, not merely an elect few. Chastity also carries with it the notion of someone's living out a life of integrated sexuality. Our mainstream culture has so divorced sexuality from personality that sexual expression has come to be considered as something merely recreational, rather than as an expression of who we are deep inside ourselves. In this way the culture suggests that sex is akin to playing baseball, when its really more like making art.

When someone creates art he or she shares something very deep from within oneself, and there is a sense of sharing self. But playing baseball is something one just does and can be shallow about, little more than recreation. When sex tends to be seen as merely something fun to do or as a way of getting to another end, it can be very difficult to understand or commit to the decision to abstain.

The practical question

Among men and women living with same-sex attraction, the notion of committing to chastity suffers because first, the teaching is seen as difficult; second, it is seen as "boring"; and third, it appears woefully unreal and isolating. How can I commit to something so difficult, one might reasonably ask, if it seems that to do so means going against the tide alone? For some, living an actively homosexual life has been all they have known for years. Choosing to set out on such a path would get them little support from some of their friends and even active opposition from others.

An increasing number of men and women who find themselves in this boat turn for support to an organization called Courage. Founded almost twenty years ago by Father John Harvey, a priest with the Oblates of St. Francis de Sales, Courage offers an environment of support, prayer, and friendship for men and women with same-sex attraction who seek to live chastely in a world which does not value chastity (information on contacting Courage is provided at the end of this book).

Father Harvey began his work with priests and religious struggling with sexual identity and chastity issues more than forty years ago. At that time, terms like "homosexual" were never heard and Webster's still listed "happy or joyful" as the first meaning of the word gay. Harvey's work with the men struggling to integrate a confused sexual identity within a broader religious or faithful Catholic life brought home to him the power that support groups can have in helping people confront some deep-seated tendency or habit. Support groups tended to break down the walls of isolation around men living with same-sex attraction and offered the tremendously useful gift of perspective to individual men struggling with their problems. In 1980, Father Harvey assembled a small group of lay Catholic men in a parish on the Lower East Side of Manhattan and helped the men found Courage, the Roman Catholic Church's only Vatican-approved ministry to people living with same-sex attraction.

It was not an easy birth. After all, such a thing had never been tried before. And there was such a stigma attached at that time to homosexuality that some Catholics were scandalized that the Archdiocese of New York, under whose auspices Courage was founded, reached out to Catholics living with same-sex attraction at all. Yet together that first small group founded the organization and came up with the Goals of Courage which have guided the organization ever since:

> 1. To live chaste lives in accordance with the Roman Catholic Church's teaching on homosexuality.
>
> 2. To dedicate one's life to Christ through service to others, spiritual reading, prayer, meditation, individual spiritual direction, frequent attendance at Mass, and the frequent reception of the sacraments of Penance and Holy Eucharist.
>
> 3. To foster a spirit of fellowship in which all may share thoughts and experiences, and so ensure that no one will have to face the problems of homosexuality alone.
>
> 4. To be mindful of the truth that chaste friendships are not only possible but necessary in a celibate Christian life and in doing so provide encouragement to one another in forming and sustaining them.

5. To live lives that may serve as good examples to others.

Since then Courage has grown to be sixty-four groups in six countries and has helped thousands of men and women to more fully integrate their sexuality into a life of virtue and to come to a point of both interior and exterior chastity. But there is some confusion about the organization, and the misunderstandings need to be addressed:

Courage is not an orientation change group. Courage does not require anyone coming to its meetings or getting support to commit to diminishing their same-sex attraction or changing it to a more heterosexual focus. If individual members wish to try such a course, their Courage groups will support them, but it's not a requirement.

Courage is not an organization of perfectionists! The first men that Father Harvey helped to form Courage did not do so to create a society of the folks who had already made it. Courage members are not required to be living chastely when they arrive and some may never arrive at that point. All Courage requires is that its members commit to trying to live the goals. The goals are goals, after all, things people aim toward and for. They are not grades for work already done.

Courage is not "rigid." Courage is faithful to the teaching of the Catholic Church that is true, but Courage is not only about living chastely. Courage is about becoming better Christians. Courage is about growth, integration, and joy and about using the teaching of the Church to help get there.

Courage is not anti-gay. In fact, Courage is not particularly anti-anything in the sense of feeling the need to denounce things or continually address the "issue" of same-sex attraction. Courage remains intensely personal. Members have included former gay activists and married men for whom the members of their support groups are the only people on earth who know their struggle to live chastely. It *is* true that Courage is about choices and in that sense one course of action has to win out over another. Encouraging members to choose Mass or prayer over gay bars and one-night-stands might be seen by some as "anti-gay," but its not as though, in an abstract sense, Courage formally goes out and denounces patrons of gay bars or people who do one-night-stands.

But while Courage does a good job providing support, the organization is still young, and not every diocese in the United States and around the world has a Courage chapter. For someone who doesn't have a Courage chapter nearby, and doesn't feel he or she can start one, there are some practical things individuals might do to find support for living chastely. I will expand on these themes later in the book, but here they are in a nutshell:

First, don't be afraid. Don't be daunted or discouraged. When I first began contemplating living chastely, just contemplating the idea was like wrestling a huge gorilla that had taken over a corner of my life. It's really not that big. Make a clear resolution that living chastely will be a value in your life and is something you will strive to do. Living a chaste life will require a singular, consistent commitment. It's not something you start "on a lark," so to speak.

Second, recommit to the sacraments and to a life of prayer, particularly the sacraments of reconciliation and the Blessed Sacrament if you are Catholic. (I would urge non-Catholics to seek out forms for examinations of conscience and communions appropriate to their denominations.) As they start out in this life, many people find that chastity is not something they live out themselves, but something God lives out with and in them. Remember that Christ told His disciples that if they wished to see the Kingdom of God, they would first have to become as "little children." Prayer is the link Christ uses to nurture and sustain those very little children who seek to follow him with the deep purity of heart that chastity requires. In addition, honest examinations of conscience provide a vehicle people can use to get to know themselves better and begin to interpret the patterns of desire which make trying to live chastely difficult. Many people living with same-sex attraction who try to live chastely find that desire for same-sex sexual contact is rarely merely desire, but often can be understood as a reaction to something else happening in their lives. A regular program of examining conscience can help discover those patterns.

Third, tell somebody! For many men and women living with same-sex attraction, this will be the hardest step. But I am deeply convinced that, especially if one has begun acting-out at all, particularly acting out in "anonymous" venues (cruising certain areas, visiting adult book stores, movie theaters, or certain bars), telling one, two, or three other people can be absolutely essential. Over the years I have discovered that isolation and loneliness are among the biggest enemies of chastity in the lives of many people, whether same-sex attracted or not. Telling people you know love and support you can do a lot to make chastity much less a mountain and much more a molehill.

Finally, recognize chastity is a "long-haul" virtue. Although there are always exceptions that prove the rule, most people do not decide to be chaste one day and find they have achieved the virtue the next day. Be firm and consistent in your commitment to the virtue, but be gentle with yourself too. By simply seeking to attain the virtue, you have taken the most important step — whether or not you ever actually live the virtue perfectly. Remember Christ's promise; "come to me all you who are heavy laden and I will give you rest." Everyone, who seeks, finds and everyone, who knocks, discovers the door open to them.

CHAPTER NINE

What's love got to do with it?

Despite the preponderance of evidence that promiscuity characterizes sexually active same-sex relationships, few activists, outside of the truly "lavender left," are prepared to defend one-night stands. Rather, what gets taken up in many quarters is a cry for the Church and society to better understand and even bless sexually active same-sex *love*. Dignity's statement on sexual ethics, for example, asserts: "All humans are created in God's own image and likeness. Since humans were not made to be alone (see Genesis 2:18), as we seek and express intimacy and love we show God's image in action," adding later:

> Although we agree that a sexual ethic centered solely on procreation in the context of heterosexual marriage is not relevant to our experience as gays and lesbians, the criteria we use for sexual decisions are not so easily identified. *We say that we respond to Christ's call to be loving when our primary concern is for the quality of our relationships. The values on which we base our rela-*

tionships come through clearly: mutual respect, caring, compassion, trust, understanding, and generosity [emphasis added]. What emerges from our experience and reflection is an emphasis on persons and on actions that further personal and spiritual growth. We hear a call to an intimacy in relationships that links sexuality and spirituality. It is a call that Christians identify with Jesus, who challenged the disciples to love God totally and to love all others as themselves (Matthew 22:34-40). It is a call that Christians recognize as the ongoing presence of the Spirit. . . . Generally, we seek relationships that are whole and not just the expression of genital sexuality.

But a summary of 5,100 web sites found through an Internet search on the term "gay love" reveals the gay community's and broader culture's confusion about love most poignantly. The overwhelming majority of those sites appear to offer either pornography or advice on relationships, with many of the latter advertising books whose covers promised both titillation and advice. Alyson Publications' *Love Between Men: Enhancing Intimacy & Keeping Your Relationship Alive,* for example, has a cover whose title is arranged along with two naked men in a strategically draped embrace, presumably so that the book can be sold on some mainstream shelves without a brown paper wrapping. It appears to be widely assumed that "gay love" really has a lot to do with same-sex activity and overlooks the question: Just what is *love*, after all? What is "love between men" or "love between women" for that matter? Are same-sex relationships that are sexually active really loving? This chapter seeks to shed at least a little light on the nature and demands of love.

A poverty of language

Peter Kreeft has observed that one can gauge the importance of a thing by how many counterfeits it has inspired. Few people, after all, go to the trouble of counterfeiting paper clips or staples. Compact discs and videos of movies get counterfeited more often because they are more valuable. Occasionally some museum or collector will lose a lot of money buying a counterfeit piece of art or purported document. The greater the value something has, the more likely that someone will try to fake it. This is especially true concerning love, the one thing in the universe that has more value than anything but God. Love has lots of counterfeits. Many relationships, acts, ideas, policies, and homilies that claim love as their basis and end do not reflect or understand real love.

The poverty of language, at least in popular English, greases the culture's skid into confusion. For example, do we really mean to say that we feel and intend equivalent things about our spouse, children, friends, pets, movies, and ice cream when we say we "love" them all? The term "unconditional love" gets tossed about a lot these days but gets practiced very little. The degree of self-sacrifice it demands would likely earn us a scolding from the folks who preach the importance of "self-love." "Self-love" itself often gets tossed out as an excuse for everything from participation in support groups to self-indulgence to masturbation, an act which could be better understood as self-hating rather than loving. And what role in life should "romantic love" play?

Fortunately, anyone who wants to speak more deeply and accurately about love has access to other languages which have recognized more shades of meaning to the concept of love. The Greeks, for example, had at least four primary terms that we can use. *Eros* or erotic love; *storge*, or the love of family and familiar things like village, town, or country; *philia*, the love between friends; and *agape*, the self-sacrificing and self-aware love of God for us and our love, possibly, for one another. But if we want to use more specific terms we need to define them a bit more clearly.

Our culture imagines that it best understands *eros* or erotic love. But the leering, market-oriented approach to sex that dominates our culture has more to do with objectification, lust, and prurience than with any one of our four definitions of love. *Eros* or erotic love fuels and feeds romance but it differs from the popular culture's view of sex, which focuses so much more on bodies than on persons. "Desire" is the word in English that corresponds most closely to *eros*, but the word *eros* tends to be a consuming desire for one person or one thing. *Eros* is love with a definite, almost overpowering, objective. C.S. Lewis, the great Christian apologist and writer, used as a model of erotic love two people facing one another, looking deeply into each other's eyes and focusing entirely on each other. I find such a model useful because it recognizes the all-consuming interest each of the partners in erotic love has for the other.

Three aspects of erotic love are important for our discussion. First, a customary selfishness characterizes erotic love because *eros's* desire bases itself essentially in the *I* of the person undergoing the erotic attraction. Even if the person experiencing erotic love has disciplined his or her heart and can keep the emotion free of recognized, conscious selfishness, *eros*, by its very nature, involves at least a subconscious, psychological selfishness. There can be no other essential interpretation of the quintessential sentence of erotic love: "I want you." Second, *eros* or erotic love has less to do with freedom and decision than do the other types of love. Few people *decide* to have erotic feelings for someone else, nor can they be forced to have such. As many unrequited lovers know, to their sorrow, feelings of erotic love and their associated romantic attitudes tend to be something that happens *to* us rather than something coming *from* us. Either we have our beloved, or we don't. Third, *eros's* power and immediacy can easily lead us to forget that the person we love this way remains a person, an *I*, even as he or she is the object of our erotic interest. Nothing about erotic love has the power or authority to transform or remove the independent nature and infinite value of a human person. Every person we love erotically (or any other way for that matter) remains a person created in the image and likeness of God, and thus possess an innate value far beyond even our most hotly adoring calculus.

Storge, the second of the two terms for love, corresponds most closely to the English word "affection," and is correspondingly the least well known of the terms, even among Christians. *Storge* characterizes the feelings of love between siblings and other family members, or the feelings one might have for an especially favored or important place in life. The modern understanding of the word "affection," however, does not sufficiently address *storge*'s deeper meanings.

Storge's family associations grant it, in many ways, a certain power of familiarity and humility. Mothers nursing their children or grown children caring for aging parents are examples of *storge.* There is in this love an awareness and acceptance of quirks in personality that allows its participants to accept those elements in particular in others that they would not accept in strangers. Since families are the best examples of places where one must accept rather than choose one's acquaintances, *storge* is often associated with family life. *Storge* is the kind of love about which one might feel most private and even a little embarrassed. Lovers and friends, newlyweds, and even family members are often pleased to be seen about with one another, but how many of us might feel odd confessing an affection for someone in our circle that we know others thought an "old coot."

Another excellent English word to use in conjunction with *storge* might be the tenderness of a mother's love. Interestingly, the acceptance of others' realities — their quirks, faults, idiosyncrasies , and irritating habits — makes *storge* a strong antidote to lust. Objectifying someone through a lust-filled gaze becomes almost impossible if we will ourselves to try and see others as their mothers see them.

Finally, while all the loves can overlap in greater or lesser degrees, *storge* probably colors the others more than they color it. Particularly, in mature relationships seasoned by many years, storge can provide a pillar of support to the primary kind of love that the relationship possesses without overtaking it. Thus, long friendships have an element of *storge*, but such affection is not the friendship's core. Long-married couples, too, will probably share much *storge*, but affection is not the sum of their relationship. In many ways, *storge* is about the day-to-day stuff of love without *eros's* fireworks or the feeling of discovery that can characterize a strong friendship. However, *storge* does retain one of *eros's* characteristics — *storge* cannot usually be willed.

Philia occupies a position often seen as the "highest" of the natural terms for love. *Philia*'s closest corresponding English word is "friendship," an English word which, like love, has undergone a confusion and watering-down over the last few years. Friendship, as many contemporaries define it, often means something more closely associated with being acquaintances than friends. *Philia*, by contrast, tends to carry a greater meaning. Some people might remember the 1986 film *Stand By Me* which depicts four twelve year-old boys' adventure seeking a dead body and their discovery of far more about themselves and their friendship in the process. *Stand By Me* depicts, in a very distilled way, the loyalty, honesty, compassion, and tenderness possible in *philia*. *Philia* combines fingers pricked to form blood brotherhoods with the claims and promises of summer vacations and the trust and honesty forged in the heat of shared danger or other experience. I am reminded of a man's comment about his father's friendships from combat days. These were, he remembered, of such lasting importance to his father that if one of his friends were to cable him from across the country to say, "Come, I need you," his father would be on the next train. In many ways, *philia*'s strengths have led some to confuse or misidentifiy it with *eros*, but it is significantly different. C.S. Lewis's model for *philia* contrasts with his model for *eros*. In the model of *philia*, the two participants are focused not so much on each other as on something external to each one. They are two together pursuing a common goal outside themselves, where in *eros* the two people focus on each other.

One glaring example of the confusion about love today is the gay and lesbian activists' attempt to draft historical figures into their ranks posthumously, based upon their writings to other men or women at the time or on descriptions others wrote about them. The most notorious recent instance concerns the biblical Story of David and Jonathan. After Jonathan is killed in battle, David laments his death in the first chapter of 2 Samuel, declaring: "I am distressed for you, my brother Jonathan; very pleasant have you been to me; your love to me was wonderful, passing the love of women" (1:26). Activists seized upon this verse, claiming that it and the broader David and Jonathan story proves that "same-sex love" (by which they mean the contemporary gay variety) was present even among God's anointed. They proceed to argue that the Church should change its stance on same-sex acts. Yet an examination of the story indicates a strong relationship rooted in *philia* much more than anything guided by a disordering *eros*. Both David and Jonathan start the story at roughly the same age; though from vastly different backgrounds, both have similar interests and face a common enemy in Saul, Jonathan's father and Israel's king. There is danger, adventure, risk, loyalty, and, finally, tragedy. At the end of the tale David weeps for Jonathan as one should weep for a loss of a good friend. None of this is unusual or deserves the mischaracterization it has currently drawn. Exalting *eros* has inclined contemporary culture to water down and overlooks the power true *philia* possesses. The assertion that David and Jonathan "must have been" secret lovers says much more about our impoverished understanding of love than about the sexual inclinations of Hebrew princes.

Two factors of *philia* stand out for our discussion now. First, *philia* is completely a love we choose or will. In many ways a current popular phrase describes *philia* accurately: none of us choose our families but all of us choose our friends. This element of freedom in *philia* links it to *agape*, the supernatural transformation of love, and thus gives it a different character and depth. Second, *philia* can (and should) provide us many of the practical things we need as human beings from other people — compassion, company, understanding, shared living experiences, and time. Scripture correctly observes in Genesis that "it is not good that the man should be alone" and *philia* provides the "disinterested friendship" the *Catechism* cites as the support people living with same-sex attraction need to approach being saints.

Ironically for our discussion of specificity in love terms, our fourth specific term for love, *agape*, was the Greeks *least* specific definition of love. *Agape* meant love more generally and generically and thus was probably not used much in a culture which so prized specificity in language. But since *agape* didn't already have a specific definition, it perfectly suited the needs of early Christians who were trying to talk about an entirely new kind of love, a type of love the world had never seen before as clearly as it did in Jesus Christ. Specifically, *agape* is the love of God in all its permutations. It is God's love for us and for all His creation, our love for God in response to His love for us, and our pure love for neighbor, which is God's love for us that we accept and then reflect upon the individuals with whom we interact every day. All fall into the definition of *agape*.

Agape's role in our discussion is key but it's almost too large a topic to address. Whole books have been written about nothing else but the love of God! Yet, *agape* has certain characteristics that need to be included in our discussion of love and same-sex attraction.

First and most important, *agape* is completely a choice, an act of the will. Decision, not emotion, characterizes *agape*. No one can will themselves into erotic love, or *storge* or even *philia* (which requires some degree of reciprocity and affiliation). Yet the testimony of Scripture, the saints, and many contemporary Christians is that *agape* can and does exist in the will. St. Francis willed to love and embraced the leper even though he found leprosy repulsive. St. Martin de Porres willed to love and helped the slaves in the Spanish colony of Peru even though that love threatened his own stature and even his free state. Mother Teresa's sisters around the world routinely will to love those whom the rest of their societies have declared unlovable and even, in some cases, untouchable. "Love," as a sign in Mother Teresa's office read, "is a choice."

Second, true *agape*, supernatural *agape*, which is God's, is wholly selfless. God's love literally self-forgets and demands no reciprocation. Now, if we are wise and fully human persons, we will reciprocate God's love, for love propagates itself among healthy people. But God will not demand our love in response to His. He has loved even during the parts of our lives when we may have hated Him. In this, *agape* is superior to *philia*, for friendship still requires some reciprocation. Jesus persistently loved even the people who nailed Him to the Cross.

Agape's third characteristic is akin to the first two. Because God's love includes both self-forgetting and an act of the will, supernatural *agape* wills only what is best for the beloved. God's self-forgetfulness and will to love make it possible for God to consistently and deeply desire only what is best for us, His beloved. Although this is such a huge idea that many cannot accept it, as St. Paul wrote in the book of Romans, *everything* works to our good as His children. There will be more on this idea in chapter eleven.

The last characteristic of *agape* that we will discuss here concerns *agape*'s way of seeing. God's love sees the truth about human persons; sees us as we really are, not merely as we want to present ourselves. Consequently, *agape* sees the whole of us and seeks to interact with us at every level. There is nothing about our created being that God does not know or love and there is nothing about our created selves that God would want to ignore or slight. Although He does not love the sins we commit, He loves *us* despite our sins.

Now some readers say, "That's *God's* love. That's divine. What can that have to do with us?" While it's true that God's love can seem an impossible template for us to follow, God's grace is such that we can accept His *agape* and reflect it into the lives of the people around us. This is part of what is means to be branches in His vine. It is *agape*, His Spirit, which proceeds from the shared love of the Father and the Son, which provides the sap for the branches to use to bear fruit.

Are same-sex relationships truly loving?

Using our more precise definitions for the different types of love, can we understand same-sex relationships to express real love? If yes, then in what sense can they be seen to do so? If not, then why not? Do people living with same-sex attraction, as Dignity's statement on sexual ethics asserts, "show God's image in action" as they "seek and express intimacy and love?"

Certainly, sexually active same-sex relationships, as well as unmarried sex generally, can seem to express erotic or (its stepchild) romantic love. All the right symptoms are there. Although in many ways erotic or romantic love is the most emotion-driven and least rational of all the forms of love we discussed, it is still a kind of love and remains related at least loosely to the other types. Erotic love is akin to *agape* as half-brothers or sisters are siblings to one another. It shares at least one parent with the others, and crucially retains the others' power. *Eros* has a very different appearance and personality, however. As we briefly mentioned earlier, erotic love runs the greatest risk of being abused and distorted. Erotic love, being primarily desire, has the greatest chance of objectifying the beloved. That is to say erotic love can forget that the beloved is a person, an *I*, and thus a subject of actions, emotions, hopes, and dreams of their own. People can never, morally or truly lovingly, be made into the means which other people may use to reach their desired ends, whether those ends are sexual, social, or economic.

But given erotic love's power, doesn't this happen all the time? Doesn't all sexual expression, based upon desire as it is, objectify by definition? Well, certainly it can. Saints and the Church have long advised married men and women to undertake a periodic, honest, and complete examination of their consciences in regard to how they view and love their spouses. But, through fertility and marriage, God has also provided a certain counterbalance to the natural tendency to make of the beloved either a substitute for God (an idol) or an object (a means to a sexual or emotional end.)

When married couples make love without artificially contracepting, they channel *eros* into a deep and multifaceted love, one that works against the tendency of one to objectify the other. When a couple has decided to use natural methods to either space their pregnancies or conceive a child, they must recognize each other's full humanity whenever they express themselves sexually. A husband in this situation *cannot* see his wife primarily as means to his sexual pleasure for he has already committed — intellectually, physically, and spiritually — to reserve his sexual expression for a time set by her natural rhythms. He has already recognized her existence as a person long before they arrive in bed. Likewise a woman understands her husband as more than a "stud" or the man she desires sexually but also as the man whose love might physically alter her life by impregnating her. Each of them comprehend that the other has a role and identity beyond that urged and given highest priority by *eros*.

When heterosexual couples contracept, or when same-sex couples have sex, they take that counterbalance off the scale and make it far easier for erotic love to idolize or objectify the other. In each case, the objectification can be said to begin even before the couple shares any sexual act. In the case of the heterosexual couple, the objectification begins as soon as either the man or woman decides (whether consciously or subconsciously) that fulfilling an immediate sexual desire is more important than loving and respecting their partner as fully human, fully fertile, person. By using contraceptives to block or suppress full sexual expression, the contracepting man or woman withholds from their partner the fully human communion that the sexual act is meant to represent. Likewise, when a man or woman contemplates having sex with someone of their same sex they are doing something similar. Either consciously or subconsciously they have decided that having sex with this or that other man or woman is of more importance than considering whether such an act means they love the whole person as God created them to be. A man or a woman having sex with another man or woman still remains a man or woman, and their sexuality remains created by God to be for something far deeper and more important than merely providing the other pleasure.

Of course, this comparison has limits. Simply refusing to contracept, for example, doesn't guarantee a heterosexual couple will not objectify or dehumanize each other in some way outside the bedroom, and simply having homosexual sex doesn't preclude same-sex lovers from treating each other as fully human persons in other parts of their friendship. But insofar as the acts themselves, contracepted heterosexual sex shares with same-sex acts a much stronger possibility for objectification and dehumanization. Each in different ways departs from the true union God intended to be made possible through sexual relations. Heterosexual couples who contracept disorder an expression of a drive which, otherwise, is ordered to human good. Same-sex acts are a disordered expression of an inclination that is not and cannot be ordered to human good.

I suspect the reality that same-sex sexual acts objectify by definition and contraception tends to objectify by practice may be an important reason why many couples, both heterosexual and same-sex, have trouble maintaining their relationships for long lengths of time. Modern human beings, particularly in the First World, are terribly bored and stand frequently in need of diversion. Human beings would, in other circumstances, tend to provide much of that diversion — particularly human beings that one loved. But objectifying human beings does what the verb says it does — it turns people into objects. And objects, as so many of us know so well, invariably lose their newness and gloss over time.

I remember that when I was still sexually active this apparent dichotomy puzzled me. I knew I loved my partner on a number of different levels. I knew I found him a sexy and passionate bedmate. I knew our sex could reach real heights of emotion and desire. But then, whether passionate or merely sleepy, when the sexual act was done and all that remained was the wiping up afterward, I couldn't understand why there seemed to be such a letdown. Why did I feel so empty? Only later did I recognize that I felt so empty because the act had no meaning in the deepest parts of myself. There can be no real communion in same-sex acts, no deepest love, I have come to realize; only the experience of children playing with people they have made into toys.

The damp zone

"But aren't you guilty of the reductionism you were decrying in just the last chapter? Don't you know that there is more than sex to same-sex relationships? Aren't you overlooking a lot?" Yes, absolutely. If I stopped writing this chapter at the last line of the last section I would have been overlooking, even ignoring, a lot. Further, I suspect there are some folks out there reading this who would have felt a lot more comfortable if I had stopped there. "That's it," I imagine them thinking. "Same-sex relationships can't be truly loving. Knew it all long." But such an ending would not have been true. You see, God's love is like a rising tide. It can't be stopped, only delayed for a time (though sometimes that can be a lifetime). It finds its own level and goes where He wills it, exploiting even the smallest of cracks in its search to flood our human hearts and turn them from stone to flesh. That's why I called this section "the damp zone," because I know same-sex relationships — even those where sexual activity is taking place — have lots of room for all the other forms of love to be present and flourish. A sexually active same-sex relationship, or even a heterosexual one taking place outside of marriage, may never be soaked in God's love, but rarely is it bone-dry either. Most often I have found them to be, in varying degrees, damp.

Essentially, subject to their own human foibles, failings, and problems, of which all people have their own share, people living with same-sex attraction can pursue any of the other types of love they wish. Neither affection nor friendship nor *agape* stand closed to people living with same-sex attraction. In fact, people living with same-sex attraction who are seeking to integrate their sexuality need to be aware that their lives, like the lives of all long-term single people, quite possibly, are going to need *more* of each of these other types of love, not less. Somewhat removed as we may be from the encompassing vocation of spouse and family, same-sex-attracted men and women and other long-term singles cannot afford to take *any* of the loves for granted. *Philia*, in particular, should be cultivated as it can provide many of the good qualities of all the other loves rolled into one.

Of course there need to be some caveats in this section too. First, it has been my experience that while the other loves can grow and even flourish in the presence of disordered erotic love, they generally have done so despite the sexual activity, not because of it. I know my friendship with my former sexual partner grew by leaps and bounds *after* we stopped having sex — in a large part because our enduring friendship after the bedroom bore witness to a deepening trust between us. We both saw that we cared enough about the other's person, not just his body, to remain friends. We also ceased using sex to patch over parts of our friendship which needed more direct communication.

Second, the presence of the three other forms of love, even of a fledgling *agape,* cannot justify the actions of disordered *eros*. It's not fair, gay and lesbian activists rightly claim, to object to an entire relationship on the basis of one part. This is true. But neither is it fair or true to seek social acceptance for a disordered love, an objectifying and using love, because a relationship might contain some elements of the other loves as well.

Third, in practical terms, men (whether same-sex attracted or not) especially need to be deeply honest when deciding whether or not to pursue a friendship. *Eros* is a sneaky fox and will crawl in through a crack in the floor if he finds you vigilant at the front door. A good general rule I have found for detecting whether *eros* is having an undue influence in evaluating a friendship is something I call the "Quasimodo rule." If this guy (or girl) you are getting to know and become friendly with looked like Quasimodo, the famous Hunchback of Notre Dame, would you still want to be their friend? Ask and answer that question with clear and brutal honesty and then evaluate and act upon the results.

Sed contra

"But if same-sex relationships can have the properly ordered loves in addition to disordered *eros*, wouldn't blessing at least the effort to form long-term relationships be the Church's most compassionate course of action? Isn't your position just a tad legalistic? How many human relationships ever fully attain the standards you set anyway?"

I once had a long e-mail correspondence with a woman who asked many of these types of questions. Gradually, by getting to know me better, she had become convinced of the order and logic of many of the Church's positions on same-sex activity but still could not get past the idea that hewing to such a strong standard was "mean" and "heartless." Couldn't I admit that even though such relationships weren't perfect, they were better than one-night stands, and ought to be encouraged? I thought and prayed long and hard about the question. Answering in the positive attracted me. Such a position was very close to the position of Andrew Sullivan and other proponents of same-sex marriage. I thought of the ways such an understanding would have made my relationship's growth and change easier to take.

But in the end I had to say no, adopting such a teaching would not be any more compassionate than the current teaching — in fact less so — because it would not reflect the fullness of the truth. How, I wrote to the woman, if same-sex sexual activity objectifies and uses human beings in a disordered way, could the Church endorse even a little of it? If God created human beings in His image to have an eternal destiny with Him and to be an end unto themselves, how could any objectification be acceptable? The demands of human interaction are stringent because the reality of human nature and creation demands such a standard. God created us as persons, and not merely things.

The American Heritage Dictionary defines compassion as a "deep awareness of the suffering of another coupled with the wish to relieve it," and such a definition would appear to make a good case for allowance. But the Church's teachings, rooted in natural law, are more akin to physical laws than they are to legislation, legal opinion, or even scientific theories. They describe more than dictate. The objectification, emptiness, failed friendships, pain, and divorce (among married couples) occur because they are the natural fallout of either using an otherwise ordered drive in a disordered way or of indulging a disordered inclination. None of this would change just because the Church changed its teaching (or, for that matter, if the people doing such things left the Church as some have). Taking away the teaching — failing to call people back to their deepest humanity — would be the least truly compassionate thing to do.

Yet living in the truth is hard, and the struggle and confusion over same-sex acts have left people on all sides wounded and in need of grace. How God offers that healing is the subject of the next chapter.

CHAPTER TEN

His peace He offers

O Jerusalem, Jerusalem, killing the prophets and stoning those who are sent to you! How often would I have gathered your children together as a hen gathers her brood under her wings, and you would not! (Matthew 23:37).

Therefore, I tell you, her many sins have been forgiven — for she loved much. But he who has been forgiven little loves little (Luke 7:47).

"My son," the father said, "you are always with me, and everything I have is yours. But we had to celebrate and be glad, because this brother of yours was dead and is alive again; he was lost and is found" (Luke 15:31-32).

After love, I find more people misunderstand forgiveness than any other aspect of God. For example, many Christians share a widespread misperception that our need for forgiveness and Christ's command to forgive our neighbor, both of which we collectively repeat in prayer hundreds of thousands of times each day, means adopting a weak or "wimpy" type of love. How much more appropriate to a competitive, dog-eat-dog understanding of modern life would Jesus have been had He commanded Christians not to forgive others "seventy times seven times" but instead to "get even," or, as Machiavelli advised, to strike first. But appearances aside, mercy and its two attendants, humility and charity, are hard, muscular virtues. Engaging them regularly changes us, breaking up the hardened scabs and scars covering our hearts and preparing us for change, for the Gospel. Although the peace of Christ is the long-term goal and promise — and Christ's peace is what we get eventually — it's the kind of peace that follows thunderstorms, struggles, and hard labors. Peace rests at the Gospel's heart: but so do tears and revolution, the tears of repentant, redeemed, and relieved people and the revolution of changed and changing lives.

Few groups of people misunderstand the need of forgiveness more than those on both sides of the cultural rift over same-sex attraction and sexual behavior. People living with same-sex attraction who, like the Prodigal Son of the parable, may have strayed very far from home need forgiveness. Perhaps even more importantly, so do Christians who have taken on the parable's role of the Older Brother, the one who does not celebrate the Prodigal's return but instead reveals a deep pit of resentment, jealously, and lack of acceptance at his younger brother's homecoming. I have encountered people in both groups who have failed to understand that, like thunderstorms or hurricanes, forgiveness is an enormous and unpredictable force. When we encounter it, we cannot be sure of the outcome or of how the landscapes of our lives will look after it passes.

A peace of forgiveness: the personal dimension

In much the same way it does with love, English suffers a particular lack of adequate language when it comes to forgiveness and peace. The dictionary defines "forgive" in one of three ways. First, to excuse for a fault or an offense, to pardon. The second and third definitions include renouncing anger or resentment against another party and absolving from payment (of a debt, for example). Synonyms for the word includes terms like pardon, excuse, and condone. But none of these terms really include forgiveness's deeper dimension, of making peace among people and between people and God. The English word "peace" is fairly vaguely defined as well. To better understand what God might mean by peace and forgiveness we need to turn to Hebrew, the Scriptures' first language. Basic Hebrew etymology is a fairly easy map to read, once you have the alphabet. Hebrew organizes words around certain three-letter roots. Verbs are built upon these three-letter roots by adding certain prefixes and suffixes. Nouns and other words, in turn, are built out from the verbs. Thus it is possible to take a word and, by finding and tracing its root through its linguistic family, and other words, get a much deeper understanding of all its meanings.

Many people know that the Hebrew word for peace is "shalom." Shalom's three-letter root consists of the Hebrew letters shin-lamed-mem (the sounds of "sh," l and m). At the simplest level the three-letter verb means "to be complete or to be ended." But trace the root through its word-family and you will find more passive verbs than active ones. These verbs mean things like "to be finished," or "to be repaid," "to be accomplished" and "to be willing to be recompensed." Active verbs in the family include meanings like "to pay or recompense," "to complete or to make peace," and, finally, "to perfect yourself." These words share the notion of repayment or making whole or of setting things right. "Peace" in Hebrew and, I would argue, in the heart of God, means taking action to restore a relationship from enmity or conflict to friendship and respect. The Hebrew words almost seem to carry the notion of relationship with them, on their backs as it were. By contrast, the English words "forgive," "excuse," and "pardon" carry with them a notion of merely defining actions. One person has hurt another and asks, or doesn't ask, for forgiveness that the wounded party gives them. Did they know each other before? Will they still be friends after? English doesn't say, and the language doesn't give any hints. But the context of relationship in the Hebrew words springing from the shin-lamed-mem root is assumed and understood. Each word calls to mind two actors in the drama who have known each other before, even if just tangentially, who are connected somehow. The making of peace means restoring the relationship, even if the damage is such that it precludes the relationship continuing.

Restoring our relationship with God rests at the heart of what the vertical, or divine, personal dimension of forgiveness is all about. Christianity, at its deepest levels, concerns a relationship between God and the individual human persons and with human persons in community. God's grace, in the Christian understanding, created the relationship with God in the first place and restored the relationship after it was broken by sin. Such was the friendship hinted at in Genesis, which depicts Adam and Eve's relationship with God at such an intimate level that God "walked" in the garden with the pair and there was an accord among all creation. But Adam and Eve as individuals sinned and turned away from their relationship with God in favor of a lie that they could attain greater power and be Godlike themselves. Individually their sin belonged to them, but in a theological or archetypal way, Adam and Eve's failing broke all creation's relationship with God. Much of human history can be seen as a long series of struggles to either restore at least the human side of that friendship to what it had been or to attain the power the first lie had promised.

This is a synopsis of the broad theological canvas of forgiveness and as such it can be hard for individuals to comprehend. Readers might ask how, at the edge of the twenty-first century, can anyone write credibly of Adam and Eve? But whether one believes that every aspect of the Adam and Eve story reflects literal truth or that God used the tale to teach important truth about human beings misses the point. As G.K. Chesterton once wryly noted, the doctrine of original sin is one of the few Christian beliefs that can be confirmed by each day's headlines.

As difficult as some of its aspects might be to accept, the broad theological picture can be useful when we understand that our individual lives contain the essential conflict begun in Genesis, though written for a smaller yet no less important stage. Except for lacking the state of first innocence or original justice, each of us stands in a place similar to that of Adam and Eve. All of us wrestle with temptations to pride — a failing that many of the saints considered the source of all the other sins. Each of us has to choose to confront the failings and even wickedness in our own lives.

It's hard to explain to people who haven't done it, but confronting one's own failings and sins represents a terribly important key toward living in reality. In my own case, it wasn't that I was remarkably worse than other people were. In some things I did better than others and in some things worse, but failing to face up to how far I had strayed from the essential goodness for which God created me had left me a life filled with depression and even malice. Before confronting my own sins, my life, no matter how good it might have been in terms of what the world offered (money, sex, and power), remained drained of real color. Mine was a life lived in black and white. In much the way St. Paul had before his conversion, I spent a lot of time hurting myself by kicking against the world's essential reality (Acts 26:14). Examining my life and turning to God for help opened a door to another dimension. It's not that life afterward became a rose garden — in some ways recognizing how much road stands before us can be scary — but in a very deep way my life entered reality. Where previously my experiences — whether in suffering or joy — lacked context, now they had depth.

Pete, a friend of mine and longtime member of Alcoholics Anonymous, is fond of observing a key difference between folks who don't use a twelve-step program and those who do. The folks in the program *know* they are ill and in need of help whereas too many other people live in an illusion that they are "OK." Recognizing our failings before God and our fellow human beings brings an oddly empowering clarity to our vision, allowing us to see the often ugly but true nature of our failings. Seeing ourselves clearly is the first step toward change.

The legacy from original sin stains and mars all of our lives, whether we live with same-sex attraction or not. All of us, if we contemplate our lives honestly at all, must moan with Paul that so often we do the very things that we least want to do and fail to do the things we most want to do. That sounds depressing, but awareness of that reality can empower us to take that knowledge to Christ for forgiveness and a share of His peace. Confronting the truth about us can be rough, no doubt. As Pete has wryly commented, "I was never more self-aware than when the toilet bowl seat fell on my head." But that confrontation can set us on the right road. At the very least we can stop living in black and white and choose instead to live in color.

Barriers to peace

So, if peacemaking is such a good, why aren't more people doing it? Why might Jesus feel the need to ascribe the practice its own beatitude ("Blessed are the peacemakers")?

People resist self-reflection, regret, and apology — peace-making in short — for a number of reasons. Many of these reasons spring from pride. It can be hard to admit that we have acted wrongly, have not lived up to the normally high opinion we may have about ourselves. Pride is the ultimate reason many people persist in the abuse of alcohol, drugs, sex, and other addictions to the point where they simply can no longer function. Pride is the sickness that requires the strong antidote, for example the so-called First Step of twelve-step programs: "We admitted we were powerless over [insert substance here] — that our lives had become unmanageable."

Fear can also block peacemaking, particularly when it comes to making peace with God. It's interesting to note that many of Jesus' parables involve a landlord and servants. Coming to terms with our own failings and defects can mean taking steps to change, and change can terrify us, especially when it asks us to step out on the road following Christ without being sure of the result or of where we might be headed.

Fear of vulnerability shares a lot of similarities with fear of change as a reason people dislike making apologies. Admitting we have wronged God or another person means letting down our guard in front of them and giving up any claim to power with them. The phrases "will you forgive me" and "please forgive me" cannot, by their very nature, demand but implore. And when we say such things we open ourselves to being hurt. God or the other person, we imagine, may be very angry with what we have done. He or she may not forgive us. Apologizing means opening ourselves to the possibility of rejection.

Yet if we are in relationship with God or another person, it is *essential* we practice seeking forgiveness. Seeking forgiveness provides the occasions of risk-taking that often move our friendships to deeper, more intimate levels. When we experience the risk of saying "will you forgive me" and hear the response, "yes, I will" or even "what you have done hurt me a great deal but yes, I will forgive you," our knowledge of and trust in the other person has grown. Conversely, if we ask forgiveness and do not get it, we may not have heard the answer we desired but we have still learned a good deal about our relationship with the other person. Of course when we ask forgiveness of God we can have a good deal of confidence in the answer. "As far as the East is from the West," said God to one of the prophets, "is as far as I will remove Israel's sins from her." In many places in the Gospel Jesus shocks disbelieving crowds by openly forgiving sins. God at least is deeply inclined to forgive even when what our friends, family, or other people may not.

Forgiveness and love

So far most of this chapter has concerned elements of forgiveness that apply to everyone. But I think seeking God's forgiveness has an even greater importance for people living with same-sex attraction — particularly if they have been sexually active for a time. I don't say this because I presume that same-sex sins are universally worse than other sins. I don't. Such judgments are not my place. I contend that forgiveness is especially important to those living with same-sex attraction because same-sex attraction is still deeply socially stigmatizing and isolating. God's forgiveness is the only sure source people living with same-sex attraction have for unconditional love.

One day while Jesus sat at table in the home of a Pharisee named Simon, a woman who had been a prostitute approached Him. Kneeling before Him, she wept over His feet and used her tears to wash them, then her hair to dry them. Simon, observing all this, thought to himself, "Aha, if this man were truly a prophet he would know the nature of this woman and would not have let her approach." In response to Simon's thoughts, Jesus posed the famous question about forgiveness. If a landlord had two debtors, Jesus asked, one of whom owed him a small sum and the other a sum about ten times the first, and he forgave them both their debts, which did Simon suppose would be the more grateful? The one who had been forgiven the greater sum, Simon replied. You are right, Jesus said, adding that those who have been forgiven much, love much and those who have been forgiven little, love little.

Now, I have to admit that when I first read of this incident in the Gospel I had some hard questions about it. What had the woman done, I wondered? Was what she did so much worse than the hard heart of the Pharisee sitting next to Jesus? Later, as I pondered the passage more deeply, I realized the key difference we could discern between the woman and Simon was one of *awareness* of sins. The woman knew her sins, had asked forgiveness and been forgiven. Simon, by contrast, still thought himself righteous in the manner of many of the religious men of his time. His self-righteousness blinded him to the reality of his own sins, effectively blocking any request for forgiveness and cutting him off from the deep well of love awaiting in the heart of the man seated next to him whom he so doubted.

Jesus powerfully links forgiveness and love. Almost all of us, if we honestly search our hearts, will be aware that we need to be forgiven much. People living with same-sex attraction in particular, told in so many ways that our sins and even our temptations are worse than others, have at various times in our lives been deeply aware of our need for forgiveness. This is not necessarily because our sins have *really* been that much worse than any others but because to simply make our way in life has so often placed us in the dock pleading our defense. So much of the time we have lacked the luxury, as toxic as it is comfortable, of socially "acceptable" sins.

People living with same-sex attraction today are among those to whom the Good News of Jesus Christ is especially relevant. We who so clearly know what it is like not to fit in, to be cast out or forgotten, to lack the love of family and acceptance of peers, have a tremendous resource, an ocean of love, waiting for us in Jesus Christ. In His eyes it doesn't matter whether our sins are as bad, better, or worse than any others. In His eyes what we may have done or even thought we have done means very little in the context of our identity as Children of God. Our sexual temptations in the eyes of our society may be a barrier to Jesus, but in His eyes they are as nothing, a gauze curtain that briefly clouds our view and which we need only ask to be removed.

This paradox is part of what makes forgiveness so difficult to understand. Peace comes not from declaring that same-sex acts "aren't really sin" or by explaining away certain difficult Scriptures on the topic. Fighting for and even attaining "rights" doesn't bring real peace of heart. If it did, people living with same-sex attraction in such "gay friendly" places as Manhattan or San Francisco should be living lives of real joy, yet visiting those places did not leave the impression that many are doing so. Peace comes from yielding. Peace comes from making ourselves vulnerable to the God who so deeply loved us that He went to death on a Cross that we might be able to approach him for mercy. "Blessed are the peacemakers" indeed, for they carry within them not only the seeds of the Gospel but also the knowledge of how to plant them deeply. Now this is not to say that I disbelieve the need to confront social structures that remain truly unjust. I acknowledge that need and even the responsibility to not be silent in the face of real injustice. But imagine what different sorts of movements might arise if they arose not from wounded people demanding redress, but from forgiven people who know the mercy and love of God?

Peace in our houses: the battle to forgive

Of course, asking peace between God and us is only one part of forgiveness. Each day millions of Christians around the world pray a version of "forgive us our sins as we forgive those who sin against us." Those words Jesus taught His disciples so long ago remind us that forgiveness has a social or horizontal dimension. In fact, in an odd way, our experience of God's forgiveness is conditional on our willingness to share it by forgiving others. In many ways I see the flow of forgiveness in my life as being akin to one of the streams that comes down from the mountains near my home. As long as the stream's course remains open as it flows, it remains clear and cold and babbling, but when something blocks it or it comes to marshy ground it slows and stagnates, losing much of its clarity and energy. Forgiveness operates in much the same way. God's mercy and forgiveness springs out from hearts that have been softened and broken, but in order to keep many of its good qualities flowing it must move from our hearts down the slopes of our lives to touch other people. In order to keep experiencing the joy of forgiveness we, in turn, must forgive.

Now I am aware that for many people, particularly many people who live with same-sex attraction, this side of forgiveness may be terribly difficult. Over the course of my life lived with other people of same-sex attraction, I have become aware of wounds which appear so grievous that I cannot imagine how it would be possible for anyone to forgive them. Friendships have not merely slipped away or faded after the disclosures of same-sex attraction but have instead ended suddenly or even violently. Men and women have entered into relationships that ring with promises of fidelity and real love and have awoken later in a nightmare of abandonment. Various forms of abuse, name-calling, rejection, isolation, and despair have sometimes deeply characterized the lives of men and women living with same-sex attraction.

In many cases this abuse continues even now as some people living with same-sex attraction in conflict with their families feel alternately drawn to and repulsed by the very same people with whom they share such a long and difficult history. Writing this today, I can imagine their incredulity. "How, with all this water under the bridge, in the light of all that has happened, how can you possibly talk of forgiveness?"

I talk about forgiveness because I must. Resentments really are the ways we punish ourselves for others' failings. It's as though God gives us a practical way to see and understand our prayers lived out. God's forgiveness runs like a stream of clear water through our hearts, spirits, and lives, but our resentments, our refusal to forgive others for their failings toward us, so often preclude our drinking or sometimes even recognizing that water! There are a couple of examples of what I mean: one drawn from Scripture and the noted author Father Henri Nouwen and the other from contemporary American life.

In his book the *Return of the Prodigal Son*, Nouwen writes of how it is possible to be as lost staying home as it is to have left. This phenomenon he calls the "lostness of the elder son," linking it with the part of the story from which I quoted at the top of the chapter, that of the Father begging the eldest son to enter into his joy for having had his brother found. Nouwen writes:

> The lostness of the elder son, however, is much harder to identify. After all, he did all the right things. He was obedient, dutiful, law-abiding and hardworking. People respected him, admired him, praised him and likely considered him a model son. Outwardly the eldest son was faultless. But when confronted by his Father's joy at the return of the younger brother, a dark power erupts in him and boils to the surface. Suddenly there becomes glaringly visible a resentful, proud, unkind, selfish person, one that remained deeply hidden even though it had been growing stronger and more powerful over the years.

It is vastly important that people living with same-sex attraction who reconcile with God then move to reconcile with others in their lives. Not to do so risks ignoring the forgiveness and love of God which that reconciliation brings us. A second example, this one from contemporary life: Paul D.

I've heard about Paul D. for years but, as of this writing at least, we haven't had the chance to meet. A Catholic of long-standing, Paul regularly scandalized other Catholic friends of mine with the way his life outwardly was lived by the Church but inwardly (and often outwardly) seethed with anger and resentment. On many of the current controversies in the Church Paul was both orthodox and merciless. When I heard of his antics, often from people who shared his theology if not his spirituality, the stories brought to mind a pinched and weary soul. Then, one day over brunch, someone asked if the assembled crowd had seen what had happened to Paul D. No, what? everyone asked. Well, it seemed Paul had undergone a great change. The person relating this to the group said that on several occasions he had the chance to run into Paul socially and in business and, in each case, had found light and laughter where there had previously been only serious resentment. Not once, the companion related, had Paul snarled. When speaking on topics of Church controversy, his tone was one of understanding and mercy rather than of resentment and anger. His very soul, I imagined, sounded lighter and freer. Later it came out that Paul's mother, from whom he had long been estranged, had died, but not before Paul had been able to reconcile with her. It seems that reconciling that significant relationship had worked a huge change in Paul's soul and enabled him to connect with the mercy and love available to him.

It sounds paradoxical, but in many ways it can profit us to treat forgiveness initially as almost a discipline — that is to say something that feels less like a natural grace and more like a characteristic we must self-consciously practice. If we search our hearts diligently and become aware of tendencies in ourselves to hold onto hurts or to wallow in anger, we may need to be strict

169

with ourselves about seeking out those we understand to have hurt us and reconciling the hurt. Sometimes, perhaps many times, we will be wrong and find that the hurt was not meant in malice or that we may have misperceived or misunderstood the hurt. At other times we may also find that we were the ones to have done the hurting and not realized it. In any case, the principle remains that forgiveness given must become forgiveness shared if we wish to tap into its deep reservoir of love.

Ninevah rediscovered: forgiveness and the Church

Of course forgiveness is a two-way street and people on both sides of the cultural rift over same-sex attraction have a lot of forgiving and seeking forgiveness to do. Churches, particularly, have some long fences to mend. At the risk of painting with too broad a brush, I feel pastors and priests have often failed to challenge their congregations on the questions of interior attitude and real love, preferring to accept convenient stereotypes about same-sex-attracted people. Many times Christians have failed to understand that empathy means joining someone in the midst of their life and hurt and helping them there — not standing a ways off to shout criticism or even an occasional suggestion. Often, sometimes in my presence, Christians have tolerated the use of slurs and other derogatory terms for people living with same-sex attraction far longer than even ignorance would allow.

It pains me to write, in the summer of 1999, that so many same-sex-attracted men and women I meet report that they most often do not go to Church because overwhelmingly they feel they do not "belong" there. Occasionally I ask for specifics: what do you mean by "feel you don't belong there"? Responses include things like "I feel like everybody is looking at me" and "I can almost feel the disapproval" and "I think I make people uncomfortable." Jesus spent an awful lot of His time among men and women who made the religious of His day very uncomfortable and I cannot believe He finds our failure to offer His love pleasing. For too long, Christians, both individually and in Churches, have done a poor job in this area, but there are some very practical things both can do to help better the situation.

First, we can check any hint of superiority at the door. I remember a national Courage conference several years ago where a youth minister with a heart for promoting the Church's teaching on same-sex attraction came to speak. He himself does not live with same-sex attraction and worried that he might come across as self-righteous or superior. He began not by talking about the issues surrounding same-sex attraction but by outlining his own struggles with chastity as a younger and more immature Christian and of his battles to make the virtue more real in his life. His instincts in this regard proved correct, for when he began the meat of his discussion, it was not in any way as a religious educator (good) talking to a bunch of sinners (bad). Instead he spoke as one struggling Christian to other struggling Christians and his words touched his listeners quite deeply. More Christians need to be aware when speaking to same-sex-attracted people that there needs to be a far greater heart for truth in humility than for shows of righteousness.

The second thing Christians can do better is akin to the first. Christians can and should watch their language on this topic. For example, it's quite common even today to hear Christians say something about "living the gay lifestyle." Yet very few men and women living with same-sex attraction that I have met would say they were "living the gay lifestyle." Much more likely they would explain, if given the chance, that they are living their lives and that their lives include active homosexuality in large part because that has been what has made the most sense for them at the time and in their own personal context. The phrase "living the gay lifestyle" tends, in my opinion, to demean and dismiss what for many people has been a very deep and personal struggle over how they live their lives. I am firmly convinced that no two people come to same-sex attraction in exactly the same way, no two people live it out in exactly the same way, and no two people think about it in exactly the same terms.

Likewise, Christians can and should stop talking about people living with same-sex attraction as though they have somehow been stamped out with a cookie cutter. I am wary of the phrases "gays want" or "the gay agenda is," no matter who uses them. These types of phrases suggest that somehow those living with same-sex attraction communicate with one another through secret codes or metal plates in their brains. The only "gay agendas" which I have found have been ones articulated by various gay and lesbian organizations and many, if not most, of those disagree with one another as to priorities, strategies, and tactics. In that sense it is every bit as proper to speak of "Christian agendas" and mean the different topic areas addressed by public Christian groups. Also in terms of language, it would be helpful if Christian churches or groups would cease using people living with same-sex attraction as fundraising tools. No fundraising letter, in my opinion, can do justice to the nuance, difficulty, and pain bound up in most people's experience of same-sex attraction, and it borders on immoral to use that experience as a mere tool to raise funds.

Fourth, Christian pastors and priests can and should look to the whole area of discipleship in people's sexual lives before singling out same-sex attraction for particular condemnation. Too often people living with same-sex attraction perceive that while Christianity teaches that sexual expression rightly belongs inside a marriage between a man and woman, all too often many Christians seem willing to excuse failures of heterosexual sins even as they loudly condemn sins by those who are same-sex attracted. To a certain extent this can be laid at the feet of the gay and lesbian rights movement that, in many cases, has pushed gay and lesbian issues to a point where Churches make policy-statements that are unprepared or insufficiently thought out. The fact remains that if pastors are going to preach on same-sex sins, they had better plan to preach on adultery and premarital sex as well.

Finally, churches, no matter whether they self-identify as "liberal" or "conservative," need to start remembering that the issue of same-sex attraction concerns real people who need to either meet Jesus Christ or to be encouraged in their discipleship if they have met Him. It really doesn't do much good to condemn active homosexuality before introducing the One who provides the context for all human love. On the other hand, churches which presume to explain away Scripture's negative witness on homosexual acts or its positive message on the deep meaning of human sexuality don't do people living with same-sex attraction any favors. How demeaning it is to say to anyone, essentially, that the church thinks taking up a Cross too hard for them and that they should not even be challenged to try.

In the end, forgiveness is much more art than science. The humility, vulnerability, and grace necessary to both ask and offer forgiveness cannot be taught in a classroom or dictated by law. It can only appear as the fruit of converted hearts. It is in forgiveness, both the seeking and the offering, that the real power of the Gospel shows itself in individual and institutional lives. Even as I write this I am aware that I cannot condemn, in black and white terms, either Christians or gay and lesbian groups for seeing the other in black and white terms. The entire landscape is filled with shades of gray. I believe, for example, that there are gay and lesbian groups with misguided agendas that deeply endanger the human person, both body and soul. I know Christian groups whose response to those agendas starts with a good heart but sometimes can be more hurtful than helpful. But at the bottom line, only a small percentage of men and women on both sides share completely in those agendas or in the hurtful words than can accompany them. I believe the way forward can only be found in dealing with each other as individuals and not stereotypes. In the debates over public policies, ideas are fair game, but the people who bear the ideas must be shown respect and love.

Likewise, on the other side of the street, same-sex-attracted men and women can start doing some things that might clarify communications with Christians and contribute to greater reconciliation.

First, many of these suggestions can apply, in general, to men and women living with same-sex attraction of all theological opinions. Men and women living with same-sex attraction, to the extent they might do so, can stop looking at all Christians as though they too have been stamped out with cookie cutters. One of the oddest experiences of my life today is to be on the mailing lists of both gay and lesbian activist groups opposed to Christians and on the list of Christian groups opposed to active homosexuality. As someone who has know people from both groups, I can testify that neither caricature is particularly accurate or helpful.

Second, men and women living with same-sex attraction could resolve to practice charity and not to be overly sensitive. The overwhelming majority of Christians who have said hurtful things to me in the past have done so out of ignorance, not malice. I made it a point, when I used to "come out" to Christians, to expect questions and try to build in some time to answer them. The important thing is that men and women from both sides of the discussion over same-sex attraction feel free to share their concerns and to seek answers to questions.

Finally, and perhaps most difficult to do, men and women living with same-sex attraction can respond with forgiveness when Christians, both as individuals and as churches, begin to seek forgiveness, reconciliation, and greater communication. Same-sex-attracted men and women might remember that reaching out can be as difficult for Christians as it is for non-Christians, and that any place where forgiveness lives, God lives too. Communication animated by sensitivity and charity might be among the most powerful things people living with same-sex attraction could bring to a discussion of the topic.

CHAPTER ELEVEN

The battle for intimacy

Many people misperceive the chaste single life as one of loneliness and isolation. "I don't think I would mind living without sex too much," one thirty-something man living with same-sex attraction told me, "but I don't want to grow to be the kooky old guy living in a big house on a dark street someplace, you know?" I do know. Something very deep in human beings, deeper even than the sexual drive, fears being alone. Some people I have met, when pressed on the subject, have admitted their sexual lives are often less about sex than they are about a kind of emotional and relational calculus. Sex today, they hope, builds the relationships that they hope will sustain them later. Sexual expression, some imagine, is something they must trade for intimacy, something that can help keep the wolf of loneliness at bay. This type of attitude, while somewhat common among many in our post-modern, post-Christian, post-communal world, I have found particularly in the actively homosexual community, where relationships so often seem ephemeral, grounded less in what are internal realities than on external appearance. While I do not want to generalize too broadly, I have found that many men and women living with same-sex attraction have sex lives that are less about sex than about the search for real and sustained intimacy.

The pit of loneliness

Loneliness contributes uniquely to human suffering. The experience of loneliness can be seen as universal, as every human being, at some point, will feel the stab of being lonely. At the same time, few human beings experience loneliness in precisely the same way and, in this regard, loneliness has a deeply personal dimension. Loneliness denies us even solidarity in the experience of itself. The same things that make me feel lonely will not be precisely the same things that make you feel lonely.

I have long thought that loneliness draws much of its power from the reality of human beginnings and endings. We, as human beings, are born alone and will die that way. No one could have really been with us during our birth. Nor will anyone be able to be with us as we leave this life for the next. And we deeply fear being alone at these points of great change, and we wish, often passionately, that we not be. As Dylan Thomas wrote in *Do Not Go Gently Into that Good Night*, his powerful poem about his father's impending death, something inside many of us desperately wants to "rage against the dying of the light."

Loneliness contributes deeply to human suffering, particularly in first-world societies, where materialism often masks the importance of human connections. I recall the story of a friend of mine who lives in a very upscale Northern California suburb. She returned from her teaching job one afternoon to find her next-door neighbor on her lawn, weeping. "What's wrong? May I help?" my friend asked as she approached the weeping woman, lifting her up and inviting her in to share a cup of tea. Over a steaming mug the woman, a relatively recent (three years) Indian immigrant to the United States, told of how she had come to the United States to marry. In a relatively short time she had moved from her relatively poor but very extended Indian family in New Delhi to a wealthy but terribly isolating home in the United States. On the one hand the woman felt grateful to have moved from a small, cramped living arrangement around so many relatives to one that had so much space, modern conveniences, and distractions. But on the other hand, none of those things could mask how terribly empty she found her beautiful new home or how very difficult she found integrating into a society that based itself on such a radical notion of personal autonomy and freedom. Many Americans fail to grasp, she discovered, that doing things "their way" often means doing things alone.

I have found similar experiences in my travels in the developing world. In January, 1998, I traveled to Peru to document the stories of women maimed and killed by a government forced sterilization campaign. I interviewed Felipe Gonzales, a man whose wife, Juana, had been killed by complications of a surgical sterilization procedure she had not wanted. Felipe and three children still lived, as they had with Juana, in a house of mud and sticks in a tiny Peruvian hamlet called La Legua, but now, after his wife's death, Felipe told me his situation was far worse. "We were always poor," he said, "but together we could always manage. Now, with Juana gone, I am all alone and don't know what I will be able to do." In the end, human contact may be needed to live with either wealth or poverty.

Loneliness is such a universal element to human suffering that God included it as one of the torments Christ experienced during His Passion, part of the cup Jesus asked that He not be made to drink if such could be part of His Father's will. I have long imagined that during the days of Christ's Passion, the focus of all the loneliness in the universe moved to that one tiny part of Jerusalem. Near the place where God found His friends sleeping, during His time of trial where, hours later, Jesus would cry out that His Father had forsaken Him before He died, we find an indication that He may have been making that long trip into the dark alone.

Thus loneliness remains, in a sense, inescapable. It is difficult to imagine how any human being, even one living a life fully connected to family and broader society, could live a life completely free of even the slightest tinge of occasional loneliness. It is one of the dragons living quite close to the heart of human experience.

Loneliness and same-sex attraction

Yet with all that said about the universality of loneliness, many of us living with same-sex attraction have experienced loneliness in a particular sort of way which may not resonate entirely with others who do not share our background. As one twenty-eight-year-old man living with same-sex attraction put it very eloquently in an online essay:

> This world is not meant for people like me. It's not meant for people to swallow all by their lonesome. When you look around any cafe or restaurant all you see are the couples. Men and women, their children, boys and girls, and even on a baser level, just people with other people. Old and young alike sit and eat and exchange with words the terrible arrows that have been flung at them over the past few hours and minutes. This world has from the beginning of the clock been formed and molded and shaped to take care of pairs of two, not single and lone individuals.

> The next time you are at a movie theater or a stage play, stand up and look around before the show and count the people who are not leaning over whispering in someone's ear. Take notice of all the "loners" and praise them for hanging on to life by the teeth.

> They WILL be there and you might even see me. You have [to] look at us, because we are there

too. You have to accept us, because we are there too. We live day in and day out without the precious gemstones you call your friends or spouses or children (author unknown).

It's not, I imagine, that people living with same-sex attraction experience a loneliness that is terribly different from that which others experience. But it may be that the gates to loneliness open more widely for us than for others and the barriers to intimacy and human connection may be a tad higher.

First of all, the whole phenomenon of social stigma stands in the way of many of us making deep human connections with surrounding people. Intimacy, as I will discuss later in this chapter, has a great deal to do with trust and exposure. Yet the very social stigma around same-sex attraction makes opening ourselves to that trust and exposure appear more risky for people living with same-sex attraction than I imagine it might be for others. Of course I write out of my own experience and it may be that the experience of risk in intimacy is the same for everyone, but in my life I recall the fear of exposing my own same-sex inclination to have been a particularly high barrier to overcome.

Second, as the essayist points out, something about human nature gravitates to groups and pairs, particularly pairs of men and women and groups of children. As I have written in previous chapters, encountering functional, open, loving family lives played a very important role in the gradual healing God has worked in my heart from years of different hurts, resentments, and memories. But those encounters with family life have had a down side too, as I have realized in a very deep way that what those families shared, at least as of this writing, may never be mine to share in a direct or personally intimate way. That realization has often brought with it a deep and rather brutal loneliness that is not unique to people living with same-sex attraction but to which we may be more susceptible.

Third, if the psychiatrists and psychologists in the "nurture" school of how same-sex attraction develops are correct, the experience of a particular sort of alienation and loneliness around our peers (at least in men) may be a large part of how we have become the people we are. In this regard, it may be true that a particularly wounded loneliness has been the lot of many men who experience same-sex attraction from a very early age and thus may be all that much more difficult to overturn.

Intimacy counters loneliness

While loneliness may be an unavoidable part of the human experience and may be even heightened or given a particular edge among people living with same-sex attraction, no one necessarily stands helpless in its desert. It is possible to fight against loneliness, to structure our lives to foster deep relationships and intimacy.

Intimacy, like love and forgiveness, is one of those words whose meaning we have to reclaim. These days when you hear the terms "intimate relations" or "intimate friend" what do you think they describe? All too often the broader culture assumes an "intimate friendship" means a couple having sex. "Intimate relations" in some popular magazines routinely appears as a euphemism for sexual relations. Yet this meaning, even euphemistically, doesn't appear in the dictionary definition for the term at all. The dictionary definition of the word "intimate" as an adjective includes definitions like "intrinsic or essential" or "belonging to or characterizing one's deepest nature" or "marked by very close association, contact, or familiarity" and "marked by a warm friendship developing through long association." None of the definitions includes sex — explicitly or necessarily.

Much of the misunderstanding between sex and intimacy may arise because many confuse the relationship between the two and assume a mistaken order between them. Deep intimacy can be (and in marriage should be) expressed sexually. Yet, rightly ordered, sexual expression will arise from intimacy that is already present in a relationship. Indeed, delaying sexual relations until after a marriage commitment is made allows partners the needed time for an intimate friendship to develop so that the couple's sexual life will begin in the context of intimacy. Sexual relations that take place ahead of intimacy can even preclude, particularly in male-male couplings, the development of an intimate friendship. I have lost count of the numbers of homosexually active men I have known who have experienced this. Many have gone through a period of great excitement at having found someone they feel might be the "love of their life" only to fall into disappointment when, relatively soon after the relationship becomes actively sexual, the friendship fails. They discover too late that what they sought as intimacy had been misinterpreted by the other as predominantly sexual attraction. In fact, intimate friendships don't demand sexual expression at all. Exactly what characterizes intimate friendships and how can they help to counter loneliness?

Qualities of intimate friendship

Probably the easiest definition of an intimate friend is someone else, not related by blood, for whom our existence matters significantly; someone, who is not our family *per se* but who cares whether we are around or not. In practical terms this means a person who, if they called you at a time when they expected you home and found you were not there, would wonder a bit as they hung up the phone about where you might be and hope that you are OK. At this writing, one of the more critically-acclaimed shows on television is called *Will and Grace*, a situation comedy that explores the friendship and misadventures of a heterosexual woman and a predominantly same-sex-attracted man. The show has won critical applause because its dialogue is well-written and intelligent and its entire cast appears strong. But I find the program's script intriguing as well because its dialogue between the friends rings so true. While my intimate friends and I may never have shared the *exact content* of the conversations between

Will and Grace, we have certainly shared much of their tone and attitude. The honesty, frankness, knowledge of the other, and willingness to forgive and seek forgiveness that their friendship contains reminds me very much of some of the intimate friendships in my lives and the lives of others.

A similar, though significantly more complex example can be found in the 1998 film *As Good As It Gets*. In this film Jack Nicholson plays a man living with multiple obsessive/compulsive disorders and a highly challenging personality who gradually comes to wholeness through the interaction with several other people, notably one same-sex-attracted man he initially dislikes, a neighbor with a dog. Although the complexity of this relationship appears particular to the principals involved, the movie does a good job of showing how superficial relationships with people with whom one agrees cannot always withstand the "slings and arrows" of outrageous fortune but how tangible love, even from someone objectionable, can change lives.

Here then, are some of the qualities that I believe a friendship must possess if it's going to grow from being a mere acquaintance to one of deep and lasting intimacy. I don't mean it to necessarily be an exhaustive list, and those with more experience than I at intimate friendship are welcome to add to it.

First, a relationship that is going to move from acquaintance to intimate friendship will have to be committed to honesty. Honesty forms the foundation of intimate friendship because so many other necessary qualities of intimate friendship, like risk-taking, trust, and forgiveness rely upon honesty for their very existence. By honesty I mean that quality where both parties in the friendship are willing to be authentic and open about their actions and motives in a friendship. People, to the greatest extent possible, must strive to provide in their friendships a type of transparency made popular by the computer term WYSIWYG (say whizzy-wig). WYSIWYG is an acronym that stands for What You See Is What You Get, and in friendship it will mean that each of the friends is commited to allowing the other person to get to know them honestly and completely over time.

If the pit of your stomach clenched a bit when you read about the need for honesty in friendship, you have already anticipated the second quality necessary for intimate friendships. Risk-taking could be described as the down side of honesty. Being honest means that we both acknowledge our imperfections and make ourselves willing to allow someone else to see them as well. Conversely, it also means that we make ourselves willing to confront our friends about flaws, faults, and habits etc. that they may not have confronted or been able to see. Risk-taking is difficult because it's . . . well, risky. In much the same way as forgiveness, we cannot always predict where honesty is going to take us. If I tell my friend about a bad quality or habit that I know I have and may even need his help with, what will he say? Will he still want to be my friend? Or how will he react if I bring up something about him that he needs to recognize?

Many people find honesty and risk-taking very difficult, but believe me, they are absolutely essential in the development of am intimate friendship. Two of my intimate friendships (and another moving toward greater intimacy) developed only very slowly for years because the other people hated risk-taking and were convinced that if I "knew the real truth" about them our friendships would end. Of course, they were wrong and, in retrospect after they had told me, they realized how they had inadvertently undervalued my commitment to the friendship by assuming a harsh or mean-spirited reaction to their revelation.

A friendship where both parties commit themselves to honesty and risk-taking will eventually develop the next quality essential to intimate friendships: trust. Trust characterizes and builds intimate friendships but it also can be seen as one of the fruits of intimate friendship.

Other people may disagree with me, but I think having people in one's life whom one can trust and rely upon is absolutely essential to growing as a person. I have come to believe that deep trust — the kind proclaimed publicly in marriage vows, for example — reflects in a profound way some of the deepest and most important aspects of our relationship with God. I believe this shattering of trust or of belief in trust may be among the worst and most persistent of the results of the First World's current passion for divorce. In so many developed countries now, whole generations of men and women have learned from the wreckage of their parents' marriages that trust may be something nice to think about but really doesn't exist outside of daydreams. In the midst of their first-world wealth, their loss represents real poverty for, in a very real sense, without intimate friendships, what is left to life?

In my own life this has been very true. I never realized how little trust I had in others until I began to experience growth in trust itself. A couple of years ago, my friend Mike asked me to take up soccer again. Even though I had not played in years, was thirty-four years old and out of shape, I agreed to try even though I expected not to be able to do it. As I stepped out onto the field for the first time in almost twenty years it hit me: I didn't believe I could do this, but Mike believed I could do this, and I trusted Mike. So, I was out on the field.

The trust of intimate friendship, in the words of Scripture, celebrates when friends celebrate and weeps when they weep. It does not count the cost but pours itself out for the other. In a mature, intimate friendship both parties know the other well enough that if their car broke down at 3:00 A.M. on a snowy morning, they each could call the other for assistance and a place to stay. A story is told of a junior high basketball team somewhere in Indiana. One of the team's players, age thirteen, had been stricken with leukemia and forced into a hospital for an extended stay. His chemotherapy had cost him all his hair. His teammates were briefed on his condition and the fact of his likely changed appearance before he came back to school. His best friend, also on the team, felt so badly for him and how he would feel returning to school bald that he went to his parents and then to all the other boys in his class and on the basketball team. If his friend was going to have to be bald for a time, he told them, then he wanted to be bald as well. Cut off all my hair, he said, and asked his other classmates and teammates if they would shave their heads as well. And they did. When you think of how sensitive to appearance we often are at age thirteen and fourteen, of how we worry about how we look and whether we stand out in crowds, you realize what it must have cost those boys to take such a step. Intimate friendship sees past the mere surfaces of people and gives from the heart.

Because perfection still eludes human beings, trust both permits and requires intimate friendship's next quality: forgiveness. Now I am not going to re-present all of the chapter on forgiveness over again but, in this context, I will note that forgiveness both accelerates the growth of trust and can help cement ties that have been damaged by one or both people's failure. We trust our intimate friends, but sometimes they fail us, for they are as human as we are. Forgiveness provides both the salve and the glue that can keep such a failure from destroying a friendship that may have taken years to develop. I recall seeing a sad situation as an adolescent. Two women had been friends for many years, a friendship that had seen them through calamities and sorrows of almost every description. But the friendship foundered when one friend began to drink and could not or would not see the problems her abuse of alcohol caused, even when her close friend tried to help her see. They parted company over the issue and, even when the drinking friend faced up to the situation and overcame it, neither one felt willing or able to seek or grant forgiveness. The friendship died.

The reality of this situation leads me to the last of my list of qualities of intimate friendship: a willingness to continue. Intimate friendships share a quality with all intimate relationships; they require work and time. Both parties to a friendship must constantly commit to one another and to the friendship, be willing to keep seeing the friendship grow and change and, if necessary, go through greater challenges of risk-taking and honesty to reach deeper levels of trust.

185

How does intimacy relate to chastity?

At this point a few people may be asking, why bother? Intimate friendships sound like a lot of work to me and if they don't work out it sounds as if they can hurt. Both concerns are accurate. Building and maintaining intimate friendships can take a lot of work and can hurt us if they fail. But the alternative, in my opinion, is far worse.

At the heart of intimate friendship is a mix of the *agape* and *philia* love that I wrote about a few chapters ago. These kinds of love both sustain and change us, as human beings. Neither is risk-free and neither will force itself upon us. Yet if we don't open ourselves up to that intimacy, we run the risk of living what I have come to call "donut lives" — lives which have an outward appearance of normality and growth but which inside have little more than a hole. In the words of noted Christian apologist C.S. Lewis, none of us *have* to risk love, but those who don't take such a risk may never see heaven.

In discussions with many predominantly same-sex-attracted men and women, the theme of loneliness and need for intimacy arises again and again. In fact, it seems clear that for most of these men and women the need for intimacy and closeness, trust and enduring love far overshadow the desire for sex. Living chastely, that is living without active genital sex, becomes a great deal easier when we know that we are loved and regarded.

Each weekend night (and some weekdays) near my home in Washington, D.C., gay and lesbian bars and clubs fill with people. Some of them go to hang out with friends and party, but many others go because a kind of grinding loneliness has led them there. Even as they acknowledge that the chances of finding someone for a deeper friendship will be poor in an environment so reliant on alcohol and mere appearances, they go anyway. Spending an evening searching for unlikely companionship and intimacy, even at the cost of sexual expression they may not particularly *want*, is seen as preferable to a weekend spent alone, facing a single existence in a coupled world. But the greatest contemporary social secret is that such a Faustian and unsatisfactory deal need *not* be made. Deep intimate friendships can exist without either party feeling they need to somehow pay for the privilege with their bodies.

Ironically, this message should not be anything new to the gay and lesbian community. Surviving AIDS and HIV during the 1980s and '90s has meant people, particularly predominantly same-sex-attracted men, have lived on friendship. "I have survived HIV carried on the backs of my friends," said one long-term survivor of the infection, "and those of my friends who are also infected have survived carried on mine." When family, insurance companies, medical strategies, and social conventions failed, many who had spent much of their adult life in the gay male community found friendship the only treasure that remained.

Intimacy in and of itself can never completely defeat the occasional loneliness that, as I described at the beginning of the chapter, afflicts everyone from time to time. Yet, the presence of intimate friendships in our lives can make that loneliness more occasional than regular and more bearable than not.

Something needs to be said here about touch. It's almost inevitable, when I have spoken on this close relationship between intimate friendships and chastity, that someone has raised their hand and asked about touch in such friendships. Are hugs in bounds? Kisses? Cuddling? What, at the bottom line, are the guidelines.

It's a valid question. Touch is very important for human beings. In the early days of AIDS I got involved with trying to address the numbers of HIV-positive babies whose drug-addicted mothers had abandoned them in hospitals after delivery. I started to work with these kids thinking I would primarily help them get the stuff they needed, but it became clear quickly that human contact was what they really needed. Babies, a doctor told me early on, if not hugged, played with, and touched will die. People need to be touched, and sometimes the depth of a friendship extends beyond words to where a hug is all that will suffice.

As regards "guidelines," I will write here what I say from

the podium. In my experience there have been no hard and fast rules because no two friendships are exactly alike. This is why the honesty, risk-taking, and trust of intimate friendships are so important. Both parties have to be honest with each other about why they offer and receive hugs, and both parties have to trust that the other will respect their boundaries. In the end, it's a matter of conscience. Some people, perhaps most I expect, will be fine with hugs in friendship, but others may find them so disturbing to their equilibrium that they should probably not do too much hugging. People with real questions in this area should perhaps consult their confessor, pastor, or close, mature Christian friend who knows of the situation and can help discern the truth of the matter.

CHAPTER TWELVE

Chastity and sacrament

"To dedicate one's life to Christ through service to others, spiritual reading, prayer, meditation, individual spiritual direction, frequent attendance at Mass, and the frequent reception of the sacraments of Penance and Holy Eucharist." — The Second Goal of Courage

A chapter on the relationship between sacrament and the virtue of chastity can only reveal, like several other of this book's chapters, the tip of a very a large topic. Only very slowly have I come to realize that to participate in the sacraments is to share intimately and bodily in the very life of God. Anything that profound could demand the work of thousands of writers for thousands of years. Because I am not yet a saint and my readers do not possess infinite patience, I will limit my discussion to what I believe are the three most important aspects of the relationship between a sacramental life and an attempt to live chastly: the nature of sacrament, the Church as sacramental sign, and the role of sacramental confession and communion. I don't mean for this list to be the last word, but for what they are worth, here are my thoughts.

Sacraments generally and chastity

Many older Catholics today will probably recall the definition of sacraments given in the old Baltimore Catechism of their childhood: "A Sacrament is an outward sign instituted by Christ to give grace." As a definition, this is pretty clear. Sacraments, the Baltimore Catechism goes on to explain, must contain an outward visible sign (and thus be intelligible to our senses), must have been instituted by Christ, and must give grace. The most recent *Catechism of the Catholic Church* tells us that there are seven sacraments instituted by Christ: Baptism, Confirmation (or Chrismation), the Eucharist, Penance, the Anointing of the Sick, Holy Orders and Matrimony, and these sacraments are part of all of the important times of our Christian lives. From birth to death, they provide healing and direction in the life of faith, and follow the stages of our natural and spiritual lives (CCC 1210).

I believe the combination of these aspects make the sacraments essential in my attempt to live a Christian life, particularly a life lived in unmarried chastity. I don't mean to suggest that a chaste life *cannot* be lived without the sacraments. I know that many others do so day in and day out. But in my case, with my particular mix of personality and history, the fullness of the sacraments speak to me at many different levels and help make chastity a way of life. They have acted in my life as life preserver and comforter, a spur to conscience and forgiveness as well as a source of strength and encouragement.

I believe it very important to living chastely that the sacraments are *visible, intelligible signs* that relate to lived experience. My whole self — body, mind, and spirit — matters to God and, in turn, matter to me *because* I matter to God. God does not rely on merely the intellect for comprehension and communication, He draws my body in as well. God went far out of His way to make sure that, when I was baptized, I not only *understood* His love intellectually in assenting to Baptism but also *felt* it when the water splashed over my head to cleanse my soul from sin. I *felt* it again, in a profound way, when Jesus, in the person of a priest, confirmed me in faith and smeared oil on my face in much the same way as the prophet Nathan did to make a shepherd boy king and as God has been doing to His anointed for centuries. I *hear* it when I hear Jesus, again in the person of a priest, tell me many the same things He told the adulterous woman and the man with a crippled hand: I do not condemn you, your sins are forgiven, go and sin no more. I *taste* and *drink* it when I literally and mysteriously take Him into myself in the forms of bread and wine. The fact that I am a unity of body, soul, and spirit matters so deeply because Jesus Christ crossed an infinite distance to become a human being like me. All these outward and visible sacramental signs speak to that reality because they serve to remind me, over and over again, that I cannot compartmentalize my life or myself. I cannot, for example, assert that the David sitting in Church on Sunday is a different man from the one who chooses to do what is right or, to my sorrow, what is wrong. The sacraments will not allow me to do that. Even if I could lie or intellectually delude myself into believing that some aspect of sexual sin or other moral failing was "acceptable" or "OK for me," my own body testifies and bears witness against that falsehood. My stepfather occasionally describes the difference between driving a car and riding a motorcycle to be akin to the difference between looking at or watching a picture and actually *being* in the picture. Living a sacramental life is like that. It is living in reality as opposed to merely watching it.

I find that living in reality helps me seek chastity for another reason. On one level, the sacraments make it clear that my body as well as my mind and spirit belong to God. But on another level, the bodily connection with the sacraments helps reinforce my identity as a Child of God and secures my place at the feet of my Father. Perhaps I am too much an optimist, but my own experience in my life has been that relatively few people genuinely choose to do what they know to be wrong. Some do, it's true, but many others choose to put other things which *appear* to be good ahead of what they may or may not know to be *truly* good. This mistake becomes a lot easier to make if one forgets, or if one has never been told, about who we really are as human beings. The way the sacraments emphasize a bodily knowledge of faith's experience, the way kneeling for absolution *feels* on my old knee injury, the *taste* of communion under the species of bread and wine, or the *sight* of sunlight exploding through the colors of a stained glass window when the cloud cover passes away — all these reinforce my identity as a Christian, as someone seeking to follow Christ and hoping for heaven. They make it that much harder to forget who I really am and what I am really about.

As visible signs, the sacraments also give immediacy to my relationship with Christ. Church architecture, or at least old church architecture, provides a good example. Trinity Church, where Nicholas baptized me, is a very low Anglican structure and has little of a Catholic sensibility in either its exterior architecture or interior decoration. Good preaching, music, and fellowship afterward marked the worship I shared there, yet the experience remained somehow disembodied, particularly at times when the congregation didn't celebrate Eucharist, offering Morning Prayer instead. I don't mean to suggest that Christ was not there at those times, because He clearly was. Where two or more are gathered in my name, Jesus said, I am there with them, whether in Cathedral or auditorium. Yet, something marvelously tangible speaks out from the architecture of an old Catholic church building with a traditionally Catholic interior serving as the bosom for the celebration of Christ in the sacraments. Meeting Christ there, in the presence of icons and statues of the saints, meeting Him so tangibly in the words of absolution or in the Body of Christ, sets the experience firmly in time and space. As I will discuss later, it is *that* moment, in *that* place that I meet the Risen Lord.

The Church, in her very existence, provides me the second important sacramental assistant to living a chaste life, albeit a more frustrating one. *The Catechism of the Catholic Church* puts it, in part, in this way:

"The Church, in Christ, is like a sacrament — a sign and instrument, that is, of communion with God and of unity among all men" [*LG* 1]. The Church's first purpose is to be the sacrament of the *inner union of men with God*. Because men's communion with one another is rooted in that union with God, the Church is also the sacrament of the *unity of the human race*. In her, this unity is already begun, since she gathers men "from every nation, from all tribes and peoples and tongues"; [*Rev* 7:9] at the same time, the Church is the "sign and instrument" of the full realization of the unity yet to come (775).

As sacrament, the Church is Christ's instrument. "She is taken up by him also as the instrument for the salvation of all," "the universal sacrament of salvation," by which Christ is "at once manifesting and actualizing the mystery of God's love for men" [*LG* 9 § 2, 48 § 2: *GS* 45 § 1]. The Church "is the visible plan of God's love for humanity," because God desires "that the whole human race may become one People of God, form one Body of Christ, and be built up into one temple of the Holy Spirit" [Paul VI, June 22, 1973; *AG* 7 § 2; cf. *LG* 17] (776).

Essentially then it is the Church, not merely the theoretical, easily idealized, blueprint Church of the *Catechism* but the impractical, faulty, flesh-and-bones Church of my Christian friends, acquaintances, and people I dislike that helps to strengthen my attempts to live a chaste Christian life. I find this a deep and ironic mystery. How can something be a sacrament and yet be so frustrating?

As I suggested in the last chapter, chastity would be a most difficult virtue to attain in isolation. I know that, over the years, the Church has supported communities of hermits called *lauras* (the idea sounds almost oxymoronic). In a laura, individual hermits live most of the day apart in individual hermitages but still come together to celebrate Mass, collect mail, and sometimes share a meal. I know that some of the saints have been canonized for sanctity attained living just this sort of life. Yet, I still believe that for me, and perhaps for most Christians, a virtuous life would be harder, not easier, to attain as a hermit — though perhaps less frustrating.

The Church as sacrament in my life serves as a mortar and pestle of virtue, grinding away my ego: selfishness, greed, impatience, and lust are ground between the Holy Spirit's relentless call for holiness and the hard surfaces of other Christians and non-Christians alike. It's a brutal and persistent but necessary grinding. Of what use would the virtues of patience and self-control be, for example, if there were no one in my life with whom to practice them — even though I do so imperfectly? And without other flawed people (and others) in my life, how would such virtues come to be perfected?

In much the same way as the sacraments serve to remind me of my bodily faith, so too does the Church as sacrament serve to remind of the necessary practicality of faith. It would be all too easy to come to a mistaken *belief* about living a virtuous life if I were to try to rate the depth of my virtue by how well I perform external actions, by how many rosaries I pray, or how many sacramentals I use. Jesus found people with a very similar attitude in His day and He called them "whitewashed tombs." But living daily in the flesh-and-blood Church, and adopting simple disciplines like a regular examination of conscience, keeps me aware of my true position in seeking virtue. Examining my conscience reveals individual rights and wrongs, of course, but more important are the trends, patterns, and *habits* that a regular examination exposes. Human beings have long labeled themselves as "creatures of habit," yet many people do not fully comprehend how powerful an influence our habits are in our lives, whether for good or ill. Living my life with other Christians brings me back on track when I tend to slip and keeps me centered on where I need to be. I want to make it clear how important such centering is, even as I sometimes find it very frustrating.

Writing about other people's sanctifying influence in a book like this might come across as somehow simplistic, but in reality it is quite difficult and profound — particularly when helping to encourage chastity. I don't believe anyone finds the evaluation of his or her own actions through the eyes of others to be either easy or especially satisfying. How much simpler it is to complain and justify ourselves when we are in conflict with others than to admit that the people we dislike may have a point about our behavior or our attitude. They may dislike us for a good reason. Perhaps *we* are the ones who need to change. Yet, it is precisely in that crucible of community that I hear the message of change most clearly — if I open my ears enough to listen. Recognizing the voice of God in other people helps me recognize *their* identity as Children of God and as people complexly created in His image. This vastly helps the battle for chastity. Because objectification of others is one of the sharpest contrasts between lust and genuine love, living in the crucible of other people is the single strongest deterrent to allowing lust to flatten anyone from their three-dimensional complexity into a two-dimensional dishonest caricature that lust wants to see.

Of course there are practical steps to take when an examination of conscience reveals some of the problems created while living in the crucible. First, I try to apologize and make amends for the way I have failed someone else. Then, after enough time for reflection has passed, I head for a nearby Church and the sacrament of penance: a ritual cleansing that the modern world almost completely misunderstands and ridicules in its miscomprehension. The *Catechism of the Catholic Church* says this about confession:

> Those who approach the sacrament of Penance
> obtain pardon from God's mercy for the offense

committed against him, and are, at the same time, reconciled with the Church which they have wounded by their sins and which by charity, by example, and by prayer labors for their conversion [*LG* 11§ 2] (1422).

It is called the *sacrament of conversion* because it makes sacramentally present Jesus' call to conversion, the first step in returning to the Father [cf. *Mk* 1:15; *Lk* 15:18] from whom one has strayed by sin.

It is called the *sacrament of Penance*, since it consecrates the Christian sinner's personal and ecclesial steps of conversion, penance, and satisfaction (1423).

Confession may hold the dubious title as the element of the Catholic Faith most discussed by stand-up comedians. The world just can't get it. Many non-Catholic Christians frequently ask why Catholics need a priest to hear a confession. "What do you need a priest for," asked one man after I had finished speaking recently, "Just get down on your knees, make confession to God and then, boom, it's all done." Others assert that confession to a priest does little more than empower priests. Still others balk at the seeming ease of it all. No *real* God, they seem to be saying, could listen to a list of sins as long as one's arm, forgive them, and then leave the sinner with nothing but a few prayers and, if he is lucky, some sound advice on how to avoid sinning again.

The practice of confession is one of those things which could be discussed, described, and depicted forever and never really be understood until one does it, but here are three of the sacrament's characteristics that speak most deeply to me and which help me in living a chaste life.

First, my confession expresses my desire to keep my conversation with God, the text of my life with Him, on a level at least as deep as it has been, if not deeper. Many people believe that the sacrament of penance happens when the penitent is in the room or the little booth (the "box" my friends and I sometimes call it) with the priest. But actually, that represents the mere *culmination* of the sacrament, the top of the mountain, the final moments as it were. Most of my experience of the sacrament, in my life at least, takes place *outside* the box or the church, sometimes two or three days before, and begins with the examination of conscience.

Most first-world people, myself included, live the busiest idle lives in the history of humankind. Very few of us must toil at farming, hunting, or gleaning for ten or twelve hours a day merely to keep food on a table or a roof over our heads. Education and technology have given us a freedom from manual labor that our ancestors would not have been able to imagine. Yet, many of us spend our treasure of free time in little more than recreation (the more virtuous of us) or dissolute lassitude (the couch potatoes). But whether watching television or mountain biking, there always seems to be something to do.

Examining my conscience, the first step of confession, represents a conscious break with that. Once every week or two weeks, for anything from twenty minutes to an hour, I find a quiet place and consciously put myself in the presence of God. Of course, all of us are in the presence of God all the time, but the key word in that last sentence is *consciously*. Most of us go about our daily lives almost entirely unaware until we make ourselves remember in whose presence we stand, or sit, or kneel. Once aware of where I am (and reminded of *who* I am), I pray briefly for God's help in reviewing the time since my last confession and then begin consciously to trace every day — asking Him to point out what I need to remember.

Intimacy encompasses examination of conscience's key concepts. Reviewing honestly my motivations and actions, I learn to take risks with God and to reap the treasure of trust such risk-taking rewards. I know that other people examine their conscience differently. Catholic publishers have produced everything from small pamphlets to whole books on the subject, and I would be surprised if any two people did it exactly the same way. But it's important to understand that in beginning the examination of conscience, one has begun the sacrament of confession. In the language of the parable of the Prodigal Son, when I examine my conscience I have remembered my Father and begun to turn toward home.

The second step, the journey home, usually takes a day but can take longer too. This is the difficult step of reflecting on what God has brought to mind in my examination of conscience and reconciling with anyone whom I might have hurt. Usually this means tracking people down for an apology and offer to make recompense. While there is no *requirement* that this be done prior to confession, I have found I remember to do it, and do it more easily, when I am on my way to the confessional than after I am absolved. As I will describe more fully later, one of the joys of confession is that the sacrament ends the tale of the sins confessed. Hatchets buried in the floor of the confessional do not linger to be dug up again, but literally vanish into the ravenous love God has for us. So, in my life at least, tracking down someone and making apology after confession would be somehow odd, sort of like granting life to a problem which I know and feel to have been left behind.

The second way confession aids chastity begins with the final part of the sacrament, with the mental, spiritual, and bodily humility required to confess one's faults and errors to another human being. This is part of the discipline that many people who ask, "Why do you need to confess to a priest?" misunderstand. As someone who has both knelt alone and prayed for forgiveness and approached a priest for absolution, I can say with confidence that approaching the confessional is infinitely harder. Prayers to God for forgiveness help one prepare for confession, of course, but if the matter ended there confession would not satisfy either justice or the real needs of the penitent. In the beginning, and for some people's entire lives, the actual confessing of sins remains a real discipline, a struggle every time. Something deep within us resents and struggles against admitting to someone else that we have made mistakes or even intentionally acted wrongly.

Yet people do confess. Not in the numbers they have previously perhaps, but in large enough numbers in my area that if you don't arrive for confession promptly you can expect to wait in line for a while. I suspect that everyone standing in line with me might give a slightly different reason for coming, but many of the reasons would find their roots in the Church's teaching that even though a priest hears my confession and speaks the words of absolution, it is Christ who absolves. That teaching, combined with the joy at *hearing* "I absolve you," draws many like a magnet.

That joy, the joy of walking out from the shaded Church into the bright light of day knowing I have been washed in the blood of the lamb and my sins forgiven, balances whatever struggle with my pride I have had to get there in the first place. Something particularly liberating happens to the spirit when Christ, through the priest, absolves. As a friend who shares the sacramental life with me wrote recently, a good confession liberates for doing good: "Your sins are forgiven *right now*, as the priest recites the formula. You and I have talked about how liberating that is. Before I used to pray, 'Lord, please forgive me please forgive me please forgive me' for days after a sexual sin, not really believing or knowing that he would. Somehow knowing that one is truly forgiven after having made a good confession liberates one to live in truth more easily."

Of course, some of the people in line with me have their minds less on confession than on the sacrament for which confession prepares; the sacrament of Eucharist, or Holy Communion. The Church teaches that one should not receive communion if one is conscious of serious sins that go without absolution. Sadly, more than a few times I have gone to confession more because I wanted Eucharist than because, at that time, I recognized confession for the good it is.

The *Catechism of the Catholic Church* says this, in part, about the Eucharist, for which it borrows St. Athanasius's term, the Great Sacrament:

> The Eucharist is "the source and summit of the
> Christian life [*LG* 11]. The other sacraments, and

indeed all ecclesiastical ministries and works of the apostolate, are bound up with the Eucharist and are oriented toward it. For in the blessed Eucharist is contained the whole spiritual good of the Church, namely Christ himself, our Pasch" [*PO* 5] (1324).

The Eucharist is the efficacious sign and sublime cause of that communion in the divine life and that unity of the People of God by which the Church is kept in being. It is the culmination both of God's action sanctifying the world in Christ and of the worship men offer to Christ and through him to the Father in the Holy Spirit" [Congregation of Rites, instruction, *Eucharisticum mysterium*, 6] (1325).

Finally, by the Eucharistic celebration we already unite ourselves with the heavenly liturgy and anticipate eternal life, when God will be all in all [Cf. *1 Cor* 15:28] (1326).

In brief, the Eucharist is the sum and summary of our faith: "Our way of thinking is attuned to the Eucharist, and the Eucharist in turn confirms our way of thinking" [St. Irenaeus, *Adv. haeres.* 4, 18, 5: PG 7/1, 1028] (1327).

Holy Communion, when Jesus Christ — who is God, the King of the Universe before whom all knees must bow and tongues confess, who humbles Himself out of love and concern to come to me in the most fragile and simple way — is the source and culmination of my entire journey as a Catholic Christian. One of the sadder confusions that has sprung up in the wake of the Second Vatican Council has been a misunderstanding about the roles of the Eucharist in our lives. Some have come to believe that love for Christ in the Eucharist must take a second place or a back seat to love of Christ in our fellow Christians and non-Christians alike. But the reality is far more mysterious, lovely, and organic. Because all the love I have for others, everything about my life, even the things that are failures and need absolution, literally everything is tied up in and blessed and made holy by the moment I meet Christ in the Eucharist.

In C.S. Lewis's short classic *The Great Divorce*, residents of Hell are allowed to travel, briefly, to the forecourt of heaven where they are but ghosts against the brilliant reality of heavenly glory. If they merely repent of what has led the to hell in the first place, they can stay and go "further up and further in" into heaven with the friends and angels who helped them come to their senses. Out of a bus full of people, sadly only one stays, one who repents of some sin of appetite which Lewis depicts as a little red lizard running back and forth across his shoulders, whispering in his ear. The whole scene of his conversion is marvelous, but right now I want to focus on only a few short lines to try to explain the mystery of God's communion with my life.

When the man and the lizard meet a fiery angel, an angel so bright and hot that his glory burned like the sun at the start of a "tyrannous summer day," the pair had already set off to go back to the bus and return to Hell. The angel offers to "quiet" the lizard and the man immediately agrees, but then has second thoughts when the angel makes it clear he means to kill the lizard. That's where we pick up the conversation:

"May I kill it?"

"Well, there is time to discuss that later."

"There is no time. May I kill it?"

"Please, I never meant to be such a nuisance."

Please — really — don't bother." "Look! It's gone to sleep of its own accord. I'm sure it will be all right now. Thanks ever so much."

"May I kill it?"

"Honestly, I don't think there is the slightest necessity for that. I'm sure I shall be able to keep it in order now. I think the gradual process would be far better than killing it."

"The gradual process is of no use at all."

"Don't you think so? Well, I'll think over what you have said very carefully. I honestly will. In fact I'd let you kill it now, but as a matter of fact I am not feeling frightfully well today. It would be silly to do it *now*. I'd need to be in good health for the operation. Some other day perhaps."

"There is no other day. All days are present now."

In chapter fifteen (you can jump ahead if you like) I will reveal the end of the encounter. But right now the important line is the last: "There is no other day. All days are present now."

In a mysterious way, each Holy Communion is, much as Lewis's angel says, encompassing not only Christ and myself as I am right now, but also all that I have ever been or, God willing, will be. All days, those that have been and those that will be, are present at that moment. Everything in my life, all my encounters, doubts, loves, losses, hopes, fears, weaknesses, strengths, all my days and nights, everything, has existed in and within my next Holy Communion. Everything has pointed me to that place and that time.

When I read in the Gospels of Jesus' encounters with people, I am filled with the same odd sense of . . . leading. Each of the

202

people Christ meets in the Gospels, it seems clear at least to me, meet Him because, in a mysterious way, they are *supposed* to meet Him. He speaks to the needs of each one He meets immediately, deeply, and permanently. Whether it is forgiving the woman caught in the act of adultery, healing the man let down through the roof, or revealing to the Samaritan woman His nature, it is as though everything in their lives has led them to that point, to meet Jesus Christ.

But what would that mean for the people who didn't meet Him? I don't know. I don't claim to have all, or even any, answers, yet this is the mystery of the Eucharist in my life. Each Eucharist is a meeting with Christ and each meeting with Christ exists, from my side at least, as the sum of everything that has gone before and provides a strength for everything that may come after. Just as each mysterious meeting with Christ in the Gospel meant a moment of conversion for those who met him, so is every Eucharist a further conversion in my life. Slowly, very slowly, in fits and starts, imperfectly, painfully, but with love and grace, the message that St. Paul wrote so long ago comes true in my life. With every communion, I live more in Him and less in myself, or rather, in a really mysterious way, my own self becomes ever more a part of Him; forgiven, cleansed, ordered, loved, and graced. In just the same way that the water is the perfect physical vehicle to express Baptism's mysterious spiritual cleaning, so too are bread and wine the perfect species to hide the Eucharist's mysterious face. In a spiritual sense, in Eucharist, God and I become one. I become one of His branches, part of His Body, one who shares in His very life.

The way the Eucharist encompasses the whole of my life takes on a special relevance when discussing chastity because, I am convinced, in order to be lived in joy, chastity must be married to strong and vibrant charity. Lived chastity means saying "no" to certain values that the world says are important: relationships based on illicit sex and objectification, a way of looking at people as means to ends, a way of living life focused exclusively on the present moment. Yet if the only word chastity speaks is "no," it risks becoming little more than a language of negativity. In order to be lived successfully, chastity must also say "yes" to relationships and to the sacrifices real friendship demands. Joyfully lived chastity means willing myself to strive to see people as Jesus sees them. Saying "no" to viewing men or women primarily in terms of sexual inclinations means saying "yes" to seeing them in their deeper selves, and offering friendship there. Meeting Jesus in the sacraments, particularly in the Eucharist, gives me the energy and attitude to live that vision, to see people as He sees them.

At their roots, the sacraments help build a chaste life because they serve as a gateway to prayer and a deeper relationship with Jesus Christ. Christ stands within all the sacraments, particularly the Eucharist, communicating His very self to me as my Lord, my brother, and my friend. Having this relationship in my life helps keep me grounded in the reality of who I am, where I am going, and what I am about in a culture which increasingly forgets its identity, why it's here, or what it is about. To paraphrase St. Paul, with Christ by my side who, or what, can stand against me?

CHAPTER THIRTEEN

A message for parents and spouses

According to the most conservative estimates of the population of same-sex-attracted men and women, and after making an educated guess at the number of parents and other family members, I estimate that something like 12 million people in the United States have a more or less direct interest in questions involving same-sex attraction. These are the folks for whom questions of same-sex marriage, AIDS/HIV, same-sex parenting, and the whole host of other issues wrapped up in questions of gender identity have more than a passing academic or political interest. Many, if not most of them are Christians, but many have found their churches or other Christian friends and family of little help when confronting their children's or spouses' gender identity questions or issues. Over the years hundreds of parents and spouses have written seeking advice about their particular situation or that of a loved one. In general, I have found many of these letters and questions boil down to central themes, and this chapter will consist of my replies to questions on those themes. I don't mean this chapter to be definitive, absolute, or final. In many cases I suspect it may provide little more than a bandage on what has been a long-standing emotional wound. But given that so little reliable material has been published on the topic, I offer this chapter as a first step. The themes are "it's not your fault; you don't have to love every*thing*"; and "it's not the end of the world."

As *Always Our Children* (AOC), a message from the National Conference of Catholic Bishops' Committee on Marriage and Family notes, many parents (and spouses) find the days after a disclosure of same-sex attraction ones of "turmoil." While this chapter cannot completely arrest the turmoil, I hope it can ease at least the heaviest of the new burdens.

It's not your fault. After embarrassment, bewilderment, fear, and a sense of shame, an almost overwhelming feeling of having "failed" their children or "failed" their spouses characterizes the letters I have received from parents and spouses of same-sex-attracted men and women. As the "nurture" model for the development of homosexual feelings has begun to gain ground on the so-called "nature" model, the numbers of parents who suffer from feelings of guilt about things they did or didn't do in their child's life appears to be growing. In many ways, a person revealing their homosexual feelings to a parent or spouse relieves him or her of the burden of hiding same-sex attraction (the "closet"), yet the disclosure can move the parent or spouse into a closet. Suddenly parents wonder, "What did we do wrong?" or "Where did we go wrong?" At the time when they badly need to discuss the situation with someone else, they often feel they cannot. As the AOC document states:

> Guilt, shame and loneliness: "If only we had . . . or had not" are words with which parents can torture themselves at this time. Regrets and disappointments rise up like ghosts from the past.

A sense of failure can lead you into a valley of shame, which, in turn, can isolate you from your children, your family, and other communities of support.

I will address the question of spouses first because, in some ways, it is the easiest to discuss intellectually even as it may be the most explosive emotionally.

Nothing I have read and no one I have known leads me to grant any credence to the claim that same-sex attraction arises because of disgust or disappointment with a particular member of the opposite sex. Although relatively few in number, I still get letters from spouses worried that something they have done has "driven" their former spouse to active homosexuality. In the case where the same-sex-attracted spouse is a man, everything in my experience and reading argues for the roots of same-sex attraction being laid many years before the age most people get married. In cases where a woman has revealed lesbian feelings to her husband, the situation can be a bit more complicated. Although I have never met a same-sex-attracted man who said he felt that way because he chose or wanted to, I have met women who have adamantly insisted that they freely chose their lesbianism. Sometimes, they have said, that they made their decision because of disappointment with men in general though never, or at least not yet, because of disappointment with any one man.

Now I don't mean this to say that feelings of guilt and confusion in the area of "blame" or "fault" are the only feelings spouses may feel. Anger at not knowing the truth for so long, feelings of insecurity and abandonment, concerns over parenting issues — all can and do have a place in the letters spouses have sent me. Yet, in this small way at least, spouses working their way through the difficulty of discovering homosexuality in their mate should not have to do so with the additional burden of feeling guilty for a "role" they fear they might have played in their spouse's same-sex attraction.

Parents of children who announce a same-sex attraction or in whom they perceive such an attraction face a significantly different struggle. First, as Christian parents, they often feel a high degree of responsibility for the spiritual welfare of their children and worry that their children's same-sex attraction will lead to damnation. Second, because as parents they have generally had a greater impact in the life of the person who begins to experience homosexual feeling and they have not behaved perfectly, they can sometimes feel an almost paralyzing guilt and denial. The challenge for parents of people living with homosexuality is to learn about same-sex attraction, confront problems (perhaps long standing) with their children who live with same-sex attraction, and accept their imperfections as parents. Yet, even though the things they have done and have not done may have harmed their children, it's important that parents keep their roles in perspective and not take on too much responsibility for the ways their children's gender identity may have developed. The bottom line is that how human sexuality and gender identity develop remains a mystery. I have yet to meet a parent who set out to influence their son or daughter into having homosexual feelings or, had they known they were doing so, would not have stopped immediately. Although everyone must accept responsibility for their mistakes, there is a difference between accidents and deeds done for which one is culpable. The former is part of the cost of being human beings, essentially good-hearted but flawed. The latter are the only actions for which one must accept accountability and perhaps seek a priest for absolution. While I believe parents and other adults play a role in the development of gender identity, I don't believe they are, at the deepest level, solely responsible for how that identity develops.

Parents must make this distinction and get this matter of responsibility versus culpability sorted out because, often, confusion over these feelings can drive parents into adopting stances toward their children which are simultaneously incoherent and not in their children's truly best interest.

The spiritual dimension

First, parents whose children are same-sex attracted need to understand that their children are no more candidates for heaven or hell than any of their non-same-sex-attracted children. While I do not want to minimize or inappropriately downplay the challenges a same-sex attraction carries in contemporary American culture, parents of same-sex-attracted kids *must* keep in mind that the spiritual fates of their children are not predetermined or preordained. They have free will just as everyone else does and, in the words of the immortal Yogi Berra: "It ain't over till it's over."

However, that doesn't mean parents should be complacent. C.S. Lewis's model for the spiritual journey contains a road, as many do, but in Lewis's model the road is not straight but forks often with many decisions to be made. Each fork, each decision, Lewis says, leads one closer to or farther from heaven, and parents can definitely play a role in helping their same-sex-attracted children keep choosing the heaven-bound road.

The most important thing parents of same-sex-attracted children can do is the same as what they must do for their heterosexually attracted kids: pray every day for them. Approach the throne of grace every day carrying your children, remind heaven of how much they mean to you, and implore heaven for sufficient grace and mercy on their behalf.

Second, never give up on your children — even if they are adults and seem, quite literally, "hell bent." I know of several sets of parents in just this situation who have consciously adopted St. Augustine's mother, St. Monica, as a role model and patron on their long and lonely road. St. Monica prayed and fasted and persisted for years in imploring heaven for her son's sake before she finally saw him accept Christ.

Third, broaden and deepen your own spiritual life. Particularly once past the days immediately after your children's revelation of same-sex attraction, which can be very awkward, most parents continue the relationship with their children. Your being members of small Christian communities like volunteer corps, prayer groups, etc., can help you introduce your child to other Christians that he or she may not be able to meet anywhere else. Getting to know Christianity's variety and diversity was an important part of my coming to take Christ more seriously in my life.

Fourth, find some support! Many parents in this position feel terribly isolated and unable to share their feelings of concern and grief about their children's spiritual lives with other parents. Some parents have found membership in a fledgling support group made up of parents in a similar position an important element of their ongoing struggle. Courage, the Church's chastity-based support group for men and women living with same-sex attraction, has such a group called Encourage in the United States. Contact information may be found in the Courage appendix at the end of the book.

The bottom line is to keep on going and never give up on your children. In the vast majority of cases, your children know that you love them and want what is truly best for their lives. An actively homosexual life cannot provide eternal happiness and often fails to offer even temporal happiness. When the gay parade comes to a halt in your children's lives, they will need all the true and authentic love that a parent can offer. Keeping the temporal relationship with your children as open and healthy as possible can give them a place to go when so many other doors appear shut tight.

Keeping the relationship healthy

I recall a rally in Boston, Massachusetts, held to celebrate that state's program of Gay Straight Alliances (GSAs). GSAs are groups of students who self-identify as gay and friends who do not. They are meant to provide support for children living with same-sex attraction in a school environment gay and lesbian activists assert is "hostile." During the course of the rally a father approached the microphone to express how "proud" he felt of his sixteen-year-old daughter who is self-identified as lesbian, and to plead, in a joking way, for some of the "good looking" girls at the event to consider dating her. Now aside from the embarrassment I expect this father caused his daughter, I question the source of the Father's "pride" and whether affirming his daughter's lesbianism is really in her best interest.

"Pride" used to be associated with things people *did*, rather than expressions of pleasure or satisfaction with an inborn identity or quality. Should a child making a decision about gender identity at early age be something of which a parent should feel *proud*? What happens later if, as others have done, she reassesses her decision and chooses to base her identity on something else? What if she discovers later that a man, one man in particular, *does* have a role in her life? Ironically, if she decides to pursue that path she may be, in fact, rebelling against her parent's vision of her life.

While I didn't interview the father at the microphone, I gathered from comments I later overheard that one of his predominant emotions was fear, fear of doing or saying something which might make his daughter's life more difficult. In short, I felt from his comments that he may have fallen into a very common trap that ensnares many parents. If I love my child, the parent reasons, and I may have already played a role in the development of their homosexual feelings, I must love the life choices they make.

You don't have to love *everything*. Perhaps the most extreme example of this way of thinking can be found in the organization Parents and Friends of Lesbians and Gays (PFLAG). PFLAG is a significant gay and lesbian rights organization and advocacy group. PFLAG claims the membership of 70,000 households and 400 affiliates "worldwide." PFLAG exists, as its name suggests, to promote:

> The health and well-being of gay, lesbian, bisexual, and transgendered persons, their families and friends through: support, to cope with an ad-

verse society; education, to enlighten an ill-informed public; and advocacy, to end discrimination and to secure equal civil rights. Parents, Families and Friends of Lesbians and Gays provides opportunity for dialogue about sexual orientation and gender identity, and acts to create a society that is healthy and respectful of human diversity.

In practice this means PFLAG accepts, apparently unquestioningly and despite the small mountain of peer-reviewed evidence to the contrary, the belief that homosexual behavior is little more than a healthy alternative to active and presumably moral (i.e. taking place in the context of marriage) heterosexual behavior. "Being gay is as natural, normal, and healthy as being straight," advises *Being Yourself*, a PFLAG pamphlet for young people who experience same-sex attraction, and supporting children who accept that a gay or lesbian identity means working to support an active and public homosexuality. "But in other cases you must recognize that discrimination based on sexual orientation is hurtful in a unique way," advises *Our Daughters and Sons*, a pamphlet for parents whose children have self-identified as gay, lesbian, or bisexual: "Here, you can support your child by educating yourself as thoroughly as possible about homosexuality and by helping to bring it out of hiding in our society. It's the hiding that allows the prejudice and discrimination to survive."

Of course, to a degree PFLAG is correct. It's always better for both parents *and* children to accept and address the facts of a given situation as they find them. But accepting and addressing the reality of same-sex attraction doesn't mean that parents must or should conclude that active homosexuality is necessarily good or right for their kids. Gay and lesbian rights activists, including PFLAG, strive for a sort of equivalency. Homosexuality is merely an alternate form of human sexuality, in a way just as purple is can be considered a color in the spectrum of red colors or yellow autumn leaves can be considered a variation on brown leaves. But active homosexual behavior, as I have come to know and as documented extensively by Thomas Schmidt in *Straight and Narrow,* is not equivalent. It's not equally good. And parents should not feel compelled to put aside the common sense they have attained over what, in most cases, is years of parenting in a call to "support" their kids who live with same-sex attraction.

I have found that most parents with whom I have corresponded instinctively know this, but sometimes need to hear it affirmed by other parents or other kids. The example I use is of the four-year-old, the red crayon, and the new wallpaper.

Imagine that you are a parent of a four-year-old, your first, who is the apple of eye and among the greatest treasures of your life. Like many young families you struggle to see bills paid and to gradually improve you, and your family's living conditions. For a couple of years now you have been scrimping extra funds together to replace the really dirty and stained old wallpaper in the front hall and, finally, you have managed to get it done. It's beautiful, white and gold. Your neighbors have seen it, your mom has come over to see it, and your in-laws will see it at Christmas. One small goal among your family's many goals has been achieved. Then one evening you realize you haven't seen your four-year-old in a while. With alarm you hear her high-pitched giggle coming from the hallway where the new wallpaper almost glows with perfection in the afternoon shadows. Hurrying to the hall you round the corner and your heart sinks. There she stands, in four-year-old pride, red crayon in hand, with a good five feet of the hall covered to her height with red crayon scribbling. Now, at that moment most parents acknowledge that they still love that child with all their being. That child is still their treasure, the apple of their eyes, their joy. Yet most parents would also acknowledge that they couldn't honestly look at their child and say, "good job!" At that moment loving their child does not equal endorsing her behavior. Loving HER does not mean that you have to love what she has done or is doing.

Writing it this way makes it seem very simple, and there may be any number of people reading this who say, "Of course I knew that." But, somehow, when it comes to questions of homo-sexual activity and gender identity, parents' thinking becomes muddled. Parents who have corresponded with me have often been caught off guard by a child's revelation. Often they feel sharply conflicting emotions that may add to the burden of guilt which they may have already started to carry (and which, I pointed out above, they need to shed). I have noticed in a few cases that the revelation of a child's same-sex attraction seems to have caused parents to deeply question some of the very values and experi-ence of parenthood that they will need to address the new rela-tionship with their child.

Children's attitudes can have a significant impact on par-ents' processes of coming to grips with the knowledge of their same-sex identity. Unfortunately, some children are not above employing a sort of emotional blackmail to coerce approval of behavior from parents who may not be otherwise inclined to of-fer it. Boiled down, the child's message can often be a variation on the theme "love me, love what I do." This can leave parents feeling torn between what they deeply believe to be true and the pull on their hearts to love their children. Parents need to resist this trap — even though the struggle to clarify feelings and com-munication with same-sex-attracted children can mean enduring a period of conflict and discomfort along the way. Over the years the meetings and letters from parents have revealed two general themes among families that seem to have been able to make the transition from the conflict and confusion of discovering a same-sex attraction in a child to a relative peace. These parents who write may not approve or condone how their children live, but their relationships are such where both parties accept and under-stand each other and the parents do not feel they have had to stifle their own consciences.

First, establish clear identity and boundaries. Parents who have written me and seem to have made the transition recognize that they are not responsible for their children's decisions. They don't need to affirm everything, and they don't have responsibility for everything in their children's lives. "[Coming to terms with our son's homosexuality] was hard for us," one mother wrote, "because we were also just beginning to come to terms with his being an adult. When he told us he was gay we wanted to rush in and fix him or make his life different. It was hard to realize we really couldn't do that anymore. He had to make some decisions himself. We could and did advise. He didn't have to take our advice."

Parents' understanding of themselves and their security in parenthood appears to be crucial because that is what has allowed parents to set the boundaries they need to remain secure in their own identity and in the remaining parental responsibilities toward other minor children that they may have. Most often parents write me about boundary conflicts with same-sex-attracted children which have to do with seeming, or actual, endorsement of homosexual activity. Often it is the revelation of a new same-sex partner in the child's life whom the child wants to introduce to the family, invite to family events, and with whom they would like to share a bedroom when visiting. No two families handle these issues the same way but, in general, parents who have come through the experience feeling successful have taken the time during the course of the conflict to reassess and reassure one another of who they are as parents and what they are about. That, in turn, has enabled them to be comfortable with the decisions that have made about what they will or will not endorse or approve.

"When my husband and I talked about Chris wanting to bring his boyfriend to meet the family at Christmas," wrote one Midwestern mother, "we already had the experience of one of his older sisters wanting to bring her boyfriend into the house and sleep in the same room with him. We nixed that so it wasn't too hard to tell Chris that we would meet the boy but that if they stayed overnight he was going to have to stay in his old room and we could put his friend in the nice back guest room."

Parents' feeling secure in their identities is often very important when sometimes the revelation of homosexuality can pit siblings or other family members against each other. One set of Florida parents, for example, found themselves torn between a

215

daughter's desire to introduce a new girlfriend at a family reunion and her siblings' concern about suddenly having to explain "girlfriends" to their minor children. "It looked like the whole reunion would fall apart," the mother wrote, "until Jack [her husband] hit upon the idea of having Rachel arrive and meet everybody on an afternoon when most of the kids were going up to the lake to swim."

Second, be honest with each other and with your children about how you feel. Although some parents have found it difficult and worry that it might be counterproductive, most of the parents I have met who have reconciled themselves to a child's having a degree of same-sex attraction have done so by being honest, even when it hurt. The *Always Our Children* document notes:

> There are two important things to keep in mind as you try to sort out your feelings. First, listen to them. They can contain clues leading to a fuller discovery of God's will for you. Second, because some feelings can be confusing or conflicting, it is not necessary to act upon all of them. Acknowledging them may be sufficient, but it may also be necessary to talk about your feelings. Do not expect that all tensions can or will be resolved.

Most parents find this easier to read than to do, yet its absolutely essential that emotions be shared, confronted, acknowledged, and addressed if the relationship is going to flourish over the long term. Emotions must be confronted because they must also be clarified. For example, it is not unusual for parents to feel a deep sense of disappointment when their child reveals a same-sex attraction or, particularly, announces that he or she has accepted a gay or lesbian identity. Sometimes, without even being conscious of what they are doing, parents adopt beliefs about their children's lives, expectations for how they are going to be. The revelation of a same-sex attraction can make those expectations evident just at the moment they appear most fleeting. In the space of a few hours a parent can go from a realization that —

though they might not have admitted it even to themselves — they really *did* expect one day to dangle grandchildren off their knees, to the reality that they may never see such grandchildren. Disappointment is a natural reaction, but it must be confronted, and perhaps discussed, because it's very important the children not feel that *they* are a disappointment or that their parents have or will stop loving them. Confronting an emotion like disappointment can clarify that it is not disappointment with the *person* that is being expressed, but disappointment at perceived lost opportunities.

In a way, being honest with emotions is akin to the old American saying that "good fences make good neighbors." Honestly confronted and acknowledged emotions make communication easier, even when the emotions are difficult. Honestly expressed emotions in the wake of a child's revelation about same-sex identity can lay a groundwork of trust for later discussions of possibly thorny questions of behavior, affirmation, and endorsement. It becomes a lot easier to confront later problems surrounding gender identity and same-sex attraction when all the parties can trust the others to discuss honestly what they are feeling, thinking, and desiring.

Finally, a child or a spouse having a same-sex attraction is not the end of the world. Although increased societal discussion of the topic has meant I get fewer completely despairing letters from parents, some still experience feelings of deep mourning and loss at the revelation of same-sex attraction in a child. In the words of one classic letter from almost four years ago, a mother expressed this so well: "What can I do? My son's life is over. I have failed him." But this is not true. Her son's life is not over and she has not failed him. Here, in a longer form, is what I wrote her:

> First, your children are still your children, and still love you. If anything right now your son (or your daughter) worries that you may love him/her less because of what they have told you. When I told my mother and father of my own homosexuality, my mother cried and my father went

into denial. Neither one realized that my telling them represented not my wish to pull away from them but to draw closer. Children do not tell their parents about their same-sex attraction because they want to *hurt* the parents but because they want to stop lying to them about something they consider very central to who they are.

Second, same-sex attraction should not be considered as defining your son, daughter, or spouse. A child who tells a parent of a same-sex attraction is still the same child as before the revelation. All the child or spouse's talents, skills, education, personality, experience, and flaws are still there. The son who is a good scholar is still a good scholar. The daughter who writes well still writes well. The husband and father who works with his hands and enjoys teaching his children these skills will still do that. All that has changed is that you know more about them than you might have previously. Realizing people are more than the sum of their sexual desires is an important realization because many in society now wish to define people, particularly young people, by whether or not they experience same-sex attraction. (How common the metaphysical question: are you "straight, gay, or bi" has exploded even onto such unlikely venues as playgrounds, soccer fields, and baseball diamonds!) The fact is that someone might experience some degree of same-sex attraction but nobody *is* that attraction.

Acknowledging this will also help parents and spouses realize that life for their loved ones is not "over" because of same-sex attraction. I know of several marriages that persevere and even flourish in the wake of a revealed same-sex attraction. It is not an exaggeration to state that there are successful people living with same-sex attraction in every branch of human economic, social, or political endeavor. If your son, daughter, or spouse has told you recently of their same-sex attraction, do not automatically assume life will be miserable or a failure. Your children's fate still rests in their hands and they still need your help.

Potential pitfalls and support

It saddens me to say that I know of a number of parent-child relationships which have not fared well after the child (or in one case the parent) revealed his or her homosexuality. There is probably no easy way to express how very . . . difficult it can be to steer a family through such emotional shoals. In this regard it can be useful for both parents and children to prioritize the familial relationships which exist after the revelation.

First, it is important to recognize that relationships are not likely to be the same — we hope they will be stronger, but they will certainly not be the same. Outer circles of family — the uncles, aunts, cousins, etc. — may never accept or support the same-sex child or parent in the same way that the nuclear family might. In many families this is the way it will be, though I think that the process through which families adjust to the news allows for improvement over time.

Second, creativity plays a large role in structuring family events so that everyone can attend, no matter how they feel about same-sex attraction. Even though it may be unlikely that families may be able to bring everyone together in the same room at the same time, it is reasonable to hope that, over time, a number of different events can encompass everyone.

Although it is a generalization, I have found that a lot depends upon what sort of relationship existed before the child revealed a same-sex attraction. If the relationship with the parent was generally good before the same-sex attraction was revealed, it was probably not hurt or may have even been strengthened by the revelation. However, revealing homosexuality in a relationship that was not strong to begin with often simply made it worse.

A lot seems to have depended on parents taking the long view and committing to communication over a long time period. Support from other parents who share Catholic values and are in a similar situation with their children can also be very useful.

CHAPTER FOURTEEN

Bread, not stones

> What man of you, if his son asks him for bread,
> will give him a stone? Or if he asks for a fish,
> will give him a serpent? If you then, who are
> evil, know how to give good gifts to your chil-
> dren, how much more will your Father who is in
> heaven give good things to those who ask him!
> (Matthew 7: 9-11).

Sitting with His disciples on the mountaintop, Jesus pulls
from them an analogy, which through much of human history
must have seemed a "no brainer." Surrounded by parents, Jesus
pointed out that all of them, however flawed, try to do what is
good for their children. How much better then will God their Father, who has no flaws, treat them if they will only ask? Yet it's
unclear, were Jesus to use the same analogy today, that He would
have found it nearly as effective. Most twentieth-century American or other whichFirst World adults still want to do well by children, but far fewer have a clear idea of just what that is.

Across the United States and in other developed nations,

gay and lesbian activists have begun trying to "mainstream" or normalize same-sex attraction and homosexual identity in the nation's public and parochial schools. Speaking generally, their approach moves along four avenues:

> • First, mount a concerted and organized effort to restrict school texts to only those which present active homosexuality in a "gay positive" light.

> • Second, attempt to place in schools adult or "peer counselors" who approve of homosexual behavior and affirm a more or less exclusively homosexual identity.

> • Third, campaign to introduce materials that take a benign view of active homosexuality into school libraries.

> • Fourth, attempt to force schoolteachers and administrators to support the "gay positive" view of active homosexuality.

One such group is an Oakland, California-based group called Public Education Regarding Sexual Orientation Nationally, otherwise known as the PERSON Project. Although one of the smallest of the relatively new activist groups, they have hit the ground running with the release of a 481-page "organizing manual" for activists who wish to organize for what they understand as support for same-sex-attracted students and young people.

The manual is a state-by-state guide to curricula suggestion-and-approval processes. It includes information on how each state adopts curriculum changes; the names of key education officials in each state; the names, addresses, phone and fax numbers of members of educational boards; sample letters suggesting how to contact them; and the names and account reps for publishing companies serving that state's school system. It's an extremely targeted and comprehensive organizing tool.

PERSON's overall platform declares any disapproval of active homosexuality to be "homophobic" and any desire to shield children from approval of active homosexuality to be censorship. "It was inevitable that the LGBT [lesbian, gay, bisexual, and transgender] rights battle would eventually move into the classroom," the manual says. "It has not only to do with censorship and the repression of a certain type of knowledge, but even more ominous, it's an attempt to regulate and render invisible a whole group of people."

Fighting harassment and "homophobia" by including gay-friendly peer groups or adult counselors is one of the primary agendas of the Gay, Lesbian and Straight Education Network (GLSEN). Working out of a main office in New York City since 1990 and consisting of at least twenty chapters around the nation (with more in forming), the Education Network is the oldest and largest of the relatively new activist groups targeting youth.

The group outlines its most basic attempt to lobby for support groups and "positive role models" for homosexually inclined students is in a brochure called *What You Can Do*. This brochure, which is aimed at school teachers and administrators, urges them to (among other things) provide "role models" in the form of teachers, coaches, and administrators who are openly living an actively homosexual life. If such teachers cannot be found, the brochure instructs, speakers from outside the school who affirm homosexual activity should be brought in as an "interim" step until "openly gay and lesbian faculty" can be hired.

The Education Network also wants administrators to provide peer support groups to students who may have homosexual inclinations, particularly along the lines of "Gay Straight Alliances." Such groups "have been the key" to creating an atmosphere of peer support and acceptance in the schools, the Education Network notes. These, in particular, have been very effectively organized and are growing across the country, piggybacking on a federal law (the so-called Equal Access Act) that courts have interpreted to mean that if the school provides extracurricular clubs for some they must do so for all, including gay support groups.

Of course most reasonable people would not object to the

entirety of these groups' agendas. No one should go to school feeling threatened, harassed, or otherwise discouraged by his or her peers or teachers. Certainly no one should be beaten or otherwise attacked. Yet, from the perspective of later life and as someone who grew up with same-sex attraction, I have to question sharply some of the agenda items which these groups present as part and parcel with concerns for student safety. Specifically I am concerned, and I think parents should be concerned, about these developments:

First, these groups may serve to cement children into an identity rooted in same-sex attraction far earlier than might otherwise happen. I have often wondered if, in my own life, I wouldn't have been far better off waiting to enter the Gay and Lesbian Student Union until I had achieved a greater level of emotional maturity — and I was in my twenties when I stepped through that door. Second, by reinforcing the notion that sexual identities are fixed or static, such groups neglect the reality that a significant percentage of self-identified gay or lesbian young people would like to see their same-sex attraction diminish or disappear, if possible. Third, these groups' materials seem to be uniformly naïve about homosexual sex and its downsides. Aside from the obligatory warnings to have "safe-sex" (which, according to surveys, young gay men appear to be ignoring), there appears to be no recognition of the personal or emotional cost of homosexual activity that I discussed at greater length in the first chapter. Finally, by focusing so early on sexual identity questions, young people neglect developing their broader personalities and characters. In short, joining a group early in life that focuses so much on sexual identity can be a short ticket to early ghettoization and, I believe, can stunt personal growth. Advocates of mainstreaming homosexuality in the schools cannot know with metaphysical certainty that such diminishing is impossible, but their materials strongly leave that impression. In all these areas but particularly in the latter, adults of almost every social and religious stripe have begun offering young people stones when they have come seeking bread.

Support groups and sexual identity

In many youth, adolescence seems to be characterized by a certain fluidity of sexual identity. Researchers writing in the journal *Pediatrics* surveyed 34,000 students in Minnesota and found that 25 percent of students age 12 said they were "not sure" about their sexual orientation. By age seventeen, only five percent of the students were still "unsure." Almost all of the rest of those who had been unsure now felt they were heterosexual. Clearly, while responses to sexual stimuli may be relatively static — sex will probably feel good physically whether with same sex or the other sex — how we feel about sex emotionally and how we identify ourselves sexually can and does change. Boys in particular often feel as though their entire bodies are hooked on sex and can find themselves sexually stimulated by everything from mundane classroom lectures to being outdoors on a sunny day. Is it any wonder that hugs from friends, locker rooms, close male friendships, and adventures can appear very sexual or to have very sexual undertones? Yet having those experiences and feeling those feelings cannot and should not, in any sense, be enough to lead a young man into accepting a predominant or even partial homosexual identity.

I worry sometimes that parents forget what being a teenage child, particularly in the early teen years, can be like. As important as developing character, personality, virtue, good habits, talents, and skills are during that time, all these often seem to take a back seat to how teens perceive themselves socially. "Peer pressure" is often cited as a root cause for all sorts of adolescent social pathologies, everything from sexual experimentation to alcohol and other drug use and gang activity. Although some skeptics of the phenomenon, most notably radio personality Dr. Laura Schlesinger, point out that "people choose their peer groups," an undeniable drive to succeed among one's peers, to be thought cool and "together," still persists. Whether your peer group is the Junior High High Achievers or the gang who hangs out on the playground after school, I expect the drive to have them acknowledge and respect you remains more or less the same.

So what happens when youngsters, confused about sexual feelings and beginning to ponder sexual identity, are introduced to a social group designed to support them in feelings of sexual ambivalence or complete gay identity? Gay and lesbian school activists appear to be working on the assumption that gay or lesbian students already exist and feel little to no ambivalence about their identity. Yet an admittedly unscientific survey of almost 1100 under-age-25 readers of *Oasis* magazine or visitors to !OUTPROUD!, an activist site on the World Wide Web, found that 11 percent of the survey respondents indicated they were "questioning" or "unsure" about their sexual identities. Given that the target audiences of both Oasis and !OUTPROUD! are predominantly same-sex-attracted young people, that figure seems significantly high. If there is that much uncertainty among young people who, it may be reasonably inferred, have already made up their mind on the matter, how much more uncertainty exists among the broader population?

I believe that introducing an allure of social acceptance into questions of same-sex sexual identity does a disservice to young people who may be experiencing what would otherwise be passing or transitory same-sex attractions or feelings. How many youth, instead of questioning further or persisting in allowing a heterosexual identity to take root, decide relatively early, before age sixteen for example, that their sexual identity is predominantly homosexual? According to the *Oasis* survey, a full 38 percent of the young people responding to the survey reported "accepting" a predominantly same-sex-attracted "orientation" before age sixteen. A full 12 percent reported "accepting" at age twelve or thirteen, years when the Minnesota survey suggested that sexual identity ambivalence is at its highest. This can, and does, have an effect, in the words of Mark McGrath, one of the young men highlighted in GLSEN's "Level the playing field" series about homosexuality in school sports:

> Mark realized he was gay while in high school, and says sports were a big part of that discovery process. "Male bonding occurs a lot more with

athletes than non-athletes," he says. "The chance to form male friendships in sports is pretty unique." He adds that male adolescents are quite open to experimentation, and never found a lack of other athletes to experiment with.

"But so what?" activists might ask. Already many social conventions and acceptance exist to draw students in a heterosexual direction. Aren't you just expressing your dislike of homosexuality? Certainly, if one sees same-sex identity and behavior as value-neutral or even value-free, then there can be no reason for objecting to children accepting a predominantly same-sex identity early. But there is a lot of evidence to suggest that, no matter how people might feel about it, early acceptance of a same-sex attraction can lead one to self-destructive behavior earlier. In addition, there are indications that early acceptance of a same-sex identity can actually contribute to teen suicide, one of the social pathologies gay supportive groups were supposedly created to combat.

An article in the NARTH *Bulletin* cites a 1991 study detailed in *Pediatrics* which pinpoints some key elements associated with the risk of attempted suicide in homosexual teenagers. "Compared with non-attempters, attempters had more feminine gender roles, and adopted a bisexual or homosexual identity at younger ages," the researchers reported. "Attempters were more likely than peers to report sexual abuse, drug abuse, and arrests for misconduct." The researchers say that suicide attempts appear to be related to "'coming out' at a younger age, gender atypicality, low self-esteem, substance abuse, running away, involvement in prostitution, and other psychosocial morbidities." In 44 percent of cases, subjects attributed the suicide attempts to "'family problems, including conflict with family members and parents' marital discord, divorce, or alcoholism." Another noted physician concurs. "No service is done to our children by offering them lifestyle options before they are properly able to make informed choices about them," says Dr. George Rekers, professor of neuropsychiatry and a specialist in psychosexual

226

disorders at the University of South Carolina School of Medicine.

As an alternative I would suggest that schools educate their counseling staffs with the full facts about same-sex attraction and identity. Students need to have access to adults who are not specifically gay-partisan about the issue and who can provide true information about both the downsides of same-sex activity and the possibility of diminishing same-sex attraction should the young people choose to pursue that route. What I would have really appreciated as a teen living with same-sex attraction was an adult whom I felt I could really have trusted. I needed someone to talk to, but someone who in turn would not have given me an activist line on the fact but the facts themselves, or at least as best as they were known.

To their credit PFLAG, GLSEN, and other groups point out that its better not to label oneself too early, but in face of the powerful draw of group acceptance and affirmation, I suspect those sentences are more honored in theory than in practice and are really little more than boilerplate.

The impact of deciding early

Aside from the possible increase in suicidal tendencies, accepting a same-sex attraction in high school appears to place students in a real bind. According to the *Oasis* survey, 78 percent of the young people surveyed do not believe diminishing same-sex attraction or "orientation change" is possible. Yet, simultaneously, 18 percent of the survey respondents said they "would prefer to be heterosexual," or "really don't want to be" same-sex attracted or "hate" being same-sex attracted.

In a way these numbers represent the very real "blind alley" which basing identity on sexual inclination, whether homosexual or heterosexual, can represent. Defining themselves early as "gay, bi, or straight" can tend to color not only the way young people see themselves, but also they way they see their world and their behavior. In a certain behavioral sense, the crucial identity question young people must face is not over the chasm of who they find attractive but over what represents good behavior. What, in short, is the best students can do for themselves or for each other.

I worry that accepting an identity rooted in sexual attraction early eroticizes children early too, and begins to draft behavior into the investigation of identity in a way that can only further confuse the situation. Sex feels physically good, and any sort of sexual activity can be a very big deal to a young person who has never experienced any sexual contact at all. When a young person suspects they might have a predominant same-sex attraction (and again, according to the Minnesota study that represents a whopping 25 percent of kids age twelve) and then experiences same-sex activity which (1) feels good and (2) brings a strong reaction, they can easily conclude, "Oh, I must be gay." And once that assertion is made and accepted it can be as though one is on a train from which it feels very difficult, if not impossible, to disembark.

Kids who root their identity in sexuality early can place themselves in situations where those who self-identify as gay or lesbian begin modeling their behavior not on restraint, virtue, or even an adequate understanding of sexuality but instead on the sexual misbehavior ravaging youth generally. In the *Oasis* survey, a whopping 42 percent of the 963 males responding overall reported their first age of sexual contact coming before age fifteen. Among the 191 females responding overall, 35 percent reported their first sex before age fifteen. But among boys surveyed who self-identify as gay, a significantly higher percentage report first sex with someone of the same sex before age fifteen. Forty-five percent of boys who self-identified as gay in the survey reported having sex with someone of the same sex before age fifteen. Among girls who self-identify as lesbian, the number was lower than that overall, 29 percent. There are also indications from the survey that those children who self-identify as gay earlier may also have earlier sexual contact with older children or even adults. According to the survey, 60 percent of the 699 boys and young men who answered the question report their first sexual contact with another male occurred with someone older than they were. Ten percent reported that their first sexual contact with another male took place with someone who was ten years older or, in other words, an adult in almost all cases. By way of contrast, 55 percent of the 118 girls or young women who answered the question reported having first sexual contact with another older female and only two percent reported their first sexual contact as being with a woman as much as ten years older. Significantly, 27 percent of the boys and young men and 25 percent of the girls and young women who answered the question told the survey that they either wished "they had waited" for first sex or "felt they had been taken advantage of." In addition, 54 percent of the boys and young men and 43 percent of the girls and young women answered "yes" or "maybe" to the question of whether they would have sex with someone they had just met and whom they were unlikely to see again.

Again, I don't mean to draw too much from this survey. Survey organizers and publishers admit that it falls short of being a "scientific" sampling. There was no way to tell if someone lied on the survey, for example, and the sample was self-selecting to a great extent. Yet, as someone who grew up same-sex attracted and who has observed the situation of young people struggling with same-sex identity for some time, the survey report has a ring of truth. It speaks to me about the ways young people struggling with same-sex attraction may be walking away with stones when they arrive at our doors seeking bread.

Naïveté and agenda in materials for youth

I find frustrating the naïveté or an unwillingness to speak honestly and frankly to youth who may be experiencing same-sex attraction about the realities of a homosexually active life. It's not just that the hard realities of actively homosexual life are papered over — the lack of stability that characterizes so many actively gay relationships, the tyranny of the shallowness that dominates the gay social scene, the actual physical damage promiscuity can bring. Activists would object that such activity and damage does not characterize all gay and lesbian lives, and I would agree. But it *does* characterize a significant number of these lives, and youth need to know about the damage before they sign onto a way of life they may not even remotely understand.

Then there are some materials written for youth that are propagandistic in their approach. Consider the following passage taken from the Parents and Friends of Lesbians and Gays (PFLAG) brochure *Be Yourself*:

Can I Have a Family of My Own?
The Short Answer: Yes

Many gay people hold wedding ceremonies to celebrate their commitment to each other and to share their relationship with family and friends. While only a few religions, and no states, perform or witness these ceremonies, attitudes are beginning to change. More and more companies, such as Apple Computer, now treat gay partners like any other married couples, and provide health care coverage for their gay employees' partners. President Clinton's Administration has used the words "you and your significant other" instead of "you and your spouse" in recognition of gay partners.

Many gay couples are also raising children together. Some lesbians have used artificial insemination in order to conceive a child. Other gays and lesbians, who came out after they'd been involved in heterosexual relationships, are raising the children from those relationships with their gay partners. As society's attitudes continue to change, adoption of children by gay couples will also become more common. Six states permit adoption by same-sex couples. And many gays see their friends and the local gay community as their family. In most cities, there is a large and

close-knit gay community that offers the same
type of love and support we look for from our
families.

Now, without putting too fine a point on it, this has to be
among the most propagandistic passages of prose that I have ever
read. Glossed over or simply not discussed at all are the moral
controversies over gay or lesbian marriages or sexually active
same-sex relationships. Love, activists would answer. But, as I
pointed out in earlier chapters, the *nature* of love in sexually actively homosexual relationships is the subject of heated debate.
The brochure suggests job benefits and being recognized as "significant others" prove somehow that the realities of homosexually active life are changed if enough corporations and hetero-
sexuals agree they are changed. When, in reality, the circumstances
and problems of same-sex relationships haven't changed at all.
The most amazing comment is the almost passing observation
that "[s]ome lesbians have used artificial insemination in order
to conceive a child." Apparently of little concern to the authors
and concealed from younger readers are the significant questions
of whether it's fair to decide, ahead of time, that a child doesn't
need both a mother *and* father. And what happens to the child
when the lesbian relationship breaks up, which does happen.
Children born to traditional families go through horrific experiences when their parents' break up according to societal rules.
What happens when there are no rules?

The reading list from *Be Yourself* is also troubling. One of
the books suggested in *Be Yourself*'s resource section is the 1985
edition of *Young, Gay and Proud*, but the 1985 edition has gone
out of print and all three of the gay book resources consulted
recommended the 1995 edition instead.

Young, Gay and Proud's chapter "Getting Started," for example, advises:

There are all sorts of stupid rules, like that . . .
guys shouldn't wear dresses. Girls aren't sup-

posed to shave their heads. People might say that certain kinds of sex are dirty . . . we all know about all these "rules." . . . Many of them are more than just foolish — they can be destructive. . . . No one has the right to make anyone else feel bad about their sexuality or their sexual choices. . . .

"There is no right or wrong way boys or girls should act, and sex by itself never hurt anyone," the book adds. "The only rules we need are simple: do what feels right to you, and take care not to hurt anyone else. That way, maybe we can all be comfortable with being the best thing of all — ourselves."

From the chapter for teenage boys, "Doing It: Gay Men":

Learning how to give and receive love through sex is an important part of loving ourselves and becoming more comfortable with our sexuality. It also shows the straight world that we're not going to live according to their narrow-minded myths about men, women, and sex. . . . Most of all, just have a good time. Sex should be fun. . . .

From the chapter for teenage girls, "Doing It: Lesbians":

In lesbian loving, there are no rules, and we don't want any. . . . Being a lesbian means exploring. [The author proceeds to suggest that her teenage reader masturbate, specifically describing how best to do so, and suggesting techniques for mutual masturbation with a girlfriend.] "No one can tell you what is right for you, but you. . . . Sex with someone you choose, at a time and place of your choosing, can be exciting and fun . . . you're the only one that can know what you're ready for, and when.

In my opinion such advice deserves to be criticized as not merely propaganda, but as fairly self-righteous propaganda. Do the authors really believe that what girls and young women who think they may be predominantly lesbian need to know is how to masturbate themselves and other girls properly? Do boys need to be encouraged to flout the "straight world's narrow-minded myths" when so many who built their lives on a similar philosophy wound up dying?

What *is* needed?

Although many paths into same-sex attraction share certain common themes, each person's story remains significantly unique. It's hard to suggest a one-size-fits-all approach to each situation. Yet my own experience as a young person living with same-sex attraction and working with similar young people leads me to make certain general suggestions for how children who experience same-sex attraction might be given bread instead of stones. These approaches are simple on the surface but difficult in practice because they require time, empathy, and skill — qualities difficult to find in many quarters today.

Broadly speaking, I believe both the parochial and public schools betray the trust of parents and their responsibilities toward children when they neglect their role in the formation of young people into adults adequately prepared for life. In parochial schools this responsibility is particularly acute. Catholic schools exist not only to teach young people secular skills and encourage maturity; they also exist to form students spiritually and especially to reinforce good spiritual lessons children should be getting at home. Encouraging same-sex identities and activity in a few teens undermines the moral formation of *all* young people, not only those who are same-sex attracted. Young people who experience same-sex attraction do not represent another species of human being. They are not, as Chandler Burr concluded from his exhaustive research, a "separate creation." Thus it is, or should be, impossible to promulgate a separate set of moral guidelines

233

for them. Why should young people who experience same-sex attraction be offered stones — moral codes that do not reflect truth and which carry high practical costs — while young people who don't are reaffirmed in moral stances that preserve spiritual or temporal life? In practice, of course, undermining moral norms for some undermines moral norms for all. Failing to encourage spiritual maturity in some helps stunt spiritual growth in all of a school's children.

Specifically, young people who may experience same-sex attraction often need adults who *listen* to them and relate to them one-on-one. They cannot be adults who would find the reality of same-sex attraction shocking or intimidating, but should be able to model a spiritual and gender identity that is balanced, healthy, and responsible. Often such adults will not be parents but instead uncles, aunts, older siblings, cousins, or even close family friends. The important qualities of the young adult's friendship with these older models will be trust, challenge, and discovery as the older partner both affirms the younger friends' masculinity or femininity and challenges them to explore it more deeply or expand it more broadly. The role of a caring, responsible, and serious godparent could be key here. Such a person would model for his or her godchild not only what it means to be a man or woman, but also what it means to be a particularly Catholic man or woman.

Second, young people (and many school administrators) need to have stripped away the patina of propriety that is the public face of the activist gay and lesbian movement, what gay social critic Daniel Harris has called the "glad to be gay" propaganda. The world of adult active homosexuality consists of a good deal more than soft lights, sociability, and the banter of hip gay characters on television sitcoms. Certainly, the flavor of homosexual life as presented in the notorious film *Boys in the Band* is a negative stereotype, but so much of the public image of gay and lesbian life today is deeply dishonest. Young people need to know, accurately and truthfully, what actively homosexual life is like in many cases before they begin to make decisions or adopt attitudes that may color their entire lives.

Third, young men and women who experience same-sex attraction need to be reassured that their attraction need not define or limit their lives or their relationships. In addition to the inevitable concern over sex, young people who experience same-sex attraction should be actively encouraged in the skills and characteristics that are unique to them and on which they can build a unique personal identity. The point would be to encourage young people to build identities that would allow them to stand out as individuals in the face of pressure to conform to peer or social expectations. For example, a real expertise in some talent or skill that both peers and adults recognize can serve as a powerful bulwark against the pull to "be like everybody else" or to take steps into behavior that a young man or woman might otherwise not take.

Whether young people experience same-sex attraction or not, they deserve to be seen as more than mere characters in a broader societal play. I am very concerned when I hear people discuss the needs of "gay youth" as though every young person experiencing same-sex attraction has the same needs. I get even more concerned when people publish books for youth experiencing same-sex attraction which advise not what is objectively good but something that reflects the writers' or publishers' bias or agenda. Children deserve more than books purporting to teach them how to masturbate or how to pull on condoms. Children deserve to be heard, encouraged, loved, and cared for. Children, whether same sex-attracted or not, deserve bread, not stones.

CHAPTER FIFTEEN

For people living with same-sex attraction

Oh, when the saints . . . go marching in,
Oh, when the saints . . . go marching in,
Oh, Lord, I want to be in that number,
When the saints . . . go marching in.

Oh, when the sun . . . refuses to shine,
Oh, when the sun . . . refuses to shine,
Oh, Lord, I want to be in that number,
When the sun . . . refuses to shine.

Oh, when the dead . . . in Christ shall rise,
Oh, when the dead . . . in Christ shall rise,
Oh, Lord, I want to be in that number
When the dead . . . in Christ shall rise.

Writing this book closes a portion of my life. Roughly fifteen years ago as a younger, more callow, arrogant, and idealistic man I raised the curtain on my small career as a gay activist by writing in the service of a gay revolution against positions taken by Christians on the campus of a state university. Now, fifteen years later as I complete this book which Christians will publish, I lower the curtain. I only hope my experience set down here will help deliver a few from the whirlwind that I, in a small way, helped to sow.

I have found, in preparing this chapter, that fifteen years provides a good perspective from which to view a portion of one's life. Somehow this span of time feels more manageable than the twenty-five-, thirty-, or fifty-year increments by which we mark marriages or submit to reunions. At fifteen years, foothills passed appear more as uplands than the mountainous peaks under whose shadows we once cowered. With the distance of years valleys become more clearly glens than gorges and remaining heights seem, while still high, at least surmountable. Everything, it appears, gains depth from the panorama.

Fifteen years ago I wrote from a starkly black-and-white perspective. Being gay meant I wore a white hat in the drama of life. Struggling for gay rights placed me in the grand, brave, and noble traditions of women, Jewish, African-American, and Hispanic activists. It meant big ideas like "justice," "the right to love" and "the right to be who we are" animated my days, and while I shouted at the broader society from a postage-stamp stage, at least it was a stage with a good height.

Fifteen years ago, I felt homosexual identity was far more important than how I *lived* as a homosexual. I became a gay activist at the end of the sexual revolution's first wave, after the crash of falling barricades slipped into a thumping dance club beat which, in turn, lost itself in ambulance wails and funereal dirges. When forced to acknowledge the realities of problems in gay and lesbian lives, I recall viewing them more as issues rooted in other people's prejudice than anything inherently wrong with "politically correct" gay or lesbian behavior or identity at the time. If gay and lesbian lives are to be made better, I reasoned, they would come to be so by changing society's attitude toward such lives. The solution to our problems lay with society far more than it did with us, I believed, and I know many gay and lesbian activists today who still feel and think this way.

But in my case time, experience and the deaths of friends have changed me. I have learned that the stage I stand upon as a human being is far, far wider than the previous platform based on sexual orientation or identity. Issues of good or bad, moral or immoral, right or wrong have far more to do with how we live than with what temptations or inclinations we experience — and I have been forced to understand the need for nuance, motivation, and mercy in how we confront our issues or temptations.

In chapter twelve I shared the beginning of a passage from C.S. Lewis's *The Great Divorce*. Recall that in that slim conceit Lewis hypothesizes a bus, which anyone can ride, from hell to heaven. Hell's residents are free to stay in heaven if they will but confront the prevailing sin or attitude which kept them from heaven in the first place. As Lewis tells the story, out of a bus full of people only one repents of his sinful tendency. Lewis depicts this abiding and (suggested) sexual temptation as a little red lizard running back and forth across the man's shoulders, whispering in his ear. Recall that when the man and the lizard meet a fiery angel, an angel so bright and hot that his glory burned like the sun at the start of a "tyrannous summer day," the pair had already set off to go back to the bus and return to Hell. The angel offers to "quiet" the reptile and the man immediately agrees, but then has second thoughts when the angel makes it clear he means to kill the lizard. That's where we picked up the conversation, and this time I will reproduce the encounter in full. The angel begins the dialogue.

"May I kill it?"

"Well, there's time to discuss that later."
"There is no time. May I kill it?"

"Please, I never meant to be such a nuisance.

Please — really — don't bother. Look! It's gone to sleep of its own accord. I'm sure it'll be all right now. Thanks ever so much."

"May I kill it?"

"Honestly, I don't think there's the slightest necessity for that. I'm sure I shall be able to keep it in order now. I think the gradual process would be far better than killing it."

"The gradual process is of no use at all."

"Don't you think so? Well, I'll think over what you've said very carefully. I honestly will. In fact I'd let you kill it now, but as a matter of fact I'm not feeling frightfully well today. It would be silly to do it *now*. I'd need to be in good health for the operation. Some other day perhaps."

"There is no other day. All days are present now."

"Get back! You're burning me. How can I tell you to kill it? You would kill *me* if you did."

"It is not so."

"Why, you're hurting me now."

"I never said it wouldn't hurt you, I said it wouldn't kill you."

"Oh, I know. You think I'm a coward. But it isn't that. Really it isn't. I say! Let me run back by tonight's bus and get an opinion from my own doctor. I'll come again the first moment that I can."

"This moment contains all moments."

"Why are you torturing me? You are jeering at me. How *can* I let you tear me to pieces? If you wanted to help me why didn't you kill the damned thing without asking me — before I knew? It would be all over now if you had."

"I cannot kill it against your will. It is impossible. Have I your permission?"

The Angel's hands were almost closed on the Lizard, but not quite. Then the Lizard began chattering to the Ghost, so loud that I could hear what it was saying.

"Be careful," it said. "He can do what he says. He can kill me. One fatal word from you and he *will!* Then you'll be without me forever and ever. It's not natural. How could you live? You'd be only a sort of ghost, not a real man as you are now. He doesn't understand. He's only a cold, bloodless abstract thing. It may be quite natural for him, but it isn't for us. Yes, yes. I know there are no real pleasures now, only dreams. But aren't they better than nothing? And I'll be so good. I admit I've sometimes gone too far in the past, but I promise I won't do it again. I'll give you nothing but really nice dreams — all sweet and fresh and almost innocent. You might say, quite innocent. . . ."

"Have I your permission?" said the Angel to the Ghost.

"I know it will kill me."

"It won't. But supposing it did?"

"You're right. It would be better to be dead than to live with this creature."

"Then I may?"

"Damn and blast you! Go on can't you? Get it over. Do what you like," bellowed the Ghost: but ended, whimpering, "God help me. God help me."

Next moment the Ghost gave a scream of agony such as I never heard on Earth. The Burning One closed his crimson grip on the reptile: twisted it, while it bit and writhed, and then flung it, broken back, on the turf.

"Ow! That's done for me," gasped the Ghost, reeling backwards.

For a moment I could make out nothing distinctly. Then I saw, between me and the nearest bush, unmistakably solid but growing every moment solider, the upper arm and the shoulder of the man. Then, brighter still and stronger, the legs and hands. The neck and golden head materialized while I watched, and if my attention had not wavered I should have seen the actual completing of a man — an immense man, naked, not much smaller than the Angel. What distracted me was the fact that at the same moment something seemed to be happening to the Lizard. At first I thought the operation had failed. So far from dying, the creature was still struggling and even growing bigger as it struggled. And as it grew it changed. Its hinder parts grew rounder. The tail, still flickering, became a tail of hair that flickered between huge and glossy buttocks. Suddenly I started back, rubbing my eyes. What stood before me was the greatest stallion I have ever seen, silvery white but with mane and tail of gold. It was smooth and shining, rippled with swells of flesh and muscle, whinneying and stamping with its hoofs. At each stamp the land shook and the trees dindled.

The new-made man turned and clapped the new horse's neck. It nosed his bright body. Horse and master breathed each into the other's nostrils. The man turned from it, flung himself at the feet of the Burning One, and embraced them. When he rose I thought his face shone with tears, but it may have been only the liquid love and brightness (one cannot distinguish them in that country) which flowed from him. I had not long to think about it. In joyous haste the young man leaped upon the horse's back. Turning in his seat he waved a farewell, then nudged the stallion with his heels. They were off before I well knew what was happening. There was riding if you like! I came out as quickly as I could from among the bushes to follow them with my eyes; but already they were only like a shooting star far off on the green plain, and soon among the foothills of the mountains. Then, still like a star, I saw them winding up, scaling what seemed impossible steeps, and quicker every moment, till near the dim brow of the landscape, so high that I must strain my neck to see them, they vanished, bright themselves, into the rose-brightness of that everlasting morning.

I love that passage from Lewis for many different reasons. I admire the way Lewis depicted the tension leading up to making a decision to change one's life. I treasure the fact that Lewis chose to relate the dialogue between the Lizard and the Ghost, showing how long association with the Lizard left the man so handicapped that he was almost unable to do what he needed to do but that he surrendered the Lizard anyway. But I enjoy the Lizard's transformation most. Lewis writes a powerful truth when he depicts the reptile's metamorphosis from torturing and lying creature that must be carried everywhere to a beautiful and loving servant that is willing and able to carry his former victim made new master.

It is this message which I believe can speak most clearly and strongly to men and women living with some degree of same-sex attraction: the man and Lizard in Lewis's tale (and by extension ourselves) are not one and the same. We are more than the sum of our temptations, desires, or loves. The Gospel's most profound message to everyone, no matter his or her temptation, is twofold. First, we are created in the image of God, and, second, God loves us. God's love is not something we can earn more of by being extra good and it's not something He withdraws from us when we sin. God's love is only something we must choose to accept or reject. Acceptance of God's love means accepting the hard, maturing work of becoming ever more the people He meant us to be. Rejection means taking the apparently easy road off on our own. Acceptance means eventual sainthood and heaven, rejection means hell — not, I must note, by God's desire but by our choices.

So much confusion reigns about what the Church teaches about same-sex attraction that I urge every homosexually attracted person to forget what they *think* the Church teaches or what they have heard she teaches and learn instead what she *really* teaches. Just a couple of weeks ago I got a letter from a twenty-eight-year-old man who felt strongly his love for his same-sex partner with whom he was sexually active. Why, he wanted to know, couldn't the Church recognize his and his partner's love for one another and bless it? I answered that the Church already recognizes the parts of our relationships and friendships that truly love, and are truly wholesome and life giving. All those things are counted among the virtues to which all Christians are called. There is nothing wrong with them. The Church and the saints celebrate them. But that's not the same as sex, he said. Why can't the Church celebrate the sexual side of their love since he and his partner would "never" give up having sex? Heaven itself is lost in that word "never."

I don't believe love limits the lover or the beloved to only what the other wants. I came to realize that I couldn't claim to love my partner only as long as he had sex with me. Real love seeks what is best for the beloved, and respects them fully and loves them fully. What did Jesus say about love so memorably? No greater love has any man than he lay down his life for his friends. I think people living with same-sex attraction were created to love and to be loved without limits, loved for who they are and not what they can or will do.

I don't think it's helpful to fall into the trap of saying "guy-guy bad, girl-guy good." I don't think it matters nearly as much whom one claims to love as how one really loves in fact. I suspect it's much more fruitful to look at what is being called love in whatever relationship is being discussed. Is that which is *claimed* for love, in fact, all that loving?

Most people don't recognize, or want to recognize, the aspect of love that is least like a Hallmark card. Love can be awful. Love can be self-sacrifice and pain on the part of the lover for the beloved's good. After all, the greatest symbol of love on earth is not the Valentine's Day heart, but Good Friday's Cross. God, who is Infinite and Mighty, before whom every knee will bend one day and every tongue confess, and in whose presence the very stones of Jerusalem would have cried out if no one else had — *that* God crossed eternity to let Himself be beaten, spit upon, nailed to the Cross, and tortured to death so that men and women, no matter their sexual temptations or inclinations, could one day stand before Him face to face. That's love.

Christ's ennobling and terrifying message for people living with same-sex attraction is that we are created, loved, and responsible. It ennobles us because it sees in us the reality of our creation as human beings in God's image. It terrifies us because it puts the ball firmly in our court. Some Christians might try to tell us that God doesn't love us because of our same-sex attraction, but we know that's not true. God doesn't base his love on what temptations we have or don't have. Others might try to tell us that acting out our sexual desires, particularly with someone we feel we love, is also not wrong, but we know that's not true either. Love doesn't give itself away in half-measures or objectify its subjects. No, the hard truth is that love dies to self and gives itself away. Love is the Cross.

So if you have gotten nothing else from this book at all, I firmly hope that you pull from it this one, twofold lesson: that you are loved and that you can surely be one with that number when the saints come marching in. Don't let anyone dissuade you or feed you a watered-down Gospel. Don't accept any version of what Bonhoeffer called Cheap Grace. Whatever you have done in the past, matters nothing. Nor, even, does anything you are doing now. Right now, at the very moment I write this or you read it, you may be planing to do something sinful — and God still loves and seeks after you. All that matters is that you come before the Lord. So many same-sex-attracted men and women feel they don't "belong" in Church, when, in fact, that is precisely where they do belong. It doesn't matter that you may be tempted to do what is wrong. In the words of Lewis's Angel, "this moment contains all moments" and everything that has happened in your life so far, all that is good and bad, all that you have done and has been done to you, prepares you for this moment of decision. Christ is calling. His Mercy waits in a torrent, a flood for troubled souls. Will you come? Until, God willing, we meet one day face-to-face I wish you peace. And freedom.

Bibliography

"Always Our Children." United States Catholic Conference Committee on Marriage and Family, 1997.

Bonhoeffer, Dietrich, *The Cost of Discipleship.* New York: Collier Books, 1963.

Catechism of the Catholic Church. English translation for use in the United States. United States Catholic Conference, Libreria Editrice Vaticana, 1994.

Dignity, "Catholicism, Homosexuality and Dignity," brochure.

—, Task Force on Sexual Ethics, "Sexual Ethics, Experience, Growth and Challenge," document, 1989.

Kirk, Marshall and Hunter Madsen, *After the Ball: How America Will Conquer Its Fear and Hatred of Gays in the 90s.* New York: Penguin Books, 1989.

Kramer, Larry, "Sex and Sensibility," in *Advocate,* May 27, 1997.

Lewis, C.S., *The Great Divorce.* HarperCollins Ltd.: London, 1946, 1974. Rpt. by Touchstone, a division of Simon and Schuster, 1997.

McWhirter, David and Andrew Mattison, *The Male Couple: How Relationships Develop.* Englewoodcliffs, N.J.: Prentice-Hall, 1984.

Morrison, David, "At a Parting of the Ways," in *Malchus,* April, 1994.

Nouwen, Fr. Henri, *Return of the Prodigal Son: A Meditation on Fathers, Brothers, and Sons.* New York: Doubleday, 1992.

"On the Pastoral Care of Homosexual Persons," Congregation for the Doctrine of Faith, October 1986.

Paglia, Camille, "I'll Take Religion Over Gay Culture," in *Salon,* June 23, 1988.

PFLAG, *Be Yourself,* pamphlet, 1994.

PFLAG, *Our Sons and Daughters,* pamphlet, 1998.

!OutProud!/Oasis Internet Survey of Queer and Questioning Youth, sponsored by !OutProud!, the National Coalition for Gay, Lesbian, Bisexual and Transgender Youth and *Oasis* magazine, March 1998.

Rofes, Eric, *Reviving the Tribe: Regenerating Gay Men's Sexuality and Culture in the Ongoing Epidemic.* Harrington Park: Haworth Press, 1996.

Romesburg, Don, editor. *Young, Gay and Proud.* NC:NP, 1995.

Schmidt, Thomas E., *Straight and Narrow? Compassion and Clarity in the Homosexuality Debate.* Downers Grove, Ill: Intervarsity Press, 1995.

Shilts, Randy, *And the Band Played On: Politics, People, and the AIDS Epidemic.* New York: Penguin Books, 1988.

Sullivan, Andrew, "They've Changed, So They Say," *New York Times,* July 26, 1998.

Van den Aardweg,Gerard, *The Battle for Normality: A Guide for (Self-) Therapy for Homosexuality.* San Francisco: Ignatius Press, 1997.

APPENDIX ONE

An overview of Courage

Courage is the only national, Vatican-approved Catholic ministry to men and women living with same-sex attraction around the world. It's approach is primarily one of spiritual support to assist men and women living with same-sex attraction to live according to the teachings of the Church on their sexuality (which is to say chastely) and both deepen and broaden their Catholic Faith.

In 1980 Father Harvey assembled a small group of lay Catholic men in a parish on the Lower East Side of Manhattan and helped the men found Courage. Father Harvey, a priest with the Oblates of St. Francis de Sales, began working with priests and religious struggling with sexual identity and chastity issues. Harvey's work with the men struggling to integrate a confused sexual identity within a broader religious or faithful Catholic life showed him the power that support groups can have in helping people confront some deep-seated tendency or habit. He found that support groups tended to break down the walls of isolation around men living with same-sex attraction and offered the tremendously useful gift of perspective to individual men struggling with their problems.

The founding of Courage was a bold step. Never before had an open, public ministry to men and women living with same-sex attraction been tried. There was such a stigma attached to homosexuality that some Catholics were scandalized that the Archdiocese of New York, under whose auspices Courage was founded, reached out to Catholics living with same-sex attraction at all. But the group perservered, guided by the a set of goals that have defined the Courage group ever since:

1. To live chaste lives in accordance with the Roman Catholic Church's teaching on homosexuality.

2. To dedicate one's life to Christ through service to others, spiritual reading, prayer, meditation, individual spiritual direction, frequent attendance at Mass, and the frequent reception of the sacraments of Penance and Holy Eucharist.

3. To foster a spirit of fellowship in which all may share thoughts and experiences, and so ensure that no one will have to face the problems of homosexuality alone.

4. To be mindful of the truth that chaste friendships are not only possible but necessary in a celibate Christian life and in doing so provide encouragement to one another in forming and sustaining them.

5. To live lives that may serve as good examples to others.

Since 1980 Courage has grown to sixty-four groups in six countries and has helped thousands of men and women to more fully integrate their sexuality into a life of virtue and to come to a point of both interior and exterior chastity. The practical aspects offered by Courage and the Church are discussed more fully in chapter eight, but I wish to reiterate what Courage is *not* that the reader may understand more fully what Courage is:

Courage is not an orientation change group. Courage does not require anyone coming to its meetings or getting support to commit to diminishing their same-sex attraction or changing it to a more heterosexual focus. If individual members wish to try such a course their Courage groups will support them, but it's not a requirement.

Courage is not an organization of perfectionists! The first men that Father Harvey helped to form Courage did not do so to create a society of the folks who had already made it. Courage members are not required to be living chastely when they arrive and some may never arrive at that point. All Courage requires is that its members commit to trying to live the goals. The goals are goals, after all, things people aim toward and for. They are not grades for work already done.

Courage is not "rigid." Courage is faithful to the teaching of the Catholic Church, that is true, but Courage is not only about living chastely. Courage is about becoming better Christians. Courage is about growth, integration, and joy and about using the teaching of the Church to help get there.

Courage is not anti-gay. In fact, Courage is not particularly anti-anything in the sense of feeling the need to denounce things or continually address the "issue" of same-sex attraction. Courage remains intensely personal. Members have included former gay activists and married men for whom the support groups are the only people on earth who know their struggle to live chastely. It *is* true that Courage is about choices, and in that sense one course of action has to win out over another. Encouraging members to choose Mass or prayer over gay bars and one-night-stands might be seen by some as "anti-gay," but its not as though, in an abstract sense, Courage formally goes out and denounces patrons of gay bars or people who do one-night stands.

For more information on Courage, contact the Courage Central Office at (212) 268-1010, St. John the Baptist Church,

210 W. 31st Street, New York, NY, 10001. Courage maintains a comprehensive website at http://world.std.com/~courage and can be reached through e-mail: courage@world.std.com. The list below includes Courage chapters as listed on the Courage home page at the time of publication. Starting a Courage group requires only two or three committed lay men or women and a priest willing to serve as chaplain. Call the central office in New York for details. The following are Courage chapters around the world.

Australia
Courage, P.O. Box 151 Geebung, Qld. 4034. Phone: 07 3865 2464; fax: 07 3265 3301.

Canada
British Columbia, Vancouver: contact Fr. Edwin Budiman, (604) 684-5775, Guardian Angels Parish, 1161 Broughton Street, Vancouver, BC, V6G 2B3.
Manitoba, Winnipeg: contact Gilles, (204) 233-7465, P.O. Box 2655, Winnipeg, Manitoba R3C 4B3, email: gillesu@ hotmail.com.
Ontario, London: contact Christine Rose Smith (Director of Project Hope including Courage/Encourage) at (519) 439-9680 (phone or fax), or write to same: c/o Diocese of London, 1070 Waterloo Street, London, Ontario, N6A 3Y2 — Priest Advisor: Fr. Terence Runstedler (519) 539-2029.
Ontario, Ottawa: contact Fr. Jerry McCormick, (613) 725-2242, St. Elizabeth Church, 1303 Leaside Ave., Ottawa, K1Z 7R2.
Ontario, Thunder Bay: contact Fr. Scott, (807) 344-5812, c/o St. Andrew's Parish, 292 Red River Rd., Thunder Bay, Ontario, P7B 1A8.
Ontario, Toronto: contact Rev. Vaughan Quinn, O.M.I., (416) 928-5094, 141 McCaul Street, Toronto, Ontario M5T 1W3.

New Zealand
Christchurch: contact Maria, phone: 64 03 3489221 or e-mail:_ akiwi@ihug.co.nz.

The Philippines
Contact Brother Dan Healy or Fr. Richard Palumbo, Anawim Community Center, 5 Vida Doria Street, B.F. Resort Village, Las Pinas, Metro Manila, Philippines, e-mail: 74742.55@compuserve. com.

Republic of Ireland
Contact Courage, P.O. Box 108, Eglinton Street, Cork.

United Kingdom
Courage in England is called "EnCourage." There are chapters in London, Birmingham, and Manchester.

London: contact David, P.O. Box 3745, London, England N2 8LW.
Belfast: contact, Courage, P.O. Box 378, Belfast BT15, Northern Ireland.

The United States

NW Arkansas/SW Missouri: contact Joyce Fink, (501) 245-9080, COURAGE in the Ozarks.
California, Orange: contact Fr. Enrique J. Sera, (714) 751-5335, Immaculate Heart of Mary Church,1100 South Center Street, Santa Ana, CA 92704.
California, San Diego: contact Fr. Richard L. Perozich, (619) 280-0515, Our Lady of the Sacred Heart Church, 4177 Marlborough Avenue, CA 92105.
California, San Francisco: contact Fr. Lawrence Goode, (415) 333-3627.
Colorado, Denver: contact Fr. Jim Fox, (303) 466-8720.
Connecticut, Gales Ferry: contact Fr. Bill Schneider, (860) 464-7251.
Connecticut, New Haven: contact Fr. Carleton Jones, (203) 562-6193.
District of Colombia, Washington: contact Brother Dunstan, (202) 269-2300.

Florida, Miami: contact Rick, (305) 386-8985.

Florida, Ocala: contact Fr. Patrick O'Doherty, (352) 854-2181.

Florida, St. Petersberg: contact Dr. Edward Hughes, (727) 527-5776.

Florida, Sebastian: contact Fr. Timothy Sockol, (561) 589-5790.

Georgia, Gainesville: contact Fr. Bill Hoffman, (770) 534-3338.

Illinois, Chicago: contact Fr. Mykhailo Kuzma, (847) 991-0820, or Tom (630) 910-8328, or e-mail: Sedona53@aol.com.

Kentucky, Louisville: contact Jim, (502) 589-5299.

Louisiana, Layfayette: contact Robert, (318) 232-0074.

Maryland, DC/College Park: contact Fr. Robert Keffer, (301) 864-6223, 4141 Guilford Drive, College Park, MD.

Massachusetts, Boston: e-mail: BCourage@yahoo.com or write: Courage, P.O. Box 750045, Arlington, MA 02475.

Massachusetts, Lawrence: contact Fr. Albert Sylvia, (978) 681-9080 (Encourage group only at present) Contact Boston group (above) for Courage assistance.

Massachusetts, New Bedford: contact Msgr. Harrington, (508) 992-3184, Holy Name Church.

Massachusetts, Springfield: contact Fr. Zachary Grant at (413) 733-3101.

Michigan, Dearborn: contact Fr. Bob McCabe, (313) 278-5555 or Fr. John Ricardo, (313) 277-3110.

Michigan, Grand Rapids: contact Fr. James Chelich, (616) 243-0491.

Michigan, Lansing, Deacon John Cameron, (517) 342-2509 or e-mail: cameron_lansing@msn.com.

Minnesota, St. Paul: contact Fr. LeVoir, (612) 455-1302 or Kathy Laird, Office of Marriage and Family Life (612) 291-4438. (Courage is called Faith in Action in this state.)

SW Missouri/NW Arkansas: contact Joyce Fink, (501) 253-9080, Courage in the Ozarks.

New Jersey, Montclair: contact Msgr. Timothy Shugrue, (201) 744-5650 or (201) 509-7839 Immaculate Conception Church, 30 N. Fullerton Ave.

New Jersey, Trenton: contact Msgr. Thomas Gervasio, (609) 468-2589.

New Jersey, Wenonah: contact Richard, (609) 468-2589.

New Mexico, Albuquerque: contact Fr. Christopher Zugger, (505) 256-1539 or (505) 256-1787.

New York, Brooklyn, and Queens: contact Msgr. Murphy, (718) 625-0305 (also has a separate Women's Group).

New York, Buffalo: contact Fr. Paul Stellar at (716) 632-8898.

New York, Long Island: contact Courage (516) 285-3975 or Msgr. Sweeney, (516) 678-5800.

New York, Manhattan, and Queens: contact Fr. Harvey, (212) 268-1010 (Women's Group).

New York, Manhattan: contact Fr. Kowalski, (212) 682-5722 (also has a separate Women's Group).

New York, New York: contact Courage Central Office, (212)268-1010, St. John the Baptist Church 210 W. 31st Street New York NY 10001.

New York, Manhattan: contact Fr. James Lloyd, (212) 307-1808, St. Paul the Apostle, 415 W. 59th Street, New York, NY 10019.

New York, Manhattan: contact Fr. James Connolly, (212) 753-8418, St. John the Evangelist, 348 E. 55th Street.

New York, Mid-Hudson Region: contact Fr. Donald Timone, (914) 562-7664, Sacred Heart Rectory, 301 Ann St., Newburgh, NY 12550.

New York, Rochester: "Zoar" (in solidarity with Courage) contact Tom, (716) 323-1203.

New York, Staten Island: contact Jim, (718) 720-2194.

New York, Syracuse: contact Fr. Jeffrey Keefe, O.F.M., (315) 422-6233.

New York, White Plains: contact Msgr. Gallagher, (914) 963-7330, St. John the Evangelist, 148 Hamilton Ave., White Plains, NY.

North Carolina, Charlotte: contact Larry, e-mail: recovery house@juno.com.

Ohio, Steubenville: contact Fr. Ron Mohnickey, (614) 283-6403.

Ohio, Toledo: contact Lucy Abu-Absi, Family Life/Respect Office, (419) 244-6711.

Oregon, Portland: contact Fr. Vinant Sampietro, C.S.P., (503) 238-0474.

Pennsylvania, Erie: contact Fr. James Peterson, (814) 454-0891, 1701 Parade Street, Erie, PA.

Pennsylvania, Harrisburg: contact Courage, (717) 232-2169, ext. 40.

Pennsylvania, Lehigh Valley: contact Courage, (610) 866-8938, 1861 Catasauqua Rd., Bethlehem, PA 18018.

Pennsylvania, Philadelphia: contact John, (215) 587-4505, St. Peter's Rectory, Corner 5th St. & Girard Ave.

Pennsylvania, Pittsburgh: contact Fr. O'Shea, (724)745-6560.

Rhode Island, Providence: contact Rev. John Randall, (401) 421-6441.

Tennessee, Memphis: contact Rev. Charles Bauer, (901) 784-3904, 2564 Hale Avenue, Memphis, TN 38112.

Texas, Austin: contact Fr. Robert Becker, (512) 926-2552.

Texas, Beaumont: contact (Mark W. Stiles Unit), Chaplain Harry Davis, (409) 727-3070, ext. 4674, or e-mail:Deacon Al O'Brien diocese3@pernet.net.

Texas, College Station: contact Fr. Dean Wilhelm, (409) 846-5717.

Texas, Dallas/Ft.Worth: contact e-mail:couragefw@catholic.org or call (972) 938-5433.

Texas, Killen: contact Fr. Walter Matus, (817) 634-7878.

Texas, San Antonio: contact Michelle, (210) 226-8381, St. Mary's Catholic Church, 202 N. St. Mary's St., San Antonio, TX.

Virginia, Virginia Beach: contact e-mail: gregorius@juno.com.

Washington, Seattle: contact Roger at 206-766-8936 ext. 1, e-mail: courage4seattle@webtv.net.

West Virginia, Wheeling: contact Fr. O'Shea, (412) 745-6560.

Wisconsin, LaCrosse: contact Rev. John Parr, (608) 788-7700 (Courage is called Faith in Action in this state).

APPENDIX TWO

Letter to the world's bishops

Author's note: In October, 1986, the Congregation for the Doctrine of the Faith sent a letter to all Catholic bishops around the world explaining and clarifying the Church's current position on homosexuality, same-sex-attracted persons, the morality of same-sex acts, and the pastoral response to issues of same-sex attraction and activity. In some places in the world the document, called "On the Pastoral Care of Homosexual Persons,"meant a liberalizing of ecclesiastical positions and an opening of attitudes; in other places (many in the first world) the letter represented a new discipline regarding these questions. Many gay and lesbian activists roundly condemned the document. I am including the document as an appendix to this book because, in many ways, it is the fundamental statement of the Church's contemporary stand on issues of same-sex attraction. (Editor's note: Except for stylistic changes, including the Americanization of Briticisms, the text has been reproduced verbatim.)

Letter to the Bishops of the Catholic Church
October 1, 1986

1. The issue of homosexuality and the moral evaluation of homosexual acts have increasingly become a matter of public debate, even in Catholic circles. Since this debate often advances arguments and makes assertions inconsistent with the teaching of the Catholic Church, it is quite rightly a cause for concern to all engaged in the pastoral ministry, and this Congregation has judged it to be of sufficiently grave and widespread importance to address to the Bishops of the Catholic Church this Letter on the Pastoral Care of Homosexual Persons.

2. Naturally, an exhaustive treatment of this complex issue cannot be attempted here, but we will focus our reflection within the distinctive context of the Catholic moral perspective. It is a perspective which finds support in the more secure findings of the natural sciences, which have their own legitimate and proper methodology and field of inquiry.

However, the Catholic moral viewpoint is founded on human reason illumined by faith and is consciously motivated by the desire to do the will of God our Father. The Church is thus in a position to learn from scientific discovery but also to transcend the horizons of science and to be confident that her more global vision does greater justice to the rich reality of the human person in his spiritual and physical dimensions, created by God and heir, by grace, to eternal life.

It is within this context, then, that it can be clearly seen that the phenomenon of homosexuality, complex as it is, and with its many consequences for society and ecclesial life, is a proper focus for the Church's pastoral care. It thus requires of her ministers attentive study, active concern and honest, theologically well-balanced counsel.

3. Explicit treatment of the problem was given in this Congregation's "Declaration on Certain Questions Concerning Sexual Ethics" of December 29, 1975. That document stressed the duty of trying to understand the homosexual condition and

noted that culpability for homosexual acts should only be judged with prudence. At the same time the Congregation took note of the distinction commonly drawn between the homosexual condition or tendency and individual homosexual actions. These were described as deprived of their essential and indispensable finality, as being "intrinsically disordered," and able in no case to be approved of (cf. n. 8, sect. 4).

In the discussion which followed the publication of the Declaration, however, an overly benign interpretation was given to the homosexual condition itself, some going so far as to call it neutral, or even good. Although the particular inclination of the homosexual person is not a sin, it is a more or less strong tendency ordered toward an intrinsic moral evil; and thus the inclination itself must be seen as an objective disorder.

Therefore special concern and pastoral attention should be directed toward those who have this condition, lest they be led to believe that the living out of this orientation in homosexual activity is a morally acceptable option. It is not.

4. An essential dimension of authentic pastoral care is the identification of causes of confusion regarding the Church's teaching. One is a new exegesis of Sacred Scripture which claims variously that Scripture has nothing to say on the subject of homosexuality, or that it somehow tacitly approves of it, or that all of its moral injunctions are so culture-bound that they are no longer applicable to contemporary life. These views are gravely erroneous and call for particular attention here.

5. It is quite true that the biblical literature owes to the different epochs in which it was written a good deal of its varied patterns of thought and expression (*Dei Verbum*,12). The Church today addresses the Gospel to a world which differs in many ways from ancient days. But the world in which the New Testament was written was already quite diverse from the situation in which the Sacred Scriptures of the Hebrew People had been written or compiled, for example.

What should be noticed is that, in the presence of such remarkable diversity, there is nevertheless a clear consistency within the Scriptures themselves on the moral issue of homosexual behavior. The Church's doctrine regarding this issue is thus based, not on isolated phrases for facile theological argument, but on the solid foundation of a constant biblical testimony. The community of faith today, in unbroken continuity with the Jewish and Christian communities within which the ancient Scriptures were written, continues to be nourished by those same Scriptures and by the Spirit of Truth whose Word they are. It is likewise essential to recognize that the Scriptures are not properly understood when they are interpreted in a way which contradicts the Church's living Tradition. To be correct, the interpretation of Scripture must be in substantial accord with that Tradition.

The Vatican Council II in *Dei Verbum* (10), put it this way: "It is clear, therefore, that in the supremely wise arrangement of God, sacred Tradition, sacred Scripture, and the Magisterium of the Church are so connected and associated that one of them cannot stand without the others. Working together, each in its own way under the action of the one Holy Spirit, they all contribute effectively to the salvation of souls." In that spirit we wish to outline briefly the biblical teaching here.

6. Providing a basic plan for understanding this entire discussion of homosexuality is the theology of creation we find in Genesis. God, in his infinite wisdom and love, brings into existence all of reality as a reflection of his goodness. He fashions mankind, male and female, in his own image and likeness. Human beings, therefore, are nothing less than the work of God himself; and in the complementarity of the sexes, they are called to reflect the inner unity of the Creator. They do this in a striking way in their cooperation with him in the transmission of life by a mutual donation of the self to the other.

In Genesis three, we find that this truth about persons being an image of God has been obscured by original sin. There inevitably follows a loss of awareness of the covenantal character of the union these persons had with God and with each other. The human body retains its "spousal significance" but this is now clouded by sin. Thus, in Genesis 19:1-11, the deterioration due to sin continues in the story of the men of Sodom. There can be no doubt of the moral judgment made there against homosexual relations. In Leviticus 18:22 and 20:13, in the course of describing the conditions necessary for belonging to the Chosen People, the author excludes from the People of God those who behave in a homosexual fashion.

Against the background of this exposition of theocratic law, an eschatological perspective is developed by St. Paul when, in 1 Corinthians 6:9, he proposes the same doctrine and lists those who behave in a homosexual fashion among those who shall not enter the Kingdom of God.

In Romans 1:18-32, still building on the moral traditions of his forebears, but in the new context of the confrontation between Christianity and the pagan society of his day, Paul uses homosexual behavior as an example of the blindness which has overcome humankind. Instead of the original harmony between Creator and creatures, the acute distortion of idolatry has led to all kinds of moral excess. Paul is at a loss to find a clearer example of this disharmony than homosexual relations. Finally, 1 Timothy one, in full continuity with the biblical position, singles out those who spread wrong doctrine and in verse ten explicitly names as sinners those who engage in homosexual acts.

7. The Church, obedient to the Lord who founded her and gave to her the sacramental life, celebrates the divine plan of the loving and live-giving union of men and women in the sacrament of marriage. It is only in the marital relationship that the use of the sexual faculty can be morally good. A person engaging in homosexual behavior therefore acts immorally.

To choose someone of the same sex for one's sexual activity is to annul the rich symbolism and meaning, not to mention the goals, of the Creator's sexual design. Homosexual activity is not a complementary union, able to transmit life; and so it thwarts the call to a life of that form of self-giving which the Gospel says is the essence of Christian living. This does not mean that homosexual persons are not often generous and giving of themselves; but when they engage in homosexual activity they confirm within themselves a disordered sexual inclination which is essentially self-indulgent.

As in every moral disorder, homosexual activity prevents one's own fulfillment and happiness by acting contrary to the creative wisdom of God. The Church, in rejecting erroneous opinions regarding homosexuality, does not limit but rather defends personal freedom and dignity realistically and authentically understood.

8. Thus, the Church's teaching today is in organic continuity with the Scriptural perspective and with her own constant Tradition. Though today's world is in many ways quite new, the Christian community senses the profound and lasting bonds which join us to those generations who have gone before us, "marked with the sign of faith."

Nevertheless, increasing numbers of people today, even within the Church, are bringing enormous pressure to bear on the Church to accept the homosexual condition as though it were not disordered and to condone homosexual activity. Those within the Church who argue in this fashion often have close ties with those with similar views outside it. These latter groups are guided by a vision opposed to the truth about the human person, which is fully disclosed in the mystery of Christ. They reflect, even if not entirely consciously, a materialistic ideology which denies the transcendent nature of the human person as well as the supernatural vocation of every individual.

The Church's ministers must ensure that homosexual persons in their care will not be misled by this point of view, so profoundly opposed to the teaching of the Church. But the risk is great and there are many who seek to create confusion regarding the Church's position, and then to use that confusion to their own advantage.

9. The movement within the Church, which takes the form of pressure groups of various names and sizes, attempts to give the impression that it represents all homosexual persons who are Catholics. As a matter of fact, its membership is by and large restricted to those who either ignore the teaching of the Church or seek somehow to undermine it. It brings together under the aegis of Catholicism homosexual persons who have no intention of abandoning their homosexual behavior. One tactic used is to protest that any and all criticism of or reservations about homosexual people, their activity and lifestyle, are simply diverse forms of unjust discrimination.

There is an effort in some countries to manipulate the Church by gaining the often well-intentioned support of her pastors with a view to changing civil-statutes and laws. This is done in order to conform to these pressure groups' concept that homosexuality is at least a completely harmless, if not an entirely good, thing. Even when the practice of homosexuality may seriously threaten the lives and well-being of a large number of people, its advocates remain undeterred and refuse to consider the magnitude of the risks involved.

The Church can never be so callous. It is true that her clear position cannot be revised by pressure from civil legislation or the trend of the moment. But she is really concerned about the many who are not represented by the pro-homosexual movement and about those who may have been tempted to believe its deceitful propaganda. She is also aware that the view that homosexual activity is equivalent to, or as acceptable as, the sexual expression of conjugal love has a direct impact on society's understanding of the nature and rights of the family and puts them in jeopardy.

10. It is deplorable that homosexual persons have been and are the object of violent malice in speech or in action. Such treatment deserves condemnation from the Church's pastors wherever it occurs. It reveals a kind of disregard for others which endangers the most fundamental principles of a healthy society. The intrinsic dignity of each person must always be respected in word, in action and in law.

But the proper reaction to crimes committed against homosexual persons should not be to claim that the homosexual condition is not disordered. When such a claim is made and when homosexual activity is consequently condoned, or when civil legislation is introduced to protect behavior to which no one has any conceivable right, neither the Church nor society at large should be surprised when other distorted notions and practices gain ground, and irrational and violent reactions increase.

11. It has been argued that the homosexual orientation in certain cases is not the result of deliberate choice; and so the homosexual person would then have no choice but to behave in a homosexual fashion. Lacking freedom, such a person, even if engaged in homosexual activity, would not be culpable.

Here, the Church's wise moral tradition is necessary since it warns against generalizations in judging individual cases. In fact, circumstances may exist, or may have existed in the past, which would reduce or remove the culpability of the individual in a given instance; or other circumstances may increase it. What is at all costs to be avoided is the unfounded and demeaning assumption that the sexual behavior of homosexual persons is always and totally compulsive and therefore inculpable. What is essential is that the fundamental liberty which characterizes the human person and gives him his dignity be recognized as belonging to the homosexual person as well. As in every conversion from evil, the abandonment of homosexual activity will require a profound collaboration of the individual with God's liberating grace.

12. What, then, are homosexual persons to do who seek to follow the Lord? Fundamentally, they are called to enact the will of God in their life by joining whatever sufferings and difficulties they experience in virtue of their condition to the sacrifice of the Lord's Cross. That Cross, for the believer, is a fruitful sacrifice since from that death come life and redemption. While any call to carry the cross or to understand a Christian's suffering in this way will predictably be met with bitter ridicule by some, it should be remembered that this is the way to eternal life for all who follow Christ.

It is, in effect, none other than the teaching of Paul the Apostle to the Galatians when he says that the Spirit produces in the lives of the faithful "love, joy, peace, patience, kindness, goodness, trustfulness, gentleness and self-control" (5:22) and further (5:24), "You cannot belong to Christ unless you crucify all self-indulgent passions and desires."

It is easily misunderstood, however, if it is merely seen as a pointless effort at self-denial. The Cross is a denial of self, but in service to the will of God himself who makes life come from death and empowers those who trust in him to practice virtue in place of vice.

To celebrate the Paschal Mystery, it is necessary to let that Mystery become imprinted in the fabric of daily life. To refuse to sacrifice one's own will in obedience to the will of the Lord is effectively to prevent salvation. Just as the Cross was central to the expression of God's redemptive love for us in Jesus, so the conformity of the self-denial of homosexual men and women with the sacrifice of the Lord will constitute for them a source of self-giving which will save them from a way of life which constantly threatens to destroy them.

Christians who are homosexual are called, as all of us are, to a chaste life. As they dedicate their lives to understanding the nature of God's personal call to them, they will be able to celebrate the Sacrament of Penance more faithfully and receive the Lord's grace so freely offered there in order to convert their lives more fully to his Way.

13. We recognize, of course, that in great measure the clear and successful communication of the Church's teaching to all the faithful, and to society at large, depends on the correct instruction and fidelity of her pastoral ministers. The Bishops have the particularly grave responsibility to see to it that their assistants in the ministry, above all the priests, are rightly informed and personally disposed to bring the teaching of the Church in its integrity to everyone.

The characteristic concern and good will exhibited by many clergy and religious in their pastoral care for homosexual persons is admirable, and, we hope, will not diminish. Such devoted ministers should have the confidence that they are faithfully following the will of the Lord by encouraging the homosexual person to lead a chaste life and by affirming that person's God-given dignity and worth.

14. With this in mind, this Congregation wishes to ask the Bishops to be especially cautious of any programs which may seek to pressure the Church to change her teaching, even while claiming not to do so. A careful examination of their public statements and the activities they promote reveals a studied ambiguity by which they attempt to mislead the pastors and the faithful. For example, they may present the teaching of the Magisterium, but only as if it were an optional source for the formation of one's conscience. Its specific authority is not recognized. Some of these

groups will use the word "Catholic" to describe either the organization or its intended members, yet they do not defend and promote the teaching of the Magisterium; indeed, they even openly attack it. While their members may claim a desire to conform their lives to the teaching of Jesus, in fact they abandon the teaching of his Church. This contradictory action should not have the support of the Bishops in any way.

15. We encourage the Bishops, then, to provide pastoral care in full accord with the teaching of the Church for homosexual persons of their dioceses. No authentic pastoral program will include organizations in which homosexual persons associate with each other without clearly stating that homosexual activity is immoral. A truly pastoral approach will appreciate the need for homosexual persons to avoid the near occasions of sin.

We would heartily encourage programs where these dangers are avoided. But we wish to make it clear that departure from the Church's teaching, or silence about it, in an effort to provide pastoral care is neither caring nor pastoral. Only what is true can ultimately be pastoral. The neglect of the Church's position prevents homosexual men and women from receiving the care they need and deserve.

An authentic pastoral program will assist homosexual persons at all levels of the spiritual life: through the sacraments, and in particular through the frequent and sincere use of the sacrament of Reconciliation, through prayer, witness, counsel and individual care. In such a way, the entire Christian community can come to recognize its own call to assist its brothers and sisters, without deluding them or isolating them.

16. From this multi-faceted approach there are numerous advantages to be gained, not the least of which is the realization that a homosexual person, as every human being, deeply needs to be nourished at many different levels simultaneously.

The human person, made in the image and likeness of God, can hardly be adequately described by a reductionist reference to his or her sexual orientation. Every one living on the face of the earth has personal problems and difficulties, but challenges to growth, strengths, talents and gifts as well. Today, the Church provides a badly needed context for the care of the human person when she refuses to consider the person as a "heterosexual" or a "homosexual" and insists that every person has a fundamental Identity: the creature of God, and by grace, his child and heir to eternal life.

17. In bringing this entire matter to the Bishops' attention, this Congregation wishes to support their efforts to assure that the teaching of the Lord and his Church on this important question be communicated fully to all the faithful.

In light of the points made above, they should decide for their own dioceses the extent to which an intervention on their part is indicated. In addition, should they consider it helpful, further coordinated action at the level of their National Bishops' Conference may be envisioned.

In a particular way, we would ask the Bishops to support, with the means at their disposal, the development of appropriate forms of pastoral care for homosexual persons. These would include the assistance of the psychological, sociological and medical sciences, in full accord with the teaching of the Church.

They are encouraged to call on the assistance of all Catholic theologians who, by teaching what the Church teaches, and by deepening their reflections on the true meaning of human sexuality and Christian marriage with the virtues it engenders, will make an important contribution in this particular area of pastoral care.

The Bishops are asked to exercise special care in the selection of pastoral ministers so that by their own high degree of spiritual and personal maturity and by their fidelity to the Magisterium, they may be of real service to homosexual persons, promoting their health and well-being in the fullest sense. Such ministers will reject theological opinions which dissent from the teaching of the Church and which, therefore, cannot be used as guidelines for pastoral care.

We encourage the Bishops to promote appropriate catechetical programs based on the truth about human sexuality in its relationship to the family as taught by the Church. Such programs should provide a good context within which to deal with the question of homosexuality.

This catechesis would also assist those families of homosexual persons to deal with this problem which affects them so deeply.

All support should be withdrawn from any organizations which seek to undermine the teaching of the Church, which are ambiguous about it, or which neglect it entirely. Such support, or even the semblance of such support, can be gravely misinterpreted. Special attention should be given to the practice of scheduling religious services and to the use of Church buildings by these groups, including the facilities of Catholic schools and colleges. To some, such permission to use Church property may seem only just and charitable; but in reality it is contradictory to the purpose for which these institutions were founded; it is misleading and often scandalous.

In assessing proposed legislation, the Bishops should keep as their uppermost concern the responsibility to defend and promote family life.

18. The Lord Jesus promised, "You shall know the truth and the truth shall set you free" (Jn. 8:32). Scripture bids us speak the truth in love (cf. Eph. 4:15).

The God who is at once truth and love calls the Church to minister to every man, woman and child with the pastoral solicitude of our compassionate Lord. It is in this spirit that we have addressed this Letter to the Bishops of the Church, with the hope that it will be of some help as they care for those whose suffering can only be intensified by error and lightened by truth.

(During an audience granted to the undersigned Prefect, His Holiness, Pope John Paul II, approved this Letter, adopted in an ordinary session of the Congregation for the Doctrine of the Faith, and ordered it to be published.)

Given at Rome, 1 October 1986.
Joseph Cardinal Ratzinger
Prefect

Alberto Bovone
Titular Archbishop of Caesarea in Numidia
Secretary

APPENDIX THREE

"Always Our Children"

Author's note: The United States Catholic Conference's Committee on Marriage and Family authored this document for parents of same-sex-attracted men and women in 1997. The 1997 version met a firestorm of controversy and criticism. Gay and lesbian activists, it came out, had been given an unprecedented role in putting the document together and the document left significant questions unclear or unanswered. The Marriage and Family Committee worked with the Bishops' Doctrine Committee and the Congregation for the Doctrine of the Faith to improve the wording of several sections of the document. In all, seven changes were made, and the revised document was issued in June of 1998.

The document remains the work of a committee of the U.S. Bishops' Conference. It carries no ecclesiastical authority or magisterial weight, but represents a worthwhile place for discussions of issues of same-sex attraction between parents and children to begin.

Always Our Children: Pastoral Message to Parents of Homosexual Children and Suggestions for Pastoral Ministers

Preface

The purpose of this pastoral message is to reach out to parents who are trying to cope with the discovery of homosexuality in a child who is an adolescent or an adult. It urges families to draw upon the reservoirs of faith, hope, and love as they face uncharted futures. It asks them to recognize that the Church offers enormous spiritual resources to strengthen and support them at this moment in their family's life and in the days to come.

This message draws upon the *Catechism of the Catholic Church*, the teaching of Pope John Paul II, statements of the Congregation for the Doctrine of the Faith, and of our own episcopal conference. The message is not a treatise on homosexuality. It is not a systematic presentation of the church's moral teaching. It does not break any new ground theologically. Rather, relying on the church's teaching as well as on our own pastoral experience, we intend to speak words of faith, hope and love to parents who need the church's loving presence at a time which may be one of the most challenging in their lives.

We also want to be helpful to priests and pastoral ministers, who often are the first ones parents or their children approach with their struggles and anxieties.

In recent years we have tried to reach out to families in difficult circumstances. Our initiatives took the form of short statements like this one which were addressed to people who thought they were beyond the church's circle of care. "Always Our Children" follows in the same tradition as these other pastoral statements.

This message is not intended for advocacy purposes or to serve a particular agenda. It is not to be understood as an endorsement of what some call a "homosexual lifestyle."

"Always Our Children" is an outstretched hand of the Bishops' Committee on Marriage and Family to parents and other family members, offering them a fresh look at the grace present in family life and the unfailing mercy of Christ our Lord.

"An even more generous, intelligent and prudent pastoral commitment modeled on the Good Shepherd is called for in cases of families which, often independent of their own wishes and through pressures of various other kinds, find themselves-faced by situations which are objectively difficult" (Pope John Paul II, "On the Family," 77).

A Critical Moment, A Time of Grace

As you begin to read this message you may feel your life is in turmoil. You and your family might be faced with one of the difficult situations of which our Holy Father speaks:

— You think your adolescent child is experiencing a same-sex attraction and/or you observe attitudes and behaviors that you find confusing or upsetting or with which you disagree.

— Your son or daughter has made it known that he or she has a homosexual orientation.

— You experience a tension between loving your child as God's precious creation and not wanting to endorse any behavior you know the Church teaches is wrong.

You need not face this painful time alone, without human assistance or God's grace. The church can be an instrument of both help and healing. This is why we bishops, as pastors and teachers, write to you.

In this pastoral message we draw upon the gift of faith as well as the sound teaching and pastoral practice of the church in order to offer loving support, reliable guidance and recommendations for ministries suited to your needs and those of your child. Our message speaks of accepting yourself, your beliefs and values, your questions and all you may be struggling with at the moment; of accepting and loving your child as a gift of God; and of accepting the full truth of God's revelation about the dignity of the human person and the meaning of human sexuality. Within the Catholic moral vision there is no contradiction among these levels of acceptance, for truth and love are not opposed. They are inseparably joined and rooted in one person, Jesus Christ, who reveals God to be ultimate truth and saving love.

We address our message also to the wider church community and especially to priests and other pastoral ministers, asking that our words be translated into attitudes and actions which follow the way of love as Christ has taught. It is through the community of his faithful that Jesus offers you hope, help and healing so that your whole family might continue to grow into the intimate community of life and love which God intends.

Accepting Yourself

Because some of you might be swept up in a tide of emotions, we focus first on feelings. Although the gift of human sexuality can be a great mystery at times, the church's teaching on homosexuality is clear. However, because the terms of that teaching have now become very personal in regard to your son or daughter, you may feel confused and conflicted.

Possibly you are experiencing many different emotions, all in varying degrees such as:

Relief: Perhaps you had sensed for some time that your son or daughter was different in some way. Now he or she has come to you and has entrusted something very significant. It may be that other siblings learned of this before you did and were reluctant to tell you. Regardless, though, a burden has been lifted. Acknowledge the possibility that your child has told you this not to hurt you or create distance, but out of love and trust and with a desire for honesty, intimacy and closer communication.

Anger: You may be feeling deceived or manipulated by your son or daughter. You could be angry with your spouse, blaming him or her for "making the child this way" — especially if there has been a difficult parent-child relationship. You might be angry with yourself for not recognizing indications of homosexuality. You could be feeling disappointment along with anger, if family members and sometimes even siblings are rejecting their homosexual brother or sister. It is just as possible to feel angry if family members or friends seem overly accepting and encouraging of homosexuality. Also — and not to be discounted — is a possible anger with God that all this is happening.

Mourning: You may now feel that your child is not exactly the same individual you once thought you knew. You envision that your son or daughter may never give you grandchildren. These lost expectations as well as the fact that homosexual persons often encounter discrimination and open hostility can cause you great sadness.

Fear: You may fear for your child's physical safety and general welfare in the face of prejudice against homosexual people. In particular, you may be afraid that others in your community might exclude or treat your child or your family with contempt. The fear of your child contracting HIV/AIDS or another sexually transmitted disease is serious and ever present. If your child is distraught, you may be concerned about attempted suicide.

Guilt, shame, and loneliness: "If only we had . . . or had not" are words with which parents can torture themselves at this time. Regrets and disappointments rise up like ghosts from the past. A sense of failure can lead you into a valley of shame which, in turn, can isolate you from your children, your family and other communities of support.

Parental protectiveness and pride: Homosexual persons often experience discrimination and acts of violence in our society. As a parent, you naturally want to shield your children from harm, regardless of their age. You may still insist: "You are always my child; nothing can ever change that. You are also a child of God, gifted and called for a purpose in God's design."

There are two important things to keep in mind as you try to sort out your feelings. First, listen to them. They can contain clues leading to a fuller discovery of God's will for you. Second, because some feelings can be confusing or conflicting, it is not necessary to act upon all of them. Acknowledging them may be sufficient, but it may also be necessary to talk about your feelings. Do not expect that all tensions can or will be resolved. The Christian life is a journey marked by perseverance and prayer. It is a path leading from where we are to where we know God is calling us.

Accepting Your Child

How can you best express your love, itself a reflection of God's unconditional love for your child? At least two things are necessary.

First, don't break off contact; don't reject your child. A shocking number of homosexual youth end up on the streets because of rejection by their families. This and other external pressures can place young people at greater risk of self-destructive behaviors like substance abuse and suicide.

Your child may need you and the family now more than ever. He or she is still the same person. This child, who has always been God's gift to you, may now be the cause of another gift: your family becoming more honest, respectful and supportive. Yes, your love can be tested by this reality, but it can also grow stronger through your struggle to respond lovingly.

The second way to communicate love is to seek appropriate help for your child and for yourself. If your son or daughter is an adolescent, it is possible that he or she may be displaying traits which cause you anxiety such as what the child is choosing to read or view in the media, intense friendships and other such observable characteristics and tendencies. What is called for on the part of parents is an approach which does not presume that your child has developed a homosexual orientation and which will help you maintain a loving relationship while you provide support, information, encouragement and moral guidance. Parents must always be vigilant about their children's behavior and exercise responsible interventions when necessary.

In many cases it may be appropriate and necessary that your child receive professional help, including counseling and spiritual direction. It is important, of course, that he or she receive such guidance willingly. Look for a therapist who has an appreciation of religious values and who understands the complex nature of sexuality. Such a person should be experienced at helping people discern the meaning of early sexual behaviors, sexual attractions, and sexual fantasies in ways that lead to more clarity and self-identity. In the course of this, however, it is essential for you to remain open to the possibility that your son or daughter is struggling to understand and accept a basic homosexual orientation.

The meaning and implications of the term homosexual orientation are not universally agreed upon. Church teaching acknowledges a distinction between a homosexual "tendency" which proves to be "transitory" and "homosexuals who are definitively such because of some kind of innate instinct" (Congregation for the Doctrine of the Faith, "Declaration on Certain Questions Concerning Sexual Ethics," 8).

In light of this possibility, therefore, it seems appropriate to understand sexual orientation (heterosexual or homosexual) as a deep-seated dimension of one's personality and to recognize its relative stability in a person. A homosexual orientation produces a stronger emotional and sexual attraction toward individuals of the same sex rather than toward those of the opposite sex. It does not totally rule out interest in, care for and attraction toward members of the opposite sex. Having a homosexual orientation does not necessarily mean a person will engage in homosexual activity.

There seems to be no single cause of a homosexual orientation. A common opinion of experts is that there are multiple factors — genetic, hormonal, and psychological - that may give rise to it. Generally, homosexual orientation is experienced as a given, not as something freely chosen. By itself, therefore, a homosexual orientation cannot be considered sinful, for morality presumes the freedom to choose.[1]

Some homosexual persons want to be known publicly as gay or lesbian. These terms often express a person's level of self-awareness and self-acceptance within society. Though you might find the terms offensive because of political or social connotations, it is necessary to be sensitive to how your son or daughter is using them. Language should not be a barrier to building trust and honest communication.

You can help a homosexual person in two general ways. First, encourage him or her to cooperate with God's grace in order to live a chaste life. Second, concentrate on the person, not on the homosexual orientation itself. This implies respecting a person's freedom to choose or refuse therapy directed toward changing a homosexual orientation. Given the present state of medical and psychological knowledge, there is no guarantee that such therapy will succeed. Thus, there may be no obligation to undertake it, though some may find it helpful.

All in all, it is essential to recall one basic truth. God loves every person as a unique individual. Sexual identity helps to define the unique persons we are. One component of our sexual identity is sexual orientation. Thus, our total personhood is more encompassing than sexual orientation. Human beings see the appearance, but the Lord looks into the heart (cf. 1 Sm. 16:7).

God does not love someone any less simply because he or she is homosexual. God's love is always and everywhere offered to those who are open to receiving it. St. Paul's words offer great hope:

"For I am convinced that neither death nor life, nor angels, nor principalities, nor present things, nor future things, nor powers, nor height, nor depth, nor any other creature will be able to separate us from the love of God in Christ Jesus our Lord" (Rom. 8:38-39).

Accepting God's Plan and the Church's Ministry

For the Christian believer, an acceptance of self and of one's homosexual child must take place within the larger context of accepting divinely revealed truth about the dignity and destiny of human persons. It is the church's responsibility to believe and teach this truth, presenting it as a comprehensive moral vision and applying this vision in particular situations through its pastoral ministries. We present the main points of that moral teaching here.

Every person has an inherent dignity because he or she is created in God's image. A deep respect for the total person leads the church to hold and teach that sexuality is a gift of God. Being created a male or a female person is an essential part of the divine plan, for it is their sexuality— a mysterious blend of spirit and body — that allows human beings to share in God's own creative love and life. [Deletion: The original text included this quotation from the *Catechism*: "Everyone . . . should acknowl-

277

edge and accept his sexual identity" (*Catechism of the Catholic Church*, 2333).]

Like all gifts from God, the power and freedom of sexuality can be channeled toward good or evil. Everyone — the homosexual and the heterosexual person — is called to personal maturity and responsibility. With the help of God's grace, everyone is called to practice the virtue of chastity in relationships. Chastity means integrating one's thoughts, feelings, and actions in the area of human sexuality in a way that values and respects one's own dignity and that of others. It is "the spiritual power which frees love from selfishness and aggression" (Pontifical Council for the Family, "The Truth and Meaning of Human Sexuality," 16).

Christ summons all his followers — whether they are married or living a single celibate life — to a higher standard of loving. This includes not only fidelity, forgiveness, hope, perseverance, and sacrifice, but also chastity, which is expressed in modesty and self-control. The chaste life is possible though not always easy, for it involves a continual effort to turn toward God and away from sin, especially with the strength of the sacraments of penance and eucharist. Indeed God expects everyone to strive for the perfection of love, but to achieve it gradually through stages of moral growth (cf. John Paul II, "On the Family," 34). To keep our feet on the path of conversion, God's grace is available to and sufficient for everyone open to receiving it.

Furthermore, as homosexual persons "dedicate their lives to understanding the nature of God's personal call to them, they will be able to celebrate the sacrament of penance more faithfully and receive the Lord's grace so freely offered there in order to convert their lives more fully to his way" (Congregation for the Doctrine of the Faith, "The Pastoral Care of Homosexual Persons," 12).

To live and love chastely is to understand that "only within marriage does sexual intercourse fully symbolize the Creator's dual design as an act of covenant love with the potential of co-creating new human life" (U.S. Catholic Conference, "Human Sexuality: A Catholic Perspective for Education and Lifelong Learning," p. 55). This is a fundamental teaching of our church about sexuality, rooted in the biblical account of man and woman created in the image of God and made for union with one another (Gn. 2-3).

Two conclusions follow. First, it is God's plan that sexual intercourse occur only within marriage between a man and a woman. Second, every act of intercourse must be open to the possible creation of new human life. Homosexual intercourse cannot fulfill these two conditions. Therefore, the Church teaches that homogenital behavior is objectively immoral, while making the important distinction between this behavior and a homosexual orientation, which is not immoral in itself.

It is also important to recognize that neither a homosexual orientation nor a heterosexual one leads inevitably to sexual activity. One's total personhood is not reducible to sexual orientation or behavior.

Respect for the God-given dignity of all persons means the recognition of human rights and responsibilities. The teaching of the Church makes it clear that the fundamental human rights of homosexual persons must be defended and that all of us must strive to eliminate any form of injustice, oppression or violence against them (cf. Congregation for the Doctrine of the Faith, "The Pastoral Care of Homosexual Persons," 10).

It is not sufficient only to avoid unjust discrimination. Homosexual persons "must be accepted with respect, compassion and sensitivity" (*Catechism of the Catholic Church*, 2358). They, as is true of every human being, need to be nourished at many different levels simultaneously.

This includes friendship, which is a way of loving and is essential to healthy human development as well as one of the richest possible human experiences. Friendship can and does thrive outside of genital sexual involvement.

The Christian community should offer its homosexual sisters and brothers understanding and pastoral care. More than 20 years ago we bishops stated that "homosexuals . . . should have an active role in the Christian community" (National Conference of Catholic Bishops [NCCB], "To Live in Christ Jesus: A Pastoral Reflection on the Moral Life," p. 19). What does this mean in practice? It means that all homosexual persons have a right to be welcomed into the community, to hear the word of God and to receive pastoral care. Homosexual persons who are living chaste lives should have opportunities to lead and serve the community. However, the Church has the right to deny public roles of service and leadership to persons, whether homosexual or heterosexual, whose public behavior openly violates its teachings.

The church recognizes the importance and urgency of ministering to persons with HIV/AIDS. Though HIV/AIDS is an epidemic affecting the whole human race, not just homosexual persons, it has had a devastating effect upon them and has brought great sorrow to many parents, families and friends.

Without condoning self-destructive behavior or denying personal responsibility, we reject the idea that HIV/AIDS is a direct punishment from God. Furthermore:

"Persons with AIDS are not distant, unfamiliar people, the objects of our mingled pity and aversion. We must keep them present to our consciousness as individuals and a community, and embrace them with unconditional love. . . . Compassion — love — toward persons infected with HIV is the only authentic Gospel response" (NCCB, "Called to Compassion and Responsibility: A Response to the HIV/AIDS Crisis").

Nothing in the Bible or in Catholic teaching can be used to

justify prejudicial or discriminatory attitudes and behaviors.[2] We reiterate here what we said in an earlier statement:

"We call on all Christians and citizens of good will to confront their own fears about homosexuality and to curb the humor and discrimination that offend homosexual persons. We understand that having a homosexual orientation brings with it enough anxiety, pain and issues related to self-acceptance without society bringing additional prejudicial treatment" ("Human Sexuality: A Catholic Perspective for Education and Lifelong Learning," p. 55).

Pastoral Recommendations

With a view toward overcoming the isolation that you or your son or daughter may be experiencing, we offer these recommendations to you as well as to priests and pastoral ministers.

To parents:

1. Accept and love yourselves as parents in order to accept and love your son or daughter. Do not blame yourselves for a homosexual orientation in your child.

2. Do everything possible to continue demonstrating love for your child. However, accepting his or her homosexual orientation does not have to include approving all related attitudes and behavioral choices. In fact, you may need to challenge certain aspects of a lifestyle which you find objectionable.

3. Urge your son or daughter to stay joined to the Catholic Faith community. If they have left the Church, urge them to return and be reconciled to the community, especially in the sacrament of penance.

4. Recommend that your son or daughter find a spiritual director/ mentor who will offer guidance in prayer and in leading a chaste and virtuous life.

5. Seek help for yourself, perhaps in the form of counseling or spiritual direction, as you strive for understanding, acceptance and inner peace. Also, consider joining a parents' support group or participating in a retreat designed for Catholic parents of homosexual children. Other people have traveled the same road as you, but may have journeyed even further. They can share effective ways of handling delicate family situations such as how to tell family members and friends about your child, how to explain homosexuality to younger children, how to relate to your son or daughter's friends in a Christian way.

6. Reach out in love and service to other parents who may be struggling with a son or daughter's homosexuality. Contact your parish about organizing a parents' support group. Your diocesan family ministry office, Catholic Charities or a special diocesan ministry to gay and lesbian persons may be able to offer assistance.

7. As you take advantage of opportunities for education and support, remember that you can only change yourself; you can only be responsible for your own beliefs and actions, not those of your adult children.

8. Put your faith completely in God, who is more powerful, more compassionate and more forgiving than we are or ever could be.

To church ministers:

1. Be available to parents and families who ask for your pastoral help, spiritual guidance and prayer.

2. Welcome homosexual persons into the faith community. Seek out those on the margins. Avoid stereotyping and condemnations. Strive first to listen. Do not presume that all homosexual persons are sexually active.

3. Learn about homosexuality and church teaching so that your preaching, teaching, and counseling will be informed and effective.

4. When speaking publicly, use the words homosexual, gay, and lesbian in honest and accurate ways.

5. Maintain a list of agencies, community groups, and counselors or other experts to whom you can refer homosexual persons or their parents and family members when they ask you for specialized assistance. Recommend agencies that operate in a manner consistent with Catholic teaching.

6. Help to establish or promote existing support groups for parents and family members.

7. Learn about HIV/AIDS so you will be more informed and compassionate in your ministry. Include prayers in the liturgy for those living with HIV/ AIDS, their caregivers, those who have died, and their families, companions, and friends. A special Mass for healing and anointing of the sick might be connected with World AIDS Awareness Day (Dec. 1) or with a local AIDS awareness program.

Conclusion

For St. Paul, love is the greatest of spiritual gifts. St. John considers love to be the most certain sign of God's presence. Jesus proposes it as the basis of his two great commandments which fulfill all the law and the prophets.

Love, too, is the continuing story of every family's life. Love can be shared, nurtured, rejected, and sometimes lost. To follow Christ's way of love is the challenge before every family today. Your family now has an added opportunity to share love and to accept love. Our church communities are likewise called to an exemplary standard of love and justice. Our homosexual sisters and brothers — indeed, all people — are summoned into responsible ways of loving.

To our homosexual brothers and sisters we offer a concluding word. This message has been an outstretched hand to your parents and families, inviting them to accept God's grace present in their lives now and to trust in the unfailing mercy of Jesus our Lord. Now we stretch out our hands and invite you to do the same. We are called to become one body, one spirit in Christ. We need one another if we are to "grow in every way into him who is the head, Christ, from whom the whole body, joined and held together by every supporting ligament, with the proper functioning of each part, brings about the body's growth and builds itself up in love" (Eph. 4:15-16).

Though at times you may feel discouraged, hurt or angry, do not walk away from your families, from the Christian community, from all those who love you. In you, God's love is revealed. You are always our children.

"There is no fear in love. . . . Perfect love drives out fear" (I Jn. 4:18).

Footnotes

1 The *Catechism of the Catholic Church* states also: "This inclination, which is objectively disordered, constitutes for most [persons with the homosexual inclination] a trial" (no. 2358).

2 In matters where sexual orientation has a clear relevance, the common good does justify its being taken into account, as noted by the Congregation for the Doctrine of the Faith in "Some Considerations Concerning the Response to Legislative Proposals on the Nondiscrimination of Homosexual Persons," 11 (1992).

Bibliography of Church Teaching

Catechism of the Catholic Church, United States Catholic Conference (USCC),1994, nos. 2357-2359.
Congregation for the Doctrine of the Faith, "Letter to the Bishops of the Catholic Church on the Pastoral Care of Homosexual Persons," 1986.

Congregation for the Doctrine of the Faith 1975 "Declaration on Certain Questions Concerning Sexual Ethics" (*Persona Humana*).

John Paul II, "The Splendor of Truth" (*Veritatis Splendor*), 1993.

John Paul II, "Apostolic Exhortation on the Family" (F*amiliaris Consortio)*, 1983.

National Conference of Catholic Bishops, "Human Sexuality: A Catholic Perspective for Education and Lifelong Learning," USCC, 1991.

National Conference of Catholic Bishops, "Called to Compassion and Responsibility: A Response to the HIV/AIDS Crisis," USCC, 1990.

National Conference of Catholic Bishops, "To Live in Christ Jesus: A Pastoral Reflection on the Moral Life," USCC, 1976.

Pontifical Council for the Family, "The Truth and Meaning of Human Sexuality," 1996.

About the author

David Morrison, thirty-six, is a writer and editor who lives, works, and worships in Washington, D.C. Morrison was a gay activist for about seven years until, in his late twenties, he gradually became disillusioned with actively gay life and, in self-acknowledged despair, turned to God. After his conversion experience Morrison grew in his knowledge and faith in Christ, at first while still homosexually active as an Anglican and, later, as he is today, a Roman Catholic committed to chastity.

In addition to writing on issues of faith, identity, sexuality, and culture, Morrison has also covered human rights and their abuse in Latin America and the use of women as experimental subjects without their informed consent in population-control programs. He has also reported on the growing schism between authentic Third World development and population control efforts, the widening gap between First and Third World health care, and the growing resistance to contraceptive imperialism around the world.

Morrison is also a regularly published columnist for *New Covenant* magazine and a frequent contributor to *Our Sunday Visitor*. In addition to these journals, Morrison's work has appeared in *The Tablet* (UK), *US Catholic,* and *This Rock*, as well as the *New York Post*, the *Washington Times,* and the *Baltimore Sun*. He has spoken on issues of sexuality, identity, faith, and culture in the U.S., Canada, the United Kingdom, Australia, and New Zealand. Copies of his articles have been reprinted in over seventeen languages worldwide.

If you would like to make comments about this book, visit David Morrison's website at http://www.beyondgay.com. Additional copies of *Beyond Gay* may be purchased from Our Sunday Visitor at http://www.osv.com or by calling OSV's toll-free number, 1-800-348-2440.

Our Sunday Visitor...
Your Source for Discovering the Riches of the Catholic Faith

Our Sunday Visitor has an extensive line of materials for young children, teens, and adults. Our books, Bibles, booklets, CD-ROMs, audios, and videos are available in bookstores worldwide.

To receive a FREE full-line catalog or for more information, call **Our Sunday Visitor** at **1-800-348-2440**. Or write, **Our Sunday Visitor** / 200 Noll Plaza / Huntington, IN 46750.

- -

Please send me: __ A catalog
Please send me materials on:
    __ Apologetics and catechetics   __ Reference works
    __ Prayer books   __ Heritage and the saints
    __ The family   __ The parish

Name_____
Address_____Apt._____
City_____State___Zip_____
Telephone (   )_____
                                                   A93BBABP

- -

Please send a friend: __ A catalog
Please send a friend materials on:
    __ Apologetics and catechetics   __ Reference works
    __ Prayer books   __ Heritage and the saints
    __ The family   __ The parish

Name_____
Address_____Apt._____
City_____State___Zip_____
Telephone (   )_____
                                                   A93BBABP

- -

Our Sunday Visitor
200 Noll Plaza
Huntington, IN 46750
1-800-348-2440
osvbooks@osv.com

Your Source for Discovering the Riches of the Catholic Faith